GREAT RELIGIONS OF THE WORLD

Saint Mary's Press
Christian Brothers Publications
Winona, Minnesota

GREAT RELIGIONS OF THE WORLD

by Sr. Loretta Pastva, SND
with Stephan Nagel and
Carl Koch, FSC

Nihil Obstat: Rev. Msgr. William T. Magee
                Censor Deputatus
                6 February 1986
Imprimatur: † Loras J. Watters, DD
                Bishop of Winona
                6 February 1986

The publishing team for this course book included Donnarae Lukitsch, editor; Joseph Stoutzenberger, consultant; Carolyn Thomas, designer and illustrator; and Mary Kraemer, production editor and indexer.

The acknowledgments continue on page 249.

ISBN: 0-88489-175-5

CONTENTS

INTRODUCTION: THE GREAT RELIGIONS AND YOUR WORLDVIEW

Deeply Different Views of the World

During the first orbital spaceflight in 1961, the Russian cosmonaut Gherman Titov was suddenly overwhelmed with a feeling of exhilaration:

> I felt elation as I had never known before in my life . . . the miracles of space before my eyes to drink in hour after hour; the realization of the most fantastic dream that [people] have ever dared to nourish in their minds. . . . I felt no later reflection or regret when, feeling as I did, I replied to a call from earth with the cry "I am Eagle! I am Eagle!"

The twentieth century will be remembered for our first ventures into space. Cosmonaut Titov's ecstatic, if not religious, experience offers us a clue to the deep significance of these endeavors. More than just technical feats, our first off-planet probes are events that have changed our worldview in a quite literal way. Especially since the first moon landing, our whole notion of the "world" now includes the moon, not just the earth. From now on we can make the moon a real part of our personal, national, commercial, and even recreational activities. You may already have included a lunar trip in your future travel plans.

The ventures that we have launched on earth toward closer contact with other societies are just as dramatic as the moon landing. Our worldviews have been challenged and changed by the strange, new cultures that we hear about daily on TV news programs. Furthermore, the ease of modern transportation brings us literally shoulder to shoulder with people of vastly different mentalities and manners. Clearly, we must learn to get along with the many people who possess worldviews that are very different from ours—just as they must learn to understand us.

The surest way of learning about other people is by getting to know their worldviews. And, as often as not, a person's worldview is rooted in religious faith. As the renowned psychologist Rollo May has stated:

> Religion is whatever the individual takes to be his [or her] ultimate concern . . . the point where a [person] has the conviction that there are values in human existence worth living and dying for.

In other words, understanding the religious faith of others puts us in touch with the deepest source of their dignity and aspirations — that is, what they consider sacred in life.

During much of the Catholic Church's history, Christians were so concerned about preserving or spreading their own religion that they did not acknowledge the wisdom and grace present in other religions. Unfortunately, by closing the door on the spiritual wealth of the other religions, the Church refused treasures that might have enriched us all. Since Vatican Council II, however, the Catholic Church has adopted a more open attitude. In fact, the council leaders went so far as to mandate the study of non-Christian religions. In the *Declaration on the Relation of the Church to Non-Christian Religions,* our church leaders wrote:

> In this age of ours, when . . . the bonds of friendship between different peoples are being strengthened, the Church examines with greater care the relation which she has to non-Christian religions. . . . The Catholic Church rejects nothing of what is true and holy in these religions. She has a high regard for the manner of life and conduct, the precepts and doctrines which, although differing in many ways from her own teaching, nevertheless often reflect a ray of that truth which enlightens all [people]. Yet she proclaims . . . Christ who is the way, the truth and the life. . . . In him, in whom God reconciled all things to himself . . . , [people] find the fulness of their religious life.

The Perils of Venturing into Other Religions

Besides launching us into new territory, this course on religions that you are beginning has other parallels with space ventures. For example, astronauts often experience queasy stomachs and dizziness during their first hours of weightlessness. Similarly, when we contemplate the fact that billions of people live out of worldviews that are very different from ours, we may find ourselves temporarily thrown off balance. Our loyalty to the Catholic Church and our human need for certainty and stability may tempt us to presume that other ways to find God are inferior and that Catholics have nothing to learn from others. Or just the reverse can happen: we may become caught up in the glamour and the mystery of other religions. As "old-timers" to Catholicism, we sometimes fail to realize that newcomers to our faith often find it just as glamorous and mysterious.

Now imagine yourself as an astronaut stepping onto an alien planet. Chances are that you would feel not only exhilarated but also fearful. Actually stepping into alien worldviews may be equally threatening. Some tough questions are raised in the process. For example: If there is one God, why are there so many religions? If people of all religions worship the same God, isn't choosing a particular religion a matter of taste rather than of truth?

Because we Christians believe in one God, such questions can be more threatening to us than they might be to others who believe in more than one deity. In a single course such as *Great Religions of the World*, we cannot hope to answer these questions fully; they continue to perplex theologians who have done years of research and reflection. Think about it for a minute: How can anyone pretend to summarize or criticize religious traditions—most of which date back thousands of years—within the confines of a semester course? To pretend to do so would be deeply dishonest and doomed to obvious failure.

Top: **Worshipers in Indonesia bringing fruit and flower offerings to a temple**

Bottom: **Fireworks marking a Hindu religious festival**

What we can successfully manage is to study the historical and theological developments of a small number of religions, presented in a way that may reflect those rays of truth described by the council leaders. Through this approach, *Great Religions of the World* can provide benefits that more than balance any queasiness you may experience initially. Let's look at these benefits for a moment.

The Benefits of Exploring Other Religions

One last analogy between this course and space adventures will help clarify the benefits of a study of other religions. Future space missions will have many purposes: they will be launched in hopes of discovering new worlds or of finding new information in order to improve technology. We too can embark on a study of other religions purely out of curiosity. Yet a course such as this one is intended to do far more than provide information about exotic people and places.

1. The first reason for studying other religions has already been mentioned—or at least implied. That is, it can **promote compassion and community.** The recognition that billions of people struggle in their quests

for God and strive seriously to fulfill the often very demanding requirements of their religions can command our admiration and respect. Also, simply learning the vocabulary and the symbols of unfamiliar religions can enable us to speak more intelligently of those other beliefs. At the same time, such learning can help us to be more precise in explaining our own beliefs to non-Christians.

2. By studying other religions, we can **find greater, not less, stability in our own faith.** Mohandas K. Gandhi, a heroic model of religious tolerance, said in his own words what the Vatican Council II leaders stated about rejecting nothing that is good in other religions:

> Reverence for other faiths need not blind us to their faults. We must be keenly alive to the defects of our own faith also. . . . Looking at all religions with an equal eye, we would not hesitate, but think it our duty to blend into our faith every acceptable feature of others' faiths.

How can learning about other religions help to build our own faith? Although the idea seems contradictory, actually it happens all the time. For example: During the early sixties, civil rights protests in the United States were organized by black Protestant ministers, notably Martin Luther King, Jr. Before long, their actions roused white ministers, among them many Catholic religious and clergy, who began living out their faith more fully.

Thus a study of the world's religions encourages us to make more conscious and meaningful recommitments to our own Catholic heritage. The fact that religion has appeared in every human society in every era implies a universal call to intimacy with God. Consciousness of this call might very well lead us to reexamine the depth and sincerity of our own religious responses. After looking at alternatives, we can choose our own religion with greater freedom and, therefore, with deeper conviction.

3. As a final benefit, the special wisdom and customs of other religions can **enrich our own religious practices and values.** For instance, familiarity with Eastern meditation can enhance our appreciation of the Christian prayer tradition, as well as add to our personal ways of praying. Religious masters of the Orient have studied human nature for forty centuries. An acquaintance with their discoveries can yield tremendously valuable insights into the operations of our minds, souls, and behaviors. Although as Catholics we confess that Christ is the way, the truth, and the life, we must also acknowledge that we can gather much from what God has sown in other vineyards.

Faith and Religion

Before we discuss this course in any more detail, let's take a moment to clarify two concepts that are fundamental to it:

- Some people say, "I believe in God, but I don't go to church." Similarly, a personal relationship with Christ appeals strongly to some individuals who will have nothing to do with organized religion.
- Other people may be faithful to worship, but their daily lives seem unaffected by any religious teachings.

To understand these apparent contradictions and to avoid confusion later in this course, we must distinguish between two words that are often used interchangeably—namely, *faith* and *religion*.

Faith is a complex term that is defined in many ways—usually as "belief" or "trust." The word *faith* is also used as a synonym for *religion*. For example, we talk about someone belonging to "another faith." More exactly, however, **religious faith is the deeply personal relationship that each of us experiences with what is sacred in life.** Thus, faith can be different for each person because we are each unique persons. We come from many backgrounds. Our personal experiences differ. Our family

training is unique. We grow up in different cultures and subcultures, in different eras of history, in different climates. All these circumstances make our faith unique, personal, and precious.

Yet, if faith is a relationship, then like all relationships it must find expression. How do we express our relationships? First there has to be some kind of coming together, as happens in a love relationship when the age-old formula "I love you" is spoken. Once together, people try to find words for their love. Sometimes, especially in love letters, the words can sound ridiculous because essentially what they are trying to say cannot be communicated in words.

A Hindu wedding

Sooner or later, then, people who are in love turn to public gestures to celebrate the relationship that gives so much meaning to their lives. A father tosses his infant daughter high in the air or wrestles with his son on the floor. Florists and jewelers have capitalized on the fact that certain signs or rituals become special to lovers: "Say it with flowers." "A diamond is forever." Ultimately, lovers wish to share themselves totally in marriage. Other people—friends, relatives, in-laws—celebrate publicly with them. The couple sets up a household and a shared way of life that benefits them and others. This tiny community sends waves of love through the world.

The working definition of religion adopted for this course has strong similarities with the human experience of marriage: **Religion is the sum total of all our attempts to celebrate our faith publicly through worship, to reflect on the story of our faith, and to live out the values of that faith as a community.**

Let's expand upon this definition of religion: Religions spring, first of all, from people who are committed to a shared faith. They attempt to put the history of their faith into **words**—in myths, scriptures, doctrines, theological commentaries, and creeds. Words, however, cannot completely capture faith because, like love, it is a mystery. So religions develop special **celebrations**—including prayers, sacrifices, meals, songs, processions, and other gestures—that help to satisfy people's deep need to express and communicate their faith. Finally, religions include values that prescribe specific ways of living as a faith-filled **community.** Usually, these values are found in rules and codes of morality.

A Three-Trait Model of Religion

Probably the easiest way to pin down the idea of religion is to look at our own religious experiences. For Catholic Christians, the celebration of the Eucharist can serve as a mini-model of religion. This sacrament contains religion's three basic traits:

1. a gathering and building of community
2. a reflecting on the truths of a shared, faith-filled vision
3. a celebrating of the mysteries of faith

1. The greeting by the priest at the beginning of the eucharistic celebration acknowledges that the community has gathered in response to the mystery of God's love as revealed in Jesus. In fact, the people who gather together are the key symbol of the sacrament, representing as they do the Body of Christ. The small gestures of peace, generosity, and faith seen at Mass provide a model of the Christian community we seek to build.

2. Then, in the first part of the Eucharist, the liturgy of the Word, the community reflects on the truth that is revealed in the scriptures (that God is a loving parent), on who they are (the children of God), and, as a consequence, on how they are to live (committed to mutual love).

3. Following that reflection on the Word, the Christian community celebrates its common faith in the liturgy of the Eucharist, worshiping with Christ in thanksgiving for all that God is and has done, seeking ever-closer communion with God and with one another.

This same model of religion is reflected in Buddhism, as summarized in what are called the Triple Gem:
• I go to the Buddha for refuge. (worship)
• I go to the Doctrine for refuge. (truths)
• I go to the Community for refuge. (community)

Many religions, including early Christianity, have used the term *way* to describe themselves. That is to say, religion must become a way of life: genuine disciples of any religion feel a strong need to devote themselves in worship, thought, and deeds to the sacred mystery that calls them to a fuller life. All of the religions that we will be discussing in this course have been powerful influences in the lives of their members, as well as in history generally.

The Great Religions

As has been said, this course can open the doors to the spiritual riches of the major religions of the world, not in order to compare or judge, but to deepen your own religious life. Our appreciation of God's goodness can be enhanced as we see it at work in the religions that will be studied in this course: Hinduism, Buddhism, Taoism, Confucianism, Shintoism, Zoroastrianism, Judaism, Islam, and, of course, Christianity.

These nine religions have been chosen out of hundreds of candidates because they are considered to be *great* religions. Certain of them—for example, Christianity and Islam—are followed by huge percentages of the world population. To be world-class, however, a religion does not need millions of followers. It is enough that a religion's teachings possess a depth and a truth that give it universal appeal or special influence.

For instance, the now little-known Zoroastrian religion at one time helped to shape Judaism. And Judaism, which today has relatively few followers, gave birth to the world's two largest religions: Christianity and

Islam. Similarly, while itself limited to India, Hinduism was the parent of Buddhism, which has strongly influenced all the societies of Asia.

Now that most of the religions we will be studying in this course have been mentioned by name, let's look at how they all fit into the course.

An Overview of This Course

The first three chapters of this course will examine the key elements of religion—worship, truth, and community—so that you may more easily recognize them in the great religions.

Chapter 1 explores worship as our response to sacred mystery. History reveals that all religions mingle magic with genuine worship, that is, worship based on a deep trust in what is sacred and mysterious in life. **Chapter 2** deals with the ways in which we come to know reality—namely, through truths that are revealed to us in nature, history, and human reason. This chapter traces, in religions past and present, the importance of myths and creeds.

Chapter 3 deals with the diverse ways in which religious communities share their faith and values. In our multicultural society it is important to recognize that there exists a wide range of religious temperaments, religious styles, and cultural expressions. As individuals, we usually go through a progression of positions with regard to our religious community. Initially, we merely exist as part of a community, experiencing it but not conscious of it as such. Then, usually in adolescence, we search out and test its wisdom for ourselves. Eventually, we may consciously claim our membership in the community and help to nurture faith in others.

By the end of these three introductory chapters, we will be ready to proceed to the separate considerations of each of the world's great religious traditions, beginning with Hinduism as the oldest and ending with the more recent and widespread religions. Obviously, these treatments must be brief. This course can provide only highlights of the histories of these world-class religions.

Chapters 4 and 5 deal with the religions that originated in India. In a region and climate that may seem uncongenial to human life, Hinduism has promoted respect for life and the study of the human spirit for over forty centuries. As a result, hundreds of millions of people have been sustained in their efforts to live meaningfully. In the teachings of Gautama the Buddha—which have spread from India to China, Korea, Japan, and even the United States—we will discover the truths that have enlightened billions of Buddhists for the last twenty-five hundred years.

Chapters 6 and 7 look at the religious foundations of the Far East. Taoism and Confucianism have shaped the Chinese culture and have influenced other Oriental peoples from 500 B.C.E.* to the present day. In

---

*As is becoming standard practice in educational publications, the abbreviations B.C.E. (before the common era) and C.E. (of the common era) will be used in place of the traditional abbreviations B.C. and A.D.

these religions—as well as in Shintoism, the religion native to Japan—special emphasis is placed on the search for spiritual harmony.

Chapters 8 through 11 treat the great religions founded in the Near East. Only a few hundred thousand people—mainly the Parsis of India—still adhere to the religious teachings of the ancient Persian leader Zoroaster. Yet the thinking of this religious genius, which makes up chapter 8, is reflected in the three great religions that originated in the Near East—namely, Judaism, Islam, and Christianity.

Judaism, followed by a small but influential minority today, has its roots in the revelation given to Moses over three thousand years ago. In chapter 9 we will find that the writings of Judaism's later prophets—Isaiah, Jeremiah, and Ezekiel—are still a source of inspiration to the Jews, as well as to Muslims and Christians.

The youngest and second largest world religion is Islam, the subject of chapter 10. Its founder, Muhammad, lived six hundred years after Christ. Islam shapes the lives of most of the peoples of the Arab countries and has spread as far as Pakistan, Indonesia, Africa, and the United States.

With minds freshened by the other great worldviews, in chapter 11 we will look at the largest and most universal religion, Christianity. United by faith in Jesus Christ, it embraces various branches—Eastern Orthodoxy, Protestantism, and Catholicism. Although Christianity has served as the foundation of Western civilization, it has transcended any particular culture or country.

Finally, the epilogue deals with the contemporary cults that are emerging in our age of transition.

A Final Word

The Jesuit anthropologist Pierre Teilhard de Chardin once wrote that our concept of God must be extended as the dimensions of our world are extended. In an era when our worldviews are being stretched geographically and even galactically, may this course launch you toward a richer grasp of sacred mystery and of our common human striving for faith. And may your reentry into the faith of our forebears be marked by the glow of rediscovery.

Facing page: **An Indonesian divinity. The statue is decorated with cloth and flower offerings.**

Above: **Japanese youths bearing a portable Shintoist shrine**

For Review:

1. What are some of the perils of stepping into the worldviews of others?
2. What are the rewards of studying other religions?
3. How is faith different from religion?
4. What are the three basic elements of religion?
5. Why can we say that a religion that does not influence one's lifestyle is no religion at all?
6. What makes a religion great?
7. Briefly describe the organization of this course.

For Reflection:

1. Compare the definitions of *faith* and *religion* given on pages 13–14 with Rollo May's statement on page 9. Is Rollo May describing faith or religion?
2. Cosmonaut Titov saw the world with an "eagle eye," and Gandhi encourages us to see religion with an "equal eye." Reflect on the contrastive meanings of these two expressions.
3. What do you hope to achieve in this course? What do you plan to put into it? Draw up a contract with yourself; describe your attitude toward this course and the kind of effort you are willing to make.

A. THE KEY ELEMENTS
OF RELIGION

1
WORSHIP:
RESPONDING TO SACRED MYSTERY

One way to learn about people's personalities is to look at their childhoods—that is, the time before they learned to mask their natural tendencies. In a similar manner, we will explore in this chapter the worship rituals of early human societies in order to discover what worship was originally.

In our modern, scientific culture, seeing is believing. But at the same time, we are aware of a presence in our lives that reaches beyond our senses—a fascinating presence that we refer to as sacred mystery. As you study the origins of worship and how it differs from magic, you may be surprised to learn that in our sophisticated and skeptical world—even among Christians—many people still believe in magic as a way to manipulate life's mysteries.

Sensing Mystery in Life

- In October, as you are driving over the brink of a hill, a sudden splash of color greets your eyes. From the woods below you, fiery reds and golds explode against the dark evergreens under a blue sky. You want to hold the beauty of this moment forever.
- At a fast-food place, a friend slips into your booth. Your casual talk develops into a moment of deep sharing. You feel profoundly understood and accepted.
- While you are baby-sitting alone and late at night, a sad and beautiful song on the radio stirs thoughts about existence—time and eternity; life and death; friendships, old and new. Your meditations fill you with ecstatic pain.

Reflect on a moment in your life like the ones described above—that is, a moment of beauty, friendship, or solitude.

At some time or another, we have all felt our spirits enlarged by the wonders of creation, by affection, or by silence. In these privileged moments, we are fascinated. Our hearts overflow with goodwill. Like Peter when he was shown Jesus transfigured in glory, we want to remain in that special place forever.

In his autobiography *The Seven Storey Mountain,* the Trappist Thomas Merton described two profound experiences that led to his conversion. One was the feeling of the spiritual presence of his deceased father in a hotel room where Merton was staying in Rome. Another experience occurred while he was viewing the great Byzantine mosaics of Christ in the basilicas of Rome. Gradually, in the depths of his being, Merton became aware of an all-loving presence that embraces even sinners. On these two occasions Merton stumbled into a sacred realm that he had not dreamed existed, and he came away transformed into a believer.

At the same time, however, elements of fear, dread, and even pain may be experienced in our encounters with mysterious events because mystery implies that some things are beyond us. For example, the gaping canyon carved out by rivers that flowed millions of years ago, the deep hush before a storm, the skyward sweep of monolithic buildings, the moving strains of a fresh song at a concert—encountering these phenomena can fill us with awe. Our feelings swim. We feel microscopic—"specks in a gigantic universe." We are pierced by the realization that our lives are not in our own hands: We were not brought into the world by our own choosing. And, ultimately, death comes whether we wish it or not.

Sometimes we experience mystery through evil. Perhaps it is an experience of physical evil—the fact that disease and disaster are no respecters of persons. The experience may be of moral evil: for example, we can be shaken by the cruelty that human beings are capable of inflicting on one another. Perhaps a sense of mystery is evoked by a public assassination or by the drawn-out sorrow of standing by helplessly as a tragedy slowly destroys someone whom we love.

For example: After retiring from a successful career as an opera singer, Beverly Sills spoke to a large audience about the mystery of her life. She had enjoyed everything—a happy marriage, excellent health, a marvelous talent, and financial success. But behind the glitter of her public image, she said, lies a profound sorrow—two severely handicapped children. Sills spoke in subdued tones of the mystery of having a totally deaf daughter, who would never hear her famous mother sing.

Thus, mystery evokes dual feelings in us: we feel fascinated by mystery but also repelled and frightened.

Mystery in a Scientific Era

History tells the story of how we have attempted to deal with nature. In the nineteenth century especially, people thought that science would soon dispense with mystery. This idea made sense at the time: science had begun to flex its muscles, to demonstrate its awesome powers of discovery and invention.

The reasoning in the last century went something like this: By applying scientific principles, we will be able to master nature. Then we can focus tremendous natural energies on helping one another economically and politically. For many people in our own century, inventions such as

Beverly Sills performing with the New York City Opera

the telephone, the radio, and the airplane, and especially the advances in medicine fed the illusion that sacred mystery is merely the product of ignorance.

Instead of abolishing mystery, however, science continues to uncover more mystery all the time. In physics, for example, the study of the atom has revealed infinitesimal worlds of apparently infinite mystery. In astronomy, the nature of cosmic black holes challenges the most fertile imaginations.

Even in the human sciences we have discovered more mystery, not less. For instance, we have many differing explanations for ordinary human experiences that we once thought we understood, such as sleep and dreams. And the overcrowding of our mental hospitals and jails demonstrates all too clearly our inability to deal with human emotions. Again, while making great strides in human understanding, the fields of sociology, anthropology, and psychology have been thwarted in explaining why some persons deprive others of their needs.

The mysteries that unfold as science probes the natural world are increasingly complex and challenging. Yet even more challenging mysteries exist. These are mysteries that cannot be measured under a microscope or viewed through a laser telescope. No physical or chemical data can explain what constitutes the heart of the universe or the deepest concerns of the human heart: Who are we? Why did life originate? Why do bad things happen to good people? Where is the universe headed? In asking these questions we are entering the realm of **sacred mysteries**—the realm of religion.

The Secret of Life

A scientist himself, Loren Eiseley wrote extensively and wonderfully about sacred mysteries. In an essay entitled "The Secret of Life," he described the boundary between science and religion:

If the day comes when the slime of the laboratory for the first time crawls under [human] direction, we shall have great need of humbleness. It will be difficult for us to believe, in our pride of achievement, that the secret of life has slipped through our fingers and eludes us still. . . .

I do not think, if someone finally twists the key successfully in the tiniest and most humble house of life . . . that the dark forces which create lights in the deep sea and living batteries in the waters of the tropical swamps, or the dread cycles of parasites, or the most noble workings of the human brain, will be much if at all revealed. Rather, I would say that if "dead" matter has reared up this curious landscape of fiddling crickets, song sparrows, and wondering [human beings], it must be plain even to the most devoted materialist that the matter of which he speaks contains amazing, if not dreadful powers, and may not impossibly be . . . "but one mask of many worn by the Great Face behind."
(The Immense Journey)

We do not have the answers to these perplexing questions. If answers exist at all, they lie with a source totally other than ourselves. Some religions call that mysterious "other" by a single name; others call upon many gods; still others prefer the label "truth" or "love." Half humorously we may even refer to the "other" as "The Force" or as "ETs." In any case, the human impulse—even in our modern age—is to respond reverently to this mystery. For many persons and for much of human history that response has been worship.

Responding to Mystery with Worship

In the powerful ending of the novel *Zorba the Greek,* the main characters react in a very human way to sacred mystery. Zorba had invested all his young boss's money in building a gigantic slide to bring timber down from a mountain. The timber was needed to reinforce the walls of an old mine that, if restored, would relieve the economy of the local community. The entire town turned out to watch the logging operation. Suddenly the slide collapsed under the weight of the logs. Everyone turned away in dejection—everyone except Zorba and the young boss.

> "I say, boss," said Zorba, suddenly aware that they had escaped untouched, "did you see the showers of sparks the thing threw out?" And wrestling each other playfully, they burst out laughing.
> "Come on, Zorba," cried the boss, "teach me to dance!"

The disaster forced Zorba and his boss to recollect that ultimately life is not about the success or failure of human projects. On the contrary, at the bottom line, life is mystery. Zorba's laughter sprang from and rang with his spirit, which was in touch with mystery. Despite his bad luck, Zorba exulted in his capacity to let go of his plans. His boss was irresistibly attracted by Zorba's freedom. So together they celebrated their mystery-filled lives in a joyful dance.

Zorba's dance is worship in its fundamental form. **Worship celebrates our need and capacity to rise above our daily experiences,** which are hemmed in by time and space and matter. To engage in worship as celebration is to share in the mystery that calls us to greater life. Worship leads us to reflect on ultimate reality and to see that there is more to life than meets the eye. Worship strikes sparks from our fragmented, routine experiences, revealing our dignity and spirit.

More specifically, Zorba's dance celebrates the mystery of **salvation**—that is, the power of the human spirit to survive apparent disaster and death. Worship in many religions celebrates the sacred mystery of salvation. For example:

- The Japanese use colorful paper dragons as large as parade floats to represent the life and power available from union with good spirits.
- The Chinese have seasonal festivals to venerate the graves of their ancestors, thereby honoring these spirits and hoping to partake in their powers.

- Christian charismatics represent their openness to the Holy Spirit by joyfully raising their arms as they pray and sing.
- Millions of Hindus bathe in the Ganges River to wash away any sins that might keep them from their goal of total absorption into Brahman.
- Hindu holy men lie on nails to visibly demonstrate the primacy of spirit.
- Incense and lotuses, frequently used symbols of spirit, are important worship symbols in many Eastern religions.
- From their beginning the Catholic sacraments have been strongly connected to this sacred mystery. In effect, each of the seven sacraments celebrates and symbolizes the suffering, dying, and rising experiences of Christians, as well as of Christ.

The celebrations or rituals of worship within a religion may take many forms, as suggested by the examples above. They include communal praying, standing, bowing, kneeling, singing, kissing, touching, washing, anointing, and robing in special garments. Private prayer and meditation can be regarded as worship, but most often worship is shared. Through the liturgy of the Word and the liturgy of the Eucharist, you are familiar with the primary worship ritual of the Catholic Church.

Because we tend to approach sacred mystery very cautiously, some form of purification is often called for—including washing, confession, penance, fasting and abstinence, the removal of clothing, or the use of fire. Worship also takes place in consecrated places at certain times, and it is often led by special ministers. Regardless of its form, however, the primary function of worship has always been to bring individuals or the community into the presence of sacred mystery.

The Origins of Worship

A companion of the British zoologist Jane Goodall once described a chimpanzee that stood as if lost in contemplation before a deep waterfall in a tropical forest. The chimp moved closer to the waterfall and began to rock, giving a round of "pant-hoot" calls. Becoming more excited, it ran back and forth, leaping in the air, calling louder, beating on trees with its fists, and running back again to the stunning sight.

Facing page: **The actor Anthony Quinn dancing in a scene from the film version of** *Zorba the Greek*

Above: **The zoologist Jane Goodall**

Left: **Hindu worshipers bathing in the Ganges River**

Unlike typical groups of chimps, which do "rain dances" when surprised by a sudden storm, this animal returned to the spot on other days as if drawn there for no other reason than to perform its ritual before the magnificent power of the falls.

We might wonder, Is this chimp's behavior similar to the way that the early ancestors of us *Homo sapiens* first responded to the wonders of the natural world? Just how and when worship originated must remain pure conjecture. Yet the first traces of human society indicate that early people everywhere worshiped consciously and deliberately.

Worship—and with it religion—seems to have emerged with the ability to recognize forces that could not be understood or mastered. Despite the distance of years, scholars of prehistoric societies have painstakingly pieced together evidence that reveals many similar worship rituals among the earliest peoples.

From the archaeological remains found in Europe, North Africa, and Asia, anthropologists recognize that religious awareness already existed in the Neanderthal nomadic tribes that roamed the earth between one hundred thousand and fifty thousand years ago. Carefully arranged stones and boulders were possibly used for purposes of worship. Inside their graves or shelters for the dead were found bones, flint tools, ornaments, and evidence of food offerings. Neanderthal paintings and sculptures were located so deep in caves that they could have served no other possible purpose than that of ritual.

Early in human history, belief in some form of afterlife seemed to prevail. Concern about the return of the dead prompted early humans to smooth the sand around graves in order to detect footprints. This same fear seems to lie behind the practice of reburying the dead. In addition, deep layers of ashes near grave sites imply that memorial meals were held regularly after the burials.

Evidence of Early Religious Practices

The chart below summarizes the possible religious practices of these very ancient peoples as well as science has been able to identify them.

100,000–50,000 B.C.E.

Neanderthal society:
the last humans of the "archaic" or older type

Evidence of belief in afterlife:
- ceremonial burials
- graves (at times filled with flowers)
- flint instruments in graves
- food offerings to the dead

Evidence of belief in spirits:
- cave-bear cult

From 50,000 B.C.E.

Cro-Magnon society:
the first "modern" type of humans, having a nomadic lifestyle

Evidence of religious rituals:
- ceremonial burials
- food offerings to the dead
- stone-lined graves
- offerings of shell ornaments and stone tools
- possibly communal meals at the grave sites
- second burials, including bones painted red to symbolize blood
- engravings, paintings, and clay sculptures found deep in the caves
- drawings depicting shamans
- sculptures of the mother goddess used in fertility rites or by clan-mother cults

From 15,000 B.C.E.

- sacrificial offerings of deer or other animals needed for existence
- offerings to the dead

From 10,000 B.C.E.
The shift begins from a nomadic to an agricultural lifestyle.

Evidence of worship of nature:
- symbols of the sun and the moon
- veneration of stones, stars, and trees

Facing page: **A prehistoric deer hunt, from a rock painting in eastern Spain**

Top: **Venus of Willendorf, a famous fertility figurine dating from about 10,000** B.C.E. **The exaggerated proportions suggest that it represented a fertility goddess.**

Bottom, left: **A male figure, a silver statuette from western Syria dating from about 1250** B.C.E.

Bottom, right: **A woman and child fertility idol, a terra-cotta figurine from southern Iraq dating from about 3500** B.C.E.

Recent evidence also suggests that early humans connected the mysteries of life and death with particular spirits. Cave bears, which were hunted at grave peril, were treated with special reverence by some clans. The bear skulls were placed on pedestals, on shelves of stone, or in niches—probably for some ritual. We do not know whether the cave-bear cult served to appease a bear spirit during ritual feasts or whether it employed a form of magic to ensure the success of the clans' hunts.

Early Religions (from 5000 B.C.E.)

If we had to rely solely on the evidence of religious belief that was left to us by the peoples who wandered the earth seven thousand years ago, we would have very little to go on. Only a few clues exist, such as the arrangements of stones for sacred worship at Stonehenge in England and a few stone tombs of more elaborate construction than earlier tombs. Yet, by studying aboriginal tribes in Australia and other cultures that have remained relatively untouched by industrialized cultures, anthropologists have been able to reconstruct the religious activities of these early religions.

Australian aborigines performing an ancient ritual dance

Generally these aboriginal societies held rituals in expectation of certain benefits—including health, offspring, good crops, and fertility. For example, the cult of the mother goddess gradually became a widespread way of seeking fertility in soil, in cattle, and in women. Other rituals celebrated annual events like the return of spring, the sowing season, and harvesttime. Also, rituals marked changes in the status of individuals, such as the installation of tribal leaders and the rites of passage for births, name-givings, initiations, betrothals, marriages, and deaths.

From the very beginning of religion, it is likely that genuine worship was mingled with magic. Even today we have a difficult time separating the two approaches to mystery. Since the distinction between worship and magic is critical to understanding religion, let's spend some time discussing it.

O Thou Great Mystery

The profound religious faith that existed in early religions is reflected in this prayer by the Native American Chief Joseph Strongwolf:

O Thou great mystery,
Creator of the universe,
Good and powerful as Thou art,
Whose powers are displayed in
The wonders of the sun and
* glories of the moon,*
And the great foliage of the forest
And the great waters of the deep,
Sign of the four winds;
Whatever four corners of the
* earth that we may meet—*
Let us be friends, pale face and
* red man,*
And when we come to the end
* of that long trail,*
And we step off into the happy
* hunting ground,*
From which no hunter ever returns,
Let us not only have faith in
* Thee—*
O Thou great mystery—
But faith in each other.
O Thou Kitchin Manito, hear us!

Joseph, chief of the Nez Percé tribe (c. 1840–1904)

Distinguishing Between Magic and Worship

We can find magic at the historical roots of both science and religion. Like religion, science began in efforts to magically harness the powers of the world. Eventually people learned that certain so-ca___ ___agical substances—foods or ointments—actually helped or cured ___ ___ience developed from these first inadvertent experiments. Even ___ Mid-dles Ages, however, European scientists still spent much ___me trying to discover the "philosophers' stone," a talisman that ___rn base metals into gold. Today science distinguishes itself fron___ requiring that scientists pursue experiments that produce measu___ repeatable results.

The distinction between magic and religion is not as easily disc___ The many evidences of magic around us today seem to contradict the t___ that magic gradually matures into worship. Voodoo, for example, has ___ planted authentic Catholic worship in certain places where that wor___ had been practiced for centuries. In other words, worship can and o___ does degenerate into magic.

One important difference between worship and magic is that **wor ship rituals are willingly and freely entered into, whereas magical prac tices are compulsive and fearful.** That is to say, magic grows out of a fearful distrust of the sacred, while worship flows from a trusting rela-tionship with mystery. This distinction carries an important implication: namely, rites that are worship for some people can be treated as merely magic acts by others. This may seem obvious to you. We have all known people who attend Mass for the wrong reasons. At some time, we have all been at Mass for reasons other than worship—merely out of fear of "missing Mass" perhaps.

An even better way to distinguish between magic and religion is to look at the purpose of each. **Magic tries to control or manipulate mystery.** The implication of this attempt to control is that human plans are more important than sacred mystery.

On the other hand, **worship accepts that what is sacred and mys-terious cannot be compelled or forced; worship is freeing.** In worship, we assume our true, if paradoxical, place in the universe—living in both dignity and dependence. An example from daily experience may help make this distinction clearer:

- Jake wanted a day off from work for personal reasons, but he knew that his employer did not easily excuse people. Jake feared asking because he expected a no. So Jake waited for the right moment, which came when his employer learned that she had won a local lottery. To doubly ensure himself of a favorable reply, Jake made his request in the presence of his employer's friends. Jake got his day off through manipulation and clever strategies that forced a positive answer. He acted primarily out of insecurity.

- If the employer's daughter Jane needed a free day, the situation might have been entirely different. She might not have acted out of fear or mistrust. Knowing that her mother was favorably disposed, Jane approached her directly, made her request, and offered real reasons. Her lived experience of her mother's goodness created a relationship that reassured her.

Because he is acting out of fear, Jake acts in manipulative ways. Jane, on the other hand, has a relationship with her mother that is freeing and empowering. Consequently, she feels free to be honest. Likewise, magic and worship have coexisted in history because mystery creates feelings both of awe and of fear.

Early Efforts to Magically Control Mystery

Many kinds of magic underlay the rites of early religions. All of them were attempts to control the sacred, however. At least five types of magic developed: imitative, black, contagious, aversive, and productive magic.

1. **Imitative magic** is based on the belief that look-alikes act alike; for instance, if someone imitates the looks and actions of a certain person or animal or cloud, that person can bring about a like action in the imitated person or object. When Cro-Magnon societies made sculptures or cave paintings of bison or bears covered with dart wounds spurting blood, they believed that the animal would magically be brought under their power in the hunt. Rolling rocks down a steep slope while beating drums and imitating sounds of thunder was believed to be an effective way to bring on a needed rainstorm. Leaping high in the air in a field of sprouting grain was supposed to encourage plant growth to the height of the leap.

2. **Black magic,** which is sometimes equated with witchcraft, also operates on the principle of imitation, but its purpose is to do evil. Stabbing a wax image of a hated enemy with pins, pointing a sharpened bone at him or her, or simply describing the desired evil (in a curse) is believed to bring about the malign effect.

3. The third form, **contagious magic,** is based on the notion that once things are joined, they will retain a magical sympathy even after separation. Thus, black magic performed on someone's cut hair or fingernails is thought to produce the intended effect on that person. Cannibalism may be seen as a form of contagious magic, in which the strength or character of an individual is acquired by consuming, for instance, the person's heart or brains.

4. In **aversive magic,** communities rid themselves of accumulated guilt by transferring it to a "scapegoat." For instance, they might symbolically load their guilt into a boat that is then set adrift on the sea. Similarly, they might sacrifice an animal to atone for the guilt.

5. Lastly, **productive magic** tries to ensure the supply of food by placating certain spirits. For instance, offerings of "firstfruits" are made to corn and vegetative deities. Likewise, the ceremonial marriages of fertility gods and goddesses are enacted, with the deities represented by human actors.

Facing page: **A Mexican ceremonial mask**

Above: **A Native American performing a buffalo dance**

In an effort to bend the earth's forces to their own benefit, early peoples mingled many types of magic with their worship. In addition to the five basic types of magic, they were led by their fears to develop a reliance on some special forms of magic: sacrifices, fetishes, and shamans.

Sacrifices

Early rituals often involved animal and human sacrifices because it was believed that both spirits and people needed the power that was present in life and blood. Insofar as people believed that the spirits must be forced to grant favors, magic as coercion entered in. The value of any offerings, especially when totally sacrificed by burning, was thought to be very high because of the cost to the offerer. Often the sacrificed animals were only partially burnt; then the roasted meat was shared with the spirit powers in a community meal.

Fetishes

As a child you may have hunted for "lucky stones" to bring you good luck. Like most children today, prehistoric peoples were **animists**—that is, they believed that inanimate or nonliving objects could be inhabited by spirits. A **fetish** (also called a talisman, charm, or amulet) is an object venerated as the dwelling place of a spirit. **Fetishism** is the belief in control over the spirits in certain objects. The story of Aladdin's magic lamp, in which a powerful genie is a slave to the owner of the lamp, is a classic tale about fetishism.

Early societies thought that colorful pebbles, oddly shaped bones, or unusual gnarled sticks would bring good fortune or would protect by frustrating the curses of one's foes. Masks functioned in a way similar to fetishes: while wearing a mask a person could take on the powers of the spirit represented by the mask.

The spirit of a fetish sometimes took on a personality for its user: it might be prayerfully addressed, presented with offerings, or even punished if it did not grant the owner's wishes.

Shamans

Another method of controlling spirits was through a **shaman**—a magic specialist, also known as a witch doctor or medicine man. This powerful individual in the community was believed to magically control the spirits. A shaman talked to the spirits, and they, in turn, talked to the community through the shaman. By means of drumbeating, dancing, self-hypnosis, chanting, and drugs, the shamans worked themselves into deep trances of spirit-possession during which their spirits were said to travel to far places to discover the intentions of the spirits or the condition of the dead. While lifted to the spirit level, the shamans were believed to establish control over the spirits of disease and death in order to drive them into people or to expel them.

Magic in Modern Society

The rise of science and technology in modern times has solved many of the mysteries that struck prehistoric peoples with dread. Nevertheless, many magical practices persist among people in all quarters of the world and at all levels of education and culture. Magic continues to exist because the ultimate questions and sacred mysteries of life continue to perplex us. A sampling of modern magical practices follows:

- An exchange student from Japan wears three small pouches suspended from cords around his neck. In them are secret objects believed to have power over the spirits. One object wards off the bad spirits. The second assures him that the good spirits will be with him in his journey away from home. The third is to ensure success in his studies. He has been instructed that if he or anyone else opens the pouches, the power of these objects will be reversed.

- A prominent U.S. businessman admits that he cannot fall asleep at night unless he says certain Jewish prayers that he learned during childhood.

- A survey of college professors notes that more than half the students in their classes place either rabbits' feet or other good luck charms on their desks during exams.

- In China, some Taoists believe that naming a weapon halts its power to injure. Therefore, great care is taken to name every weapon by which one might possibly be injured.

- The arrival of the Haitian "boat people" in the United States has made us aware that peoples of the West Indies practice **voodoo**—beliefs and rites that are African in origin but closely interwoven with rituals borrowed from the Roman Catholic Church. Voodoo includes communications with the supernatural world, bizarre cemetery ceremonies, and black magic.

- The Ku Klux Klan in the United States practices a form of black magic when they burn effigies of their avowed enemies.

- At harvesttime in France, the slaughter of a goat in Grenoble and of an ox in Pouille represents the annual killing of the spirit of vegetation.

- In some areas of Africa, public ceremonies are conducted in accord with magic ritual to bring rain or guarantee better crops.

- Today Muslim pilgrims kiss or touch the sacred Black Stone at Mecca to acquire holiness.

- The right foot of Saint Peter's statue in Rome is worn thin by kissing.

- Long revered as a deity, evergreen trees still form the center of several rituals both in homes and in public places.

- Teachers in India notice the wholesale absence of students on regular school days when, according to the stars, leaving the house may involve danger.

When you were reading about the kinds of magic earlier, you may have thought of some instances of modern magical practices in your own life—possibly in your own approach to religion. Because we consider Christianity an advanced religion, we are sometimes reluctant to see

Facing page, top: **An African warrior wearing lucky fetishes**

Facing page, bottom: **A Hindu holy man**

Above: **A member of the Ku Klux Klan in the United States**

evidence of magic within it. Yet many people who neither worship Christ nor live out Christian values insist on having their children baptized, confirmed, and instructed for Communion. Why? Because they believe that the sacraments operate mechanically—that is, magically. Other people heap up great numbers of prayers, candles, or statues in the belief that these practices will compel God to grant their wishes.

Religious Faith: A Developing Relationship of Trust

We Christians use the word *faith* to talk about our relationship with God. In any definition of the word, faith is opposed to fear. Christian faith is a relationship of absolute trust and confidence in the God of the Bible. It is to believe not only that God is present and active among us, but that God's presence proceeds from love. As one first-grade student put it when asked about the meaning of the Good News, "It means God isn't mad at us." A Christian faith relationship frees and empowers. The search for Christian faith is a long journey in which we move from fear of mystery to a trust in God as Mystery.

A commentator once said about religious faith in general that it is open to everybody but that it does not have a tidy beginning, middle, and end. We begin the journey of faith the moment we start wondering where we were before we were born, where we go when we die, and what we are here for in the meantime. Once we begin that journey, however, it changes the way we act and even the way we think about life—as we will see in the next chapter.

Answer Yes

In his journal Markings, *former secretary-general of the United Nations Dag Hammarskjöld revealed how, through a slow and painful search, he moved from faith in himself to faith in God. One entry especially described the effect of his faith relationship:*

I don't know Who—or what—put the question, I don't know when it was put. I don't even remember answering. But at some moment I did answer Yes *to Someone—or Something—and from that hour I was certain that existence is meaningful and that, therefore, my life . . . had a goal.*

For Review:

1. What feelings does mystery generate in us?
2. Cite examples of how the physical and human sciences have deepened rather than dispensed with our sense of mystery.
3. Define *worship* by using an example. Precisely what mystery did Zorba's dance deal with?
4. What are some of the earliest traces of religious awareness? In what historical eras did they emerge?
5. In what two ways can magic be distinguished from worship?
6. What are the five basic types of magic? Give examples.
7. What other magical means were used to control the spirits in early times?
8. List three examples of magic practiced today. Why does the practice of magic persist?

For Reflection:

1. Which scientific or technological discoveries of our age fill you with a sense of mystery? Reflect for a few moments on the following statement by science writer Paul Davies:

   During the last few thousand years humans have progressed from technology on the scale of hand tools . . . to major engineering projects (bridges, tunnels, dams, cities) many miles in size. If that trend is extrapolated, even at a greatly diminished pace, the time will come when the whole Earth, then the solar system, and eventually the stars will be "technologized." The galaxy itself could be remodelled by manipulation, stars moved out of their orbits, created from gas clouds, or destroyed by engineered instabilities. Black holes could be formed or controlled at will as energy sources and/or disposal devices for the effluents of cosmic society.
   And if galaxies, why not the universe?

2. What is your personal attitude toward worship? Do you experience it as celebration, as dutiful ritual, or as mere routine? Do you have many celebrations in your life? If so, what do you celebrate?
3. Is it possible to believe in God and yet not to worship? Explain your stance.
4. Is honoring sacred objects such as the Bible and the chalice a form of fetishism? Why or why not?
5. Compare the poetic statements by Chief Joseph Strongwolf and Dag Hammarskjöld (see pages 29 and 34). What meanings do these writers have in common? How do their poetic prayers differ?

2 REVELATION: LISTENING FOR ULTIMATE MEANING

In the last chapter, worship was discussed primarily as an awed response to sacred mystery. Yet worship is not the only religious response to mystery. Historically we have tended to see the universe as orderly, not as accidental or chaotic. Consequently, we seek concrete answers to our questions about how our world came to be and about where it is directed. Endlessly we probe the mysteries of time and evil, the sufferings of the innocent, our shame at wrongdoing, our insatiable greeds, and our deep longings for what is good.

Science and philosophy, as well as religion, originated in the assumption that there is order in the cosmos—mysterious though that order may be. In this chapter, we will look at the revealed truths that religion espouses, especially in contrast to the wisdom of philosophy.

Matters of the Heart

Heart, in the biblical sense of the word, is our innermost region where our spirits meet the Spirit. This sense of the term is captured by the little prince in Antoine de Saint-Exupéry's story when he declares, "It is only with the heart that one can see rightly." For it is in our hearts that moments of revelation take place. ***Revelation*** literally means "to reveal" or "to unveil." In this discussion, the term refers specifically to revealed truth concerning ourselves, the world, and God.

Revelation is not just a religious term. Apart from religion, we often have sudden and astonishing bursts of insight that change our outlooks. For instance, learning that a friend is a millionaire or perhaps a victim of incest would change—for better or worse—your view of your friend, of your relationship, or even of yourself.

Another example: Carson McCullers wrote a short story titled "Sucker," in which a sad revelation takes place. The story tells about Pete, age sixteen, and his orphaned cousin Richard, who lives with Pete and who admires him as only a twelve-year-old boy can. Pete has given Richard the nickname Sucker.

Pete's friendship with Sucker mirrors his dating relationship with a girl named Maybelle. In other words, as Pete and Maybelle's relationship deepens—at least in Pete's mind—he begins to treat Sucker in a new, friendly manner. Sucker, starved for love all his life, eagerly responds to his hero's friendliness. Later, when Maybelle loses interest in Pete, he reacts by attacking Sucker, insulting and destroying him emotionally. Subsequently, Sucker becomes a cold, tough guy. At the end of the story, Pete talks about his feelings of regret:

> More than anything I want to be easy in my mind again. And I miss the way Sucker and I were for a while in a funny, sad way that before this I never would have believed. But everything is so different that there seems to be nothing I can do to get it right. I've sometimes thought if we could have it out in a big fight that would help. But I can't fight him because he's four years younger. And another thing— sometimes this look in his eyes makes me almost believe that if Sucker could he would kill me.

The insight Pete receives—that friendships require care and attention—may have come too late for Richard's sake. Yet very likely it will transform Pete's life. Pete learns the truth by looking into the heart of the matter and, most importantly, by finding words for his experience. This is similar to the process by which religious revelation happens.

Revelation and Other Religions

In the Catholic view, all people are graced with an inner power to listen for the secrets of the sacred as these are revealed in life. We know this because of the striking similarities among the great religions of the world— including the sense of a supreme deity and the calls for conversion and compassion.

The fact that all religions are open to revelation, however, does not mean that they are "pretty much the same." Love of neighbor, for instance, does not mean the same thing in the teaching of Confucius as it does in the teaching of Jesus. Nor does Christianity today support—as do certain other religions—holy wars against religious opponents or class systems among its members. Christianity has received a unique and special revelation that is expressed in its creeds and lived out in its particular set of moral values.

Although the Christian revelation is unique, there is no doubt that we can learn from other great religions—from the breadth of understanding in Hinduism, the love of nature in Shintoism, the mysticism and meditation in Zen Buddhism, and the simplicity of Islam.

Often the difficulty in learning from other religions lies in the fact that many religions have not developed formal theologies. That is, they have not reflected critically and systematically on their own beliefs. Consequently, they have a difficult time explaining their beliefs to others. This lack complicates attempts to create genuine dialogue between most other religions and Christianity—which has a fully developed theology.

The lack of theologies has created even more difficulty for these religions when they confront modern philosophies—such as Communism. Without well-defined theological positions, these religions often appear to be naive or unhistorical. Islam's Muslims, for example, believe that their holy book, the Koran, was dictated word for word to Muhammad by an angel. Such a belief allows no room for a genuine understanding of how and why the Koran was composed.

In the remainder of this chapter, we will trace the long search for ultimate meaning in ancient religions and in modern philosophies. Both of these sources have made enormous contributions to human wisdom and to our grasp of ultimate meaning.

Mythmaking: Naming a Mystery

As children, one of the first things we do to get a handle on things is to name them. As our understanding grows, our names become more precise: *doggie* becomes *a pedigreed golden retriever; toot-toot* becomes *a six-cylinder Mercury-Lynx wagon with a stick shift.* As language developed in history, people were better able to understand and to share their faith and fears. In a similar way, dentists today carefully describe procedures to their patients beforehand. By making sense of the event, the dentist enables the patient to face the ordeal more successfully.

Early peoples regarded **dreaming** as a way of making sense out of the mysteries that surrounded them. The "dream stories" of the tribal religious leaders were the earliest form of storytelling used by all religions to explain mysteries. In fact, an important contribution of prehistoric peoples to later religions was the use of imagination in communicating religious truth and values. Today we call this activity of explaining mysteries **mythmaking.**

In its simplest form, a **myth** is a story that may contain historical fact or may be entirely fictitious. Even when it is entirely a fiction, however, a myth is never a falsehood. The reason is that a myth's purpose is to report revelation—not history or scientific fact—in a way that listeners can understand. Similarly, when we say, "It's raining cats and dogs," we are not lying. We are merely using a widely understood way of expressing a fact. The story of Sucker is even a closer example of modern mythmaking. For us to grasp the point of McCullers's story, it does not matter that Pete and Sucker are not real in the sense that we could look up their names in a telephone book. We do have to believe, however, that people like Pete and Sucker actually exist. So even "fictional" stories can be deeply rooted in reality.

Myths may just as easily be based on the lives of real people—usually people whom we think of as "larger than life." In the United States, for instance, the words and deeds of Abraham Lincoln have grown into a powerful myth that continues to guide people along the path of justice and charity. Myths, then, are accepted, effective ways of expressing truth.

The cover of a copy of the Muslim Koran

Ancient Religions and Mythmaking

As societies became more organized and tribes came together to form cities and kingdoms, the deities of fields, streams, and mountains grew into complex clans of gods that incorporated the various functions of the older tribal gods. Likewise, religious myths expanded into rich legends, sagas, dramas, and epics.

The first recorded religious myths employ both human characters, who are often remote ancestors, and godlike creatures, whose supernatural exploits serve to interpret natural events. The "dreams" of the simpler societies grew into elaborate **mythologies**—that is, groups of myths. The mythologies reflected the worldviews and the values of complex cultures in two ways:

- by explaining the mysteries of creation, nature, and human death and destiny; and
- by explaining the supernatural origins of (and so giving authority to) customs, ceremonies, and beliefs.

Religious myths from these times usually have many levels of stories in which a community and each individual could find meanings that are important to them. An example of a multileveled story is the biblical passage about Jacob's dream on his way to Haran (Genesis 28:10–16). Clearly, the revelation of God's presence at the ancient Israelite shrine of Bethel served the practical purpose of justifying Bethel's use as a place of worship. On another level, every individual Israelite who shared Jacob's faith and who worshiped at the shrine could identify with Jacob's experience. In fact, reading the story today, we who worship Jacob's God remember that God is present and is revealed to us on our own journeys through life.

The ancient civilizations of India, China, and Japan also created myths to justify the establishment of ruling dynasties and to deal with sacred mystery. The four great ancient cultures of the West that we know most about are Egypt, Babylonia (also known as Mesopotamia), Greece, and Rome. All of these cultures have left their marks on the Western world. Let's spend a few moments looking at these more familiar cultures and their mythologies.

Ancient Egypt (4200–200 B.C.E.)

Egypt possessed a warm climate, a fertile soil, and a safe position between two deserts that assured its inhabitants of a stable, orderly, and secure existence. Consequently, myths grew up about gods who, in a serene and orderly hierarchy, presided over every city, temple, and home. The dominant concerns of creation and death were reflected in the chief deities, Ra and Osiris. **Ra** was the sun god whose tears brought forth humanity and in whose divinity the pharaohs shared. **Osiris** was the god of the underworld, of eternal life, and of the renewal of life. From the size of the temples, their hieroglyphic inscriptions, and other records, we know that the rituals to the many gods of Egypt were lengthy, serene,

Jacob's Dream

Jacob left Beersheba and set out for Haran. When he had reached a certain place he passed the night there, since the sun had set. Taking one of the stones to be found at that place, he made it his pillow and lay down where he was. He had a dream: a ladder was there, standing on the ground with its top reaching to heaven; and there were angels of God going up it and coming down. And Yahweh was there, standing over him, saying, "I am Yahweh, the God of Abraham your father, and the God of Isaac. I will give to you and your descendants the land on which you are lying. Your descendants shall be like the specks of dust on the ground; you shall spread to the west and east, to the north and the south, and all the tribes of the earth shall bless themselves by you and your descendants. Be sure that I am with you; I will keep you safe wherever you go, and bring you back to this land, for I will not desert you before I have done all that I have promised you." Then Jacob awoke from his sleep and said, "Truly, Yahweh is in this place and I never knew it!"
(Genesis 28:10–16)

Top: **The Egyptian god Ra, from a tomb painting representing him with four heads that symbolize the four elements of nature**

Bottom: **The temple of Ramses II, dating from about 1250 B.C.E., with its carved rock entrance**

Facing page: **Gilgamesh watering a bull from a vase, a Babylonian cylinder seal dating from about 2400 B.C.E.**

and solemn. These rituals were presided over by a very powerful priestly class that flourished during long periods of Egypt's history.

The pyramids and sphinxes stand in mute testimony to the enormous effort and energy devoted to the burial places of the pharaohs. The Egyptians expected a joyful afterlife, believing in a paradise toward which the souls of the dead journeyed. Even after death, however, the soul needed a body as a sort of base. For this reason, attempts were made to preserve the body by mummification and to protect it in pyramids. These efforts were reserved for nobles and especially for pharaohs—who were considered to be divine.

Very few of the Egyptian myths have survived intact, but we do know that various creation stories abounded. Generally they tell of a chaotic world filled with water, from which a hill arose on which life began. This myth is no doubt derived from what the Egyptians observed each year in the flooding of the Nile River, as well as from their experience of its waters as a source of life.

Babylonia (3200–539 B.C.E.)

Babylonia was established between the Tigris and Euphrates rivers in the area now ruled by Syria and Iraq. Unlike tranquil Egypt, it was a land of constant struggle. Because it was the bridge between the Mediterranean Sea and the Far East, Babylonia was subject to frequent invasion. Its changeable climate, periodic flooding, and plagues kept the people alert to challenges; these conditions also encouraged the making of myths that were imaginative and searching but full of violence and bloodshed.

As the Babylonian villages were destroyed by wars and disasters and then rebuilt on the same sites, a complex system of gods grew up to justify the values of the new cultures. The gods were organized into a superstate with a ruling council, whose number was almost beyond counting. Myths were constantly being developed in Babylonian societies to explain the mysteries of the changing seasons, the floods, and death.

In the beginning, according to the ancient Babylonians, only fresh water and salt water existed. From the mingling of these waters came forth all of life, beginning with the gods.

The Babylonians told several stories about the creation of people, one of which underlines their rather somber view of the world. It seems that the gods were tired of the work they had to do, tilling the ground and digging canals to grow crops for food. So the water god **Enki** got the idea of making a clay figure that **Inanna,** the mother goddess, would bring to life. The result was the first human, and ever since, people have had to work to grow food for the gods, as well as themselves.

The most famous Babylonian myths are those about the great king **Gilgamesh.** Included among these stories is one of epic length that tells of Gilgamesh's failed search for immortality. *The Epic of Gilgamesh* summarizes the basic view of the Babylonians that life on earth was more important than concern about the afterlife.

The Babylonian societies tried to placate their unpredictable gods by means of elaborate rituals, magic, and prayers. To discern the will of the gods, the Babylonian priests turned to astrology and the interpretation of dreams. Indeed, the most precious attribute of these enterprising peoples was their searching spirit and openness to new religious ideas. Our own spiritual ancestor Abraham was a product of this civilization.

Classical Greece (c. 700–300 B.C.E.)

Early Greek philosophers, best represented in the life and thinking of Socrates, questioned everything, even religious myths. Thus religious faith received its first criticism. The humanistic focus that these gifted Greeks brought to civilization was extended to the gods: the Greek deities were as closely connected to human nature as they were to natural forces, such as the sun or rain. Even today classical Greek myths remain sources of universal wisdom and valid guides to human behavior. The destructiveness of vanity, for instance, is superbly presented in the story of the young **Narcissus,** who pines away looking at his own reflection in a pool.

Nevertheless, the popular Greek gods, especially as found in Homer's epic poems, were seen as aloof and corrupt. Often they allowed disaster or even sent it upon mortals out of sheer willfulness.

In the early Greek myths, the gods themselves were said to be the offspring of the universe, not the makers of it. Originally there was just chaos and the earth. Out of them emerged night and day, and sky and sea. From the union of **Gaea,** the earth goddess, and **Uranus,** the sky god, the first race of divine beings, called **Titans,** was created.

By some accounts, a Titan named **Prometheus** created the first humans out of water and earth. Other myths suggested that people shared the same divine origin as the gods. In either case, the fate of humans was not hopeful in the Greek view. Like the Egyptians, the Greeks believed that the soul lived on. Yet life after death was, for the Greeks, nothing to get excited about: The souls of the dead were only pale reflections of their former, earthly selves. Even a person's intelligence and courage disappeared at death.

Imperial Rome (27 B.C.E.–476 C.E.)

The Romans built their culture on the Greek principle of living by human reason. As a result, the religion of their empire consisted mainly

Be Happy Day and Night

The Babylonians' answer to the quest for immortality is given to Gilgamesh by a divine barmaid.

The barmaid said to him,
  to Gilgamesh:
"Gilgamesh, where are you
  wandering to?
You will not find the life you
  seek.
When the gods made mankind,
They set death aside for men,
But they kept life in their own
  hands.
So, Gilgamesh,
  do you fill your belly,
Be happy day and night,
Take pleasure every day,
Day and night dance and play.
Wear clean clothes,
Wash your head,
  bathe in water,
Attend to the child who holds
  your hand,
Let your wife be happy with
  you.
This is what man's lot is."
                  (The Epic of Gilgamesh)

of being a good citizen. The good life was to be found in good laws and good government.

The Roman gods, which were also based on Greek models, were not vivid personalities, and religious ceremonies were not personal devotions but rather civic sacrifices. Superstitious attention was paid to carrying out these rites with great precision in order to gain the desired magical effects. Roman rulers demanded that citizens participate in the religious ceremonies and even pay homage to the emperors themselves. Yet their motives had more to do with politics than religion.

Top: **Narcissus, from a painting by the Italian Renaissance artist Caravaggio**

Bottom: Venus of Milos, **a Greek sculpture dating from about 150** B.C.E.

Right: **The Roman emperor Claudius I, a statue depicting him as a god**

The Roman upper classes grew increasingly indifferent to religion and consequently to any genuine sense of worship or morality. Greed and violence prevailed, against which the pale gods of Roman mythology presented no challenge. The Romans had reduced religion to a mere phantom of itself.

Eventually, new religions began to fill the vacuum left by the characterless and joyless imperial religion. The **mystery cults,** as they were called, came from the Near East. Through their initiation rites, they provided intense emotional experiences that focused on people's desires for salvation and immortality. Clearly the time was ripe for an authentic religion that would grapple with the sacred mysteries of life. This religious hunger helps explain why Christianity was quickly established within the Roman Empire.

The Axial Period

By bringing the discussion around to Christianity, we have moved ahead of our story of religion in terms of its history. The period from 600 B.C.E. to 600 C.E. is now called the **Axial Period** (because on this "axis" of time turn all the great religious ideas of history). During this period, in every culture outstanding religious founders appeared, who discovered revelation within their heart of hearts. These great teachers included the following:

- Zoroaster   (c. 628–c. 551 B.C.E.)   Persia
- Lao-tzu   (born c. 600 B.C.E.)   China
- Confucius   (551–479 B.C.E.)   China
- Siddhartha Gautama   (c. 563–c. 483 B.C.E.)   India
- the Jewish rabbis   (586–538 B.C.E.)   Palestine
- Jesus   (6 B.C.E–30 C.E.)   Palestine
- Muhammad   (c. 570–632 C.E.)   Arabia

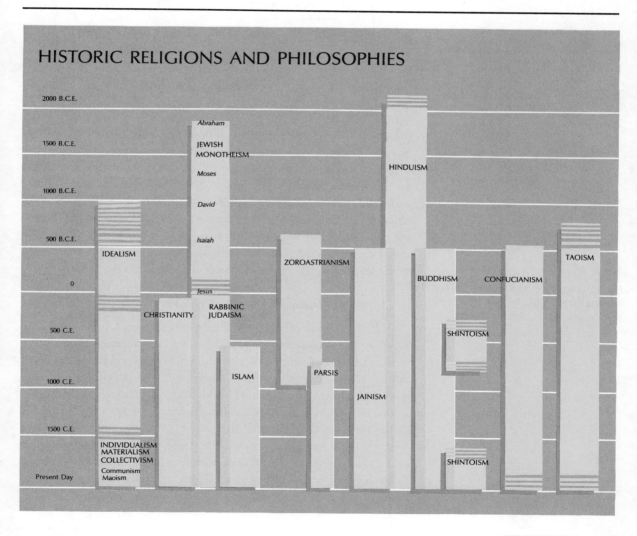

HISTORIC RELIGIONS AND PHILOSOPHIES

We will spend much of this course exploring the contributions and the insights of each of these religious leaders. Now, however, let's look at the differences between religion and philosophy—both of which study human existence and promote values. Since the time of the Axial Period, many attempts have been made to separate wisdom and values from religious faith. It seems we possess a need that is opposed to our need for religious faith—a need to appear to be independent of both communities and divinities. Henry David Thoreau, the nineteenth-century U.S. writer, put it this way: "How vigilant we are, determined not to live by faith if we can avoid it."

Philosophy as Reasoned Truth

As civilizations arose, people became more aware of their power to reason, that is, to think things out. Applying reason to the study of the universe gave impetus to science, especially to mathematics and philosophy.

The Greeks were the first to systematically study philosophy. Originally, the Greek word *philosophy* meant "the love of wisdom," but when we talk today about someone's "philosophy," we are usually referring to the person's logical viewpoint or code of behavior. Often we call people "philosophers" because they demonstrate a capacity for calm and balanced reflection.

In the widest sense of the term, everyone is a *philosopher:* we all possess some sort of perspective on the world and on how life should be lived. Sometimes nonprofessionals are called "grassroots philosophers."

As a formal discipline, philosophy stands midway between science and theology. Like science, philosophy rests on logic and factual knowledge rather than on the heartfelt wisdom that we find in myths. Yet philosophy often consists, as does theology, of reflection on subjects about which conclusive knowledge is not possible—subjects such as the meaning of life and of death. The following sections are brief portraits of some of the most powerful of these schools of thought.

Idealism: Ideas as Eternal Realities

Idealism, which originated with the Greek philosopher Plato (c. 428–c. 347 B.C.E.), sees the material world of things and events as only a dreary shadow of the real world. We can know this real world of ideas only through philosophy and intelligent reflection. In this perspective, actions are good insofar as they reflect the world of "eternal and unchanging ideas," in which virtues in pure forms have an independent existence. Christianity has been greatly influenced by this view, which emphasizes moral freedom and holds to the priority of the intellectual and spiritual over the physical and material. The Transcendentalists of the nineteenth century (including Emerson, Thoreau, and Alcott) were idealists.

Above: **Plato**

Facing page: **Socrates, a bust of the famous Greek philosopher who was Plato's teacher**

As young adults we are often idealists. Newly aware of the adult power to see life in greater breadth and depth, we become enthusiastic crusaders of high ideals. We can become painfully disillusioned, however, when life does not conform to our ideals. Gradually maturity brings with it the ability to face the fact that life is complicated and messy.

Idealism advocates the values of the mind and the spirit. At the same time, idealists sometimes build ivory towers for themselves in order to wall out life's suffering.

Materialism: What You See Is What You Get

Materialism is the view that the world is entirely dependent on matter, which is believed to be the fundamental and final reality. Whereas idealists believe in "mind over matter," strict materialists hold that our minds are merely matter—that is, our brains are controlled by heredity, chemical reactions, and physical events. Scientific technology has popularized this viewpoint, achieving amazing results by concentrating on what is observable, manageable, and predictable.

To rigorously materialistic thinkers, only that which can be subjected to the scientific method is real. By implication, then, the human spirit and the Spirit are illusions.

Our society is deeply affected by a corrupted form of materialism called **consumerism.** Consumerism goes so far as to define people in terms of what they can do or what they have. Thus, human dignity is something that is earned only by those who are productive and successful.

Materialism promotes the values of experimentation and observation. On the negative side, however, it tends to reduce everything to simplistic explanations.

Individualism: The Primacy of Choice

Individualism is the political and social philosophy that places a high value on freedom and choice. In a sense, modern industrial society has made individualists of us all by forcing so many choices on us. The individualist sees himself or herself as an end, not as a means to achieving society's purposes. Society, on the other hand, is only a means to achieve the good of the individual. And because in this view all individuals are morally equal, no one should be treated solely as a means to the well-being of another person.

Individualism advocates that the interests of each person are best served by allowing maximum freedom for choosing and achieving his or her goals. When this view is taken to the extreme, life is seen as a series of powerful moments of individual choice in which our common heritage and shared hopes are merely intruders.

The values cultivated by individualism include self-reliance, privacy, and respect for the individual. On the other hand, individualism opposes any tradition or authority.

All Things Good

Atlas, a statue of the Titan from Greek mythology who was forced to support the world on his shoulders

Plato's dialogue The Timaeus *is one of the most influential writings in Western history. Jewish, Muslim, and Christian reflections on God and on the created world have been influenced by this work. The following passage is the beginning of Timaeus' discussion of how the creator fashioned the world. Notice on what authority Plato bases his account of creation.*

> *Let me tell you then why the creator made this world of generation. He was good, and the good can never have any jealousy of anything. And being free from jealousy, he desired that all things should be as like himself as they could be. This is in the truest sense the origin of creation and of the world, as we shall do well in believing on the testimony of wise men. God desired that all things should be good and nothing bad, so far as this was attainable. Wherefore also finding the whole visible sphere not at rest, but moving in an irregular and disorderly fashion, out of disorder he brought order, considering that this was in every way better than the other. Now the deeds of the best could never be or have been other than the fairest, and the creator, reflecting on the things which are by nature visible, found that no unintelligent creature taken as a whole could ever be fairer than the intelligent taken as a whole, and again that intelligence could not be present in anything which was devoid of soul. For which reason, when he was framing the universe, he put intelligence in soul, and soul in body, that he might be the creator of a work which was by nature fairest and best. On this wise, using the language of probability, we may say that the world came into being—a living creature truly endowed with soul and intelligence by the providence of God.*

Collectivism: Utopian Visions

Collectivism is a philosophy at the foundation of many social organizations in which the individual is seen as subordinate to a social collectivity — such as state, nation, race, or social class. Diametrically opposed to individualism, collectivism asserts that the means for producing needed goods and for distributing wealth should be collectively controlled and not left to the decisions of individuals who are pursuing their own interests. Collectivism looks toward a future of equality and justice with utopian hopes.

Communism is a type of collectivism that blends the social theories of Karl Marx and Friedrich Engels. Marx saw unjust economics as the root of human suffering. He taught that an equitable distribution of the goods of the earth would come when the laboring class overthrew the dominion of the wealthy. Marx's "Kingdom of Freedom" is a society where there exists a minimum of private ownership and a totally planned economy.

Creeds and Scriptures

Philosophy has had great impact on the Western religions particularly. Early in its history, for instance, Christianity encountered Greek philosophy, which was a powerful cultural force in the Roman Empire. In order to get a fair hearing in the Greek-speaking region of the empire, the early Christians needed more than a knowledge of the Greek language: they also needed to be able to discuss the Gospel in philosophical or theological terms.

As a result, even as early as the writings of Saint Paul, we find that the revelation of Jesus as Lord has been put into language different from the story form that we associate with religious myths. Instead, in First Corinthians, Christian revelation is expressed as a **creed,** which is a list of basic beliefs stated as theological propositions. The following list shows the Gospel recast into its earliest creedal form:

- Jesus was born of the *seed of David.*
- Jesus *died,* in accordance with the scriptures, to deliver us out of the present evil age.
- Jesus *was buried.*
- Jesus *was raised* on the third day, in accordance with the scriptures.
- Jesus *is exalted* at the right hand of God, as Son of God and Lord of the living and dead.
- Jesus *will come again* as the Judge and the Savior of humanity.
- The prophecies are fulfilled, and the *new age* is begun with the coming of Christ.

Notice that this early creed still retains the outlines of a story. Creeds are often religious myths that are boiled down to an outline form.

An aside: Do not be confused in this discussion of Christianity by the use of the word *myth.* Saint Paul puts the case quite clearly for Christians: if the Resurrection did not happen, then Christian faith is in vain.

In other words, Christian revelation claims to be a truthful rendering of history. Moreover, Christian faith claims to be true not only with regard to the past; it also claims to tell about the future in the sense that the Christian story did not end with the Resurrection. The Resurrection is an ongoing story that includes us today. In much the same way, in the "Jewish story" the Exodus is not just a historical event. Rather, it is a continuing saga of hope and salvation for the followers of Judaism.

Other Kinds of Religious Writings

Religious texts include more than myths and creeds. Indeed, the majority of sacred writings is concerned with other crucial matters. Using the Christian texts as our example, let's look briefly at these additional kinds of religious writings.

Instructional Matters: These scriptural texts are intended to show how the Christian story has authority and relevance in all kinds of new situations. For example, most of Saint Paul's letters deal with building a community based on faith in Christ, that is, making the *Christ* story into the *Christian* story.

Institutional Concerns: Every enduring community must organize its activities and plan its future in order to preserve and accomplish its original intent. These concerns usually occur some time after the founding of a religion. Yet as early as the time of Saint Paul's letters—Titus and First and Second Timothy, for example—such matters as daily tasks, order, survival, and discipline were taken up.

Mature Theological Reflections: Besides the basic Christian story, much of the rest of the Nicene Creed is made up of statements that define Jesus' identity and his relationship to his Father and to the Spirit. These **doctrines,** decided upon at the First Council of Nicaea in 325 C.E., were the fruit of centuries of prayerful reflection on the scriptures—and heated debates. As such, the doctrines are considered part of Christian revelation on a par with our belief in the Resurrection.

All of these kinds of writings are considered very important when they are assembled together as the **scriptures** of a religion. Often even the book that contains such writings is considered holy. In the Islamic religion, for instance, it is considered seriously wrong to place a copy of the Koran on the floor. Similarly, placing other books on top of the Jewish Scriptures is frowned upon by Jews.

Too Many Truths?

If philosophy has influenced religion, the reverse is also true. As seen in the passages written by Plato and by Marx and Engels, myths are often found at the heart of philosophies. These myths function in much the same way as religious myths—presenting a certain worldview and promoting a particular set of values.

Karl Marx and Friedrich Engels were the fathers of Communism, which has both collectivist and materialist underpinnings. In The Communist Manifesto *(1848), they produced a document that in a very real sense became "scripture" for the worldwide Communist movement that arose in the late 1800s and early 1900s. The excerpt below, from the first part of the manifesto, sets forth the condition of the world in dramatic language, not unlike other myths.*

> The history of all hitherto existing society is the history of class struggles.
>
> Freeman and slave, patrician and plebeian, lord and serf, guild-master and journeyman, in a word, oppressor and oppressed, stood in constant opposition to one another, carried on an uninterrupted, now hidden, now open fight, a fight that each time ended either in a revolutionary reconstitution of society at large, or in the common ruin of the contending classes.
>
> In the earlier epochs of history, we find almost everywhere a complicated arrangement of society into various orders, a manifold gradation of social rank. In ancient Rome, we have patricians, knights, plebeians, slaves; in the Middle Ages, feudal lords, vassals, guild-masters, journeymen, apprentices, serfs; in almost all of these classes, again, subordinate gradations.
>
> The modern bourgeois society that has sprouted from the ruins of feudal society has not done away with class antagonisms. It has but established new classes, new conditions of oppression, new forms of struggle in place of the old ones. . . .
>
> The bourgeoisie, wherever it has got the upper hand, has put an end to all feudal, patriarchal, idyllic relations. It has pitilessly torn asunder the motley feudal ties that bound man to his "natural superiors," and has left remaining no other nexus between man and man than naked self-interest. . . .
>
> The bourgeoisie has stripped of its halo every occupation hitherto honoured and looked up to with reverent awe. It has converted the physician, the lawyer, the priest, the poet, the man of science, into its paid wage-labourers.
>
> The bourgeoisie has torn away from the family its sentimental veil, and has reduced the family relation to a mere money relation. . . .
>
> . . . Constant revolutionizing of production, uninterrupted disturbance of all social conditions, everlasting uncertainty and agitation distinguish the bourgeois epoch from all earlier ones. All fixed, fast-frozen relations, with their train of ancient and venerable prejudices and opinions are swept away, all new-formed ones become antiquated before they can ossify. All that is solid melts into air, all that is holy is profaned, and man is at last compelled to face with sober senses his real conditions of life and his relations with his kind.

Top: **Karl Marx**
Bottom: **Friedrich Engels**

In their strictest forms, all of the philosophies described above are also similar to religion in that they place absolute value on something. Specifically, idealism sets great value on human ideas; materialism, on physical reality; individualism, on choice; and collectivism, on equality. Unfortunately, whenever we place too great a moral burden on a single intellectual truth, it becomes a lie.

In contrast to philosophies, however, religious faith holds that only Mystery is absolute. In many religions, God is unknowable and independent of the physical world. Consequently, religious faith frees us from, rather than ties us to, false ideals and destructive idols.

Consider Christianity, for example, a religion that is philosophically mind-boggling. After all, it places enormous value both on the here and on the hereafter, and both on the individual and on community. The basic story of Christian faith tells about a person both divine and human, who died and then lived again. This is a deeply mysterious faith that cannot fit into any of the categories from which philosophy normally draws its truths. Like the other great religions, however, Christianity has a story to tell—a profound, hopeful story that is never-ending in the lives of its listeners.

The rain god of the Zapotec Indians of southern Mexico, a terra-cotta statue dating from about 500 C.E. The god is wearing a mask of the serpent, the symbol of superhuman knowledge.

For Review:

1. What is the biblical meaning of the term *heart?*
2. Why are myths not falsehoods? What is their purpose? How do myths accomplish their purpose?
3. Why did the myths of the ancient civilizations multiply and grow more complex than in preliterate times?
4. How might the histories and circumstances of Egypt, Babylonia, Greece, and Rome have shaped their particular mythologies?
5. Define the Axial Period.
6. How is philosophy related to science and theology?
7. Name and briefly describe four major philosophical movements. What value does each of them hold to as absolute?

For Reflection:

1. The word *god* originally meant "a call." How do the terms *call* or *calling* relate to the idea of revelation? (See 1 Samuel 3:1–18.)
2. Compare the Pygmy hymn on page 40 to the opening lines of John's Gospel. How do these passages, taken together, relate to the topic of this chapter?
3. Karl Marx said that "god-talk" of any kind is a human escape from a fundamentally inhuman world. What do you think Marx meant by that statement? Do you agree? Why, or why not?
4. To some degree we are all affected by the philosophies mentioned in this chapter: idealism, materialism, individualism, and collectivism. Which of them has the greatest effect on you? In what way? Which has the least effect on you? Why?
5. Every organization has a story at its heart: usually these are called *mission statements.* Try writing one for your family or for your school using the creedal or story outline form.
6. Catholic theologian John Dominic Crossan has suggested that the Christian story is a parable, not a myth. Parables are stories about surprising events that conflict with ordinary views of reality. In that way, they are the opposite of myths, which depict a particular worldview. In light of Crossan's insight, reflect for a few moments on the following passage from Saint Paul's First Letter to the Corinthians. In your mind is the Christian story more a myth or a parable?

   . . . Do you see now how God has shown up the foolishness of human wisdom?. . . while the Jews demand miracles and the Greeks look for wisdom, here are we preaching a crucified Christ; to the Jews an obstacle that they cannot get over, to the pagans madness, but to those who have been called, whether they are Jews or Greeks, a Christ who is the power and the wisdom of God. (1 Corinthians 1:20–24)

3
COMMUNITY: CREATING HARMONY OUT OF DIVERSITY

By definition, religion involves community. Within communities rituals and myths arise, and through communities they are handed on. In this chapter, we will discover that the founders of the great religions built on traditions within their cultures, bringing new meaning to their traditions. Moreover, as religions established new communities, they had to cope with diversity at both the cultural and the individual levels.

Community: Striving for the Common Good

In the fourth novel of his popular *Foundation* series, sci-fi writer Isaac Asimov tells the story of an awesome decision that one person had to make on behalf of the entire human race—which, at that point in the future, had colonized planets throughout the Milky Way galaxy.

What happened was this: The people of a planet called Gaia had developed telepathy to such an extent that they all thought as one being. Somewhat like bees in a beehive, every action of every person on Gaia was dedicated to the good of the entire planet. The Gaians had evolved to the point where they could not imagine acting otherwise. Furthermore, the resulting "world consciousness" was extremely powerful: the Gaians could reshape the destiny of the rest of the galaxy—if they thought it right to create a galaxy-wide community. Yet they left this decision to Golan Trevize, someone whom they trusted because of his innate instinct for rightness.

Trevize was offered two other options: He could choose a new galactic empire to be maintained by military strife. Or he could choose an empire based on mind manipulation, in which a council of brainy people would control the thinking of the leaders of each world.

In the end, Trevize chose the Gaian approach—but only because their reshaping of the galaxy's destiny would take centuries. Trevize figured there would be time to modify the Gaians' plans if it turned out that their idea of community in some way distorted human freedom.

Community as a group of people living in harmony is an ideal that is important to our society here and now—not just in Asimov's future world. Each coin minted in the United States, for example, includes the Latin inscription *e pluribus unum,* which translates as "one out of many." The motto suggests that the United States aims to build a nation united not only as states but as a people.

Modern society generally stands in need of community and harmony. Since the Industrial Revolution—which took people out of their homes to work at jobs in factories—close family ties and meaningful work have been missing from many people's lives. As Studs Terkel concluded in his documentary book titled *Working,* most people's jobs are "too small for their spirits."

More recently, the need to relocate at the whim of large corporations has further stressed family life. The impersonality of our high-tech culture, our high divorce rate, and our fear of crime and of the strangers among whom we travel every day—all these contribute to our feelings of alienation and loneliness. As never before, people are seeking to belong to small, personal groups in order to experience the community we all need. As described in the previous chapter, this desire for community has given rise to the strongest philosophical "ism" in the world today: Communism.

The idea of community is also at the heart of the great religions, and often it is linked with a belief in individual salvation. The creative tension between these twin goals of community and salvation shapes the course of every religion's history.

Religions Grow out of Communities

In the Axial Period, most of the great religious movements were sparked by a leader who was gifted with some profound insight about life. Each of these leaders attracted followers who, after a period of training, came to share that vision. Rituals and myths were employed to express certain beliefs, and rules were devised to achieve particular communal goals. New adherents, who joined the group through birth or choice, were initiated in the group's traditions, but they also brought unique gifts that helped to further shape the community's way of life.

Before the great religions became communities in their own rights, however, they belonged to communities—out of which they grew. None of the founders pulled a new religion out of a hat, so to speak. Rather, they were heavily influenced by the religions with which they were in contact. As a youth, for example, Muhammad was saturated with the stories and the teachings of the Jews and the Christians in the caravans in which he worked. He blended these stories with the tradition of his Arab ancestors, purging out of it those customs that he saw as destructive to his people.

Likewise, Gautama the Buddha's vision was an outgrowth of his dissatisfaction with the Hindu faith in which he had been reared. Gautama struggled with the question of how to be freed from the misery of endless rebirths—reincarnation being a traditional Hindu belief.

Even in the case of Jesus, it would be inaccurate to describe him as the first member of the Christian religion. He was, in fact, an initiated Jew in good standing. As a child he was reared in a Jewish home, and as a man he read from the Jewish Scriptures in the synagogue—a privilege afforded only to men over thirty years of age who were full members of the community.

Jesus observed the Jewish festivals and was completely knowledgeable of the many rules and rituals of Israel. When asked about the heart of the Mosaic Law, he was able instantly to identify it. His teaching and stories built on the Jewish Scriptures—especially in his use of such images as bread, water, figs, olives, leaven, vineyards, shepherds, and temple; and in his references to the commandments, to justice for the poor, and to prophetic and apocalyptic teachings.

From his own teachings we know that Jesus was keenly aware of the Pharisaic belief in resurrection, the Sadducees' inclination to politics, and the history of divorce in the Jewish tradition. In the climactic hours of his life, at the Last Supper, he was celebrating the Passover meal of his people. Thus, while Jesus' mission gave his religious community new significance, his mission derived its meaning from his community's worldview.

Communities Develop Moral Codes

While the great religions built upon developed traditions, they also established new practices that helped their followers to find salvation within the framework of some kind of community. Gradually, each religion developed a code of behavior for its followers. The Ten Commandments in the Jewish Scriptures and the eight Beatitudes of the Christian Scriptures are familiar moral codes. Similar codes are found in almost all religions. For example:

- According to the Hindu Scriptures, three cardinal virtues have existed since the beginning of time. Called the Three Da's, they are the virtues of restraint, giving, and compassion.

Top: **The tablets of the Ten Commandments, inscribed in Hebrew, from an illustration in a fourteenth-century manuscript**

Bottom: **The Babylonian king Hammurabi standing before the sun god Shamash. The top portion of a carving in rock dating from about 1760 B.C.E. Most of the surface of this large basalt block is carved with the Code of Hammurabi, the earliest written body of laws—laws of a very humane character.**

- For all Buddhists, the way to salvation is along the Eightfold Path, which includes right conduct, right means of livelihood, and right speech.
- Jainism, a religion derived from Hinduism, lays down Five Great Vows to which a person should aspire. These vows involve renunciations of killing, lying, stealing, sensuality, and property.

Later in this course we will look at the moral codes of each of the great religions. For now, just note that the particular code that a religion espouses depends very much on the special vision or revelation it pursues. For example, obedience is considered fundamental to morality in Islam because of its belief that life is closely directed by God. By the same token, spontaneity and humor are key moral tenets in Zen Buddhism, whose followers believe that the sacred is something one can stumble upon at any time.

The moral codes of most religions, unsurprisingly, lean toward community solidarity when tensions arise between that ideal and the ideal of individual freedom. This bias toward solidarity is built into the whole idea of *religion,* which term is itself derived from a Latin word that means "to bind." That is just what religion does: it binds us together with others in a shared vision of reality. And nothing demonstrates that binding together more than our moral codes.

Yet sometimes we mistakenly see religions (our own more so than others) as unchangeable and inflexible. We forget that religions are profoundly human organizations—deeply influenced by their members both as unique personalities and as products of particular cultures. The rest of this chapter is devoted to discussing how cultures and personalities affect religions.

Coping with Changing Cultures

Hinduism is probably the prime example of religious toleration: it encompasses an almost unlimited diversity of beliefs. Some Hindus acknowledge one supreme deity while others worship hundreds and even millions of gods. Yet all are legitimately members of the Hindu religion.

The great tolerance in Hinduism has its roots in its history. Hinduism had its origin in the emphasis of Indian natives on magic and sacrifices to a mother goddess. Then, beginning about 1500 B.C.E., Aryan invaders brought with them to India an elaborate system of sacrifices to the sky father, the earth mother, the sun god, and other deities. The merging of these two strains—the pre-Aryan religion with that of the conquerors—created classical Hinduism.

Later, in the Axial Period, there sprang up two protest movements—Buddhism and Jainism—that veered away from traditional Hindu practices toward new social behaviors that they believed would lead to salvation. While both of these religious movements threatened to replace Hinduism, in the end their beliefs were absorbed into Hinduism, which reemerged as the majority religion within India.

All the great religions can trace similar developments. Because religions dwell within the tides of history, they must constantly adapt in order to endure. In fact, their survival depends on the ability to cope both with social change from the outside and with calls for reform from within. For example, the followers of Judaism have been able to adapt to many Western countries without losing their identity. And Buddhism, although born in India, now pervades the Far East.

During its two-thousand-year history, Christianity has dealt with Jewish, Greek, Roman, medieval, and modern European cultures, among others. Perpetually, its double challenge has been to absorb all that is helpful in making Christianity understood and, at the same time, to free itself from those cultural elements that might stop the Church from realizing its mission. Each crisis that has been successfully overcome has made Christianity more of a world-class religion.

The question of who Jesus is, for instance, was answered in a different way according to the thought patterns of each culture. Notice that, while none of these interpretations denies the doctrine of Jesus as both human and divine, they do offer very different perspectives.

- For the first Jewish Christians, who were immersed in the Jewish tradition, Jesus was the sacrifice of the Passover, the new Israel, the new Moses, and the fulfillment of the Mosaic Law.
- At first the Christian community fully expected to remain a part of Judaism, but this was not to be. The Holy Spirit inspired the Apostles to proclaim Christianity to uncircumcised Gentiles—thus, in effect, to all peoples. The Council of Jerusalem in 70 C.E. was the beginning of adaptation. For the early Greek Christians, whose thinking was expressed in philosophical terms rather than in the concrete Semitic manner of stories and images, Christ was understood as the Logos, the divine Word, and the universal Principle of cosmic wisdom, perfection, and harmony.
- Later on—in a medieval society ridden by ignorance, plague, and war—Christology stressed the consoling notion of Jesus as the Ransom. He was the one who, at the price of his blood, bought our salvation.
- With the rise of commerce in Europe, Protestant Reformers interpreted Jesus in terms of justification. In other words, Jesus was the one who satisfied the debt of sin we owed to the Father.
- Riding on a crest of hope in human progress, the seventeenth and eighteenth centuries saw Christ as the King whose spiritual reign over the entire universe was to be established by the Christian Church.

Jesus, a statue representing him as the Good Shepherd, dating from the third century C.E.

For most of its history, Christianity was the basis for both Western culture and Western religion. Yet the effect of culture on religion (and vice versa) is often complicated by the fact that culture takes on the guise of religion in the same way that philosophies sometimes do, as was suggested in the previous chapter. The result of this masking is usually a secular or civil religion that competes with genuine religion.

Civil Religion Today

As we read the national news magazines and watch television, we find very few discussions of religious faith. In modern society, it is not fashionable to speak publicly of God's will. Many contemporary thinkers even believe that we cannot talk about what is beyond the human. Their attitude is that if science cannot answer a question, then it probably is not worth asking. Some thinkers believe that the Great Depression and the Second World War—including the murder of millions of Jews—extinguished the willingness of many people to believe in a world governed by a God of love. In our thoroughly materialistic and skeptical world, the possibility of the sacred disappears, and God is declared "dead."

If God were dead, then logically, wouldn't religion also die? Yet the innate need for religious faith lives on. Indeed, secular worldviews often begin to take on religious traits, such as worship rituals and moral codes.

Top: **Lenin's tomb in Moscow**

Bottom: **Members and relatives of members of the U.S. Professional Football Hall of Fame at "enshrinement ceremonies"**

Right: **The Lincoln Memorial in Washington, D.C.**

Facing page: **The U.S. flag and the burning cross, inseparable symbols of the Ku Klux Klan**

For example: The veneration paid to both Lenin's tomb in Moscow and the Lincoln Monument in Washington, D.C., has a religious flavor—even though the memorials symbolize contradictory values. Similarly, political figures usually deliver the benedictions at commemorative gatherings. We even have serious rituals of flag bearing and unfurling and of rising to sing the national anthem. Understanding President Reagan as the high priest of a civil religion helps to explain his enormous popularity.

As another example, consider this: According to some observers, the Super Bowl functions as a major religious festival in the United States. And, in fact, football does ritualize aggression—that is, it lays down rules in order to make the aggression less harmful and more of a celebration of skill and strength. In addition, pregame profiles of athletes often contain so much flattery and praise that they sound like passages from Greek mythology. Moreover, moments of silence commemorate former sports heroes, and special awards are given to players who may someday be "canonized" in "the Hall of Fame."

Of course, civil religion is not limited to the United States. Civil rituals in most Western societies try to blend the Judeo-Christian values with our experiences as citizens. As a result, they often blur the crucial distinction between patriotism and biblical faith. Every religion, in fact, must continually help its followers keep salvation separate from national interests.

Adapting to Diverse Personalities

Often persons from large families can cope better than those from small families with the diversity of personalities that we run into from day to day. Rubbing shoulders with many brothers and sisters in childhood frequently teaches tolerance.

Ultimately, we all have to learn to adapt to a variety of people: the shy and the aggressive, the prophets of doom and the morning backslappers. We learn by experience that people have different styles and tones: Some are practical sorts who move swiftly and brashly. Others are slower and more thoughtful. Likewise, organized types are balanced by geniuses of disorder.

In a similar way, one of the secrets of the vitality and longevity of the great religions is their ability to tolerate differing human temperaments. Let's take a few moments to look at the major types of human temperaments, which cut across the boundaries of country and culture.

Human temperaments are sometimes roughly classified into four personality types. In reality, very seldom does a person possess only one of these types. Usually an individual exhibits a combination of temperaments, although one may be dominant. For purposes of description, however, these temperaments in their pure form can be portrayed as follows:

The Choleric Personality: Persons with a choleric temperament are doers: they are determined, eager, self-disciplined, able to organize, and willing to take risks. This type of personality is geared to leadership and is oriented to the future. As with each temperament, this one has a dark side, as well as a bright side. Overly choleric persons tend to be bad-tempered, proud, and overbearing—too willing to use or abuse others in order to get the job done. Saint Paul was obviously a successful choleric person, whereas Hitler possessed a choleric personality of a hideous sort.

The Sanguine Personality: The positive qualities of the sanguine temperament include friendliness, wit, appreciation of beauty, and vitality. Sanguine persons are geared to work with other people and to celebrate the present moment. If choleric persons are doers, sanguine persons are feelers. The weaknesses of the sanguine personality include a tendency to be superficial, moody, and easily discouraged. The sanguine temperament is often shared by salespeople, entertainers, artists, and musicians.

The Melancholic Personality: Melancholic persons have the ability to concentrate, to go to the heart of things, to endure and persevere, and to remain calm amid adversity. Melancholics also have a tendency, however, to become depressed, to brood on the past, and to harbor grudges. Stressing knowing over feeling or doing, melancholics are usually above average in intelligence. Often they are contemplative, scholarly types, and they include in their ranks many philosophers and poets.

The Phlegmatic Personality: The positive qualities associated with the phlegmatic temperament include loyalty, endurance, and gentleness. Phlegmatics are unruffled by schedules, plans, or the flow of time and events. They are happy just being, apart from knowing, feeling, or doing. At their worst, phlegmatic persons tend to be lazy and to let life pass them by. Persons who develop mature phlegmatic personalities, however, can become skilled negotiators and diplomats who, with patience and kindness, soften the injurious elements of the other temperaments.

Temperaments Shape Religions

Obviously tensions will arise within religions merely because they include all of these "people types"—none of which would be considered irreligious except in their extreme forms. More important to this discussion is the fact that these temperaments also shape religions. That is, within religions, different "styles" exist that reflect these personality types.

1. Recently a theologian wrote about "the activist fundamentalism" within the Methodist Church, which is a Protestant Christian denomination. This activist view identifies spirituality with doing: the main task of Christianity is to reform the Church or to spread the gospel message throughout the world. This choleric style of religion can be brought to a negative extreme—that is, to a Christianity that is all crusade and no celebration, all Calvary and no Cana.

2. For other followers of a religion, feeling plays a larger role in faith than doing. Their religion must be emotional—an expression of body, heart, soul, and strength. While not ignoring the need for morality and education, these people regard worship and celebration as the primary means of expressing faith. Charismatic Christians and the Catholics of South and Central America exhibit this more sanguine religious style. The risk in these circumstances is that the religion will become merely an escape or entertainment—that is, religion without either a vital tradition or a moral code.

3. In every religion there are the philosophers—the scholars, the thinkers, and the theologians. Their style is to be concerned with education, with the way the doctrines are formulated, and with the danger of corrupting the tradition. For these people, it is imperative for religion to be personally and consciously owned and to be based on the solid rock of clear teaching. A carefully nurtured and deeply personal spiritual life is of utmost importance to them. The Catholic Church in North America, with its high priority on an educational system, represents this melancholic style.

The danger behind this religious style is the possibility of religion's becoming too intellectual. Just as philosophies sometimes become religions, religions can also become merely philosophies if they abandon their worship rituals, basic myths, and communal character. As was mentioned earlier, the sterile, intellectualized religion of imperial Rome led many of its citizens to search for an alternative that celebrated a real hope of salvation.

Top: **A Guatemalan Easter celebration**

Bottom: **A prison Bible class**

4. Throughout the history of Christianity, the controversy between grace and good works crops up continually. Essentially this is a debate between "be-ers" and doers. The phlegmatics argue that the moment we accept Jesus as Lord we are saved by his grace. The doers declare that we must do more than just *be* Christian; we must *act* like Christians. The Catholic Church affirms the need to do good works. Yet, ultimately, we cannot earn salvation by our deeds; salvation is the gift of a gracious God.

Adolescent Attitudes Toward Organized Religion

Usually we are born into a religion: we begin with a religious faith that is purely the product of our family experience. At some point, either in

Prominent Roles Within Religions

Depending on one's particular temperament, there are a variety of highly visible tasks that one can perform within most religions. Typically these roles include the following:

- ***Founder:*** *a witness of a revelation that establishes a new religion. God speaks; the founder hears. Legends grow up around his or her life. Founders normally declare that they are only messengers. Each has deeply devoted disciples who preach in the same spirit. No religion is ever founded by a group.*

- ***Prophet:*** *an enunciator or interpreter of a divine message imparted in visions or auditions. The prophet is summoned, sometimes against his or her will, to call people to true worship. Prophets are often persecuted and many times martyred by those to whom they were sent. Sometimes prophets are founders; sometimes they are not.*
- ***Mystic:*** *a person who seeks personal union with the divine. For example, a follower of the Yogic teachings seeks the "cessation of outward seeing for the sake of inner perception."*
- ***Priest:*** *a representative of the community empowered to watch over public worship, especially sacrifice. Priests protect the traditions of a religion. Priests either inherit their positions or are consecrated to them.*
- ***Religious:*** *monks or nuns who join together in communities that are dedicated to living out a religious vision. Religious orders often have their own founders who have established rules for communal life.*
- ***Reformer:*** *an innovator who protests practices that belie the original vision of a religion.*
- ***Theologian:*** *a scholar who studies religious faith, practice, and experience—especially the relationship of God to the world.*

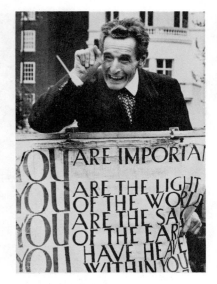

Above: **A British evangelist preaching the Gospel**

Right: **Greek Orthodox priests at a divinity school in Boston**

adolescence or in early adulthood, we begin to question the faith of our parents. We distance ourselves from their faith in order to identify our personal positions, as opposed to our parents' positions.

Just as some of us adjust to adulthood only with difficulty — in storms of emotion — while others make a more peaceful adjustment, so religious development can vary. It can occur amid traumatic upheavals of doubt and rejection, or it can take place smoothly, through gradually acquired insights. The process people go through often depends on temperament, circumstances, and training. In any case, our goal is to achieve a full experience of religious faith along with an openness to its changing nature.

To reach the goal of "owning" or becoming committed to our religion, we usually must pass through a period of searching. Included in this searching is a trying out of the different roles that are considered important in the particular religions in which we were raised. This searching period roughly corresponds to the adolescent stage of life — roughly from age thirteen to age thirty. Behind this search may be a sense of fidgeting — a sense of restlessness and discomfort.

The reasons for this fidgety feeling may not be clear even to the fidget. Sometimes a "vacation" period is needed to steady the person and to permit a more objective evaluation of his or her religious convictions.

One's entry into this searching stage is often marked by a deep need for clarification. A climate of freedom is crucial at this time to allow honest doubts and problems to surface without threat of judgment. Individuals who are genuinely searching out a new form of faith should even feel free to challenge or disagree with their religion.

Finally, some individuals may feel a need to separate completely from their religion. If the individual is being honest, even this stance must be respected. When the rich young man of the Gospel felt he could not meet the demands of Jesus' moral vision, Jesus did not try to force the youth into making a halfhearted commitment.

Some signs that one is emerging from an earlier stage of commitment include the following:

- a frustration with rules
- sharp changes in religious feeling
- a withdrawal from involvement
- rebelliousness
- an apathy toward religion
- a rejection of religious practices
- a difficulty in communicating with adults, especially those who represent religion
- an increased personal sensitivity or intensity
- painful idealism, that is, seeing easily the faults and sins of leaders and role models
- a felt need for freedom of choice
- an alternating sense of personal weakness and then strength

Among the signs that one is entering a new commitment to one's religion are these:

- an increased respect for others' sincere beliefs
- a more personal relationship with God
- a greater simplicity in religious practices and a more personal style
- an increased ability to take personal responsibility for one's religious commitment
- a greater ability to admit failure and weakness without threatening one's sense of self-worth
- more sensitivity to evil in oneself and in the world
- an increased ability for seeing the good and true in others' beliefs and views while remaining firm in one's own commitment

In summary, we can say that in order to achieve genuine community, there has to be a place in a religion for every human personality type—for the saints and the "aints," for the doers and the "don't-ers," for the heroes and the "sheroes."

Every religion includes those who sit in the stern of the ark protecting the treasures of tradition. Then there are also the upbeat, "modern" members who are way out in front on the prow of the ark. Believing in progress and impatient with tradition, they have their sights set on the future.

A wise old saying reconciles the tension between tradition and progress that is inherent in religions: "There are only two lasting things we can leave our children: one is roots, the other is wings." In every religion, the challenge is to maintain community by allowing freedom for a variety of religious styles while keeping members oriented to a common religious vision. As we now begin our study of the great religions, starting with Hinduism, we will see how powerful religious visions and styles interact with each other.

For Review:

1. How is the term *community* defined in this chapter?
2. How does Jesus' life show that he was fully committed to his community?
3. Give an example of how a moral code might be affected by a particular religious revelation.
4. What sorts of adjustments has Hinduism made in its long history? Why were the changes necessary?
5. How has our understanding of Jesus changed over the centuries?
6. What is civil religion? How does it differ from genuine religion?
7. Describe the four personality temperaments presented in this chapter. How do they correspond to the various religious styles today?

For Reflection:

1. What would you choose if you were given the options that Asimov's character had? If you could, would you choose a world of complete harmony?
2. Imagine that a friend confides that she believes in God, but that it is a private matter and no one else's business. How would you respond?
3. In what way does the following statement (from G. K. Chesterton's book *Orthodoxy*) expand upon the concept of community?

   Tradition means giving votes to the most obscure of all classes, our ancestors. It is the democracy of the dead. Tradition refuses to submit to the small and arrogant oligarchy of those who merely happen to be walking about. All democrats object to [people] being disqualified by the accident of birth; tradition objects to their being disqualified by the accident of death. . . . tradition asks us not to neglect a good man's opinion, even if he is our father.

4. Spend a few moments reflecting on the fact that Jesus was actually a Jew and not a Christian. What implications occur to you?
5. What historical image of Jesus is closest to your image? Jesus as a sacrifice? as cosmic wisdom? as a ransom? as a king?
6. Give descriptive examples of the two kinds of civil religion.
7. Which combination of the four personality types mentioned in this chapter describes you best? How does your personality shape your own style of religion?
8. Which, if any, of the signs of transition in religious commitment describe your present situation?

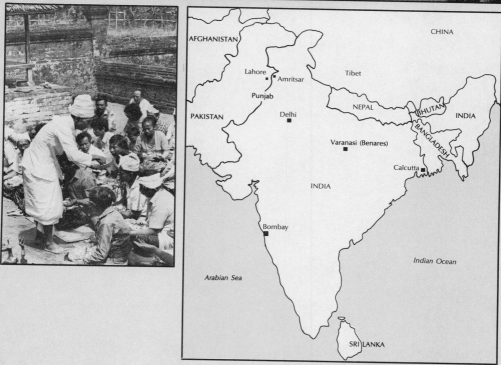

B. GREAT RELIGIONS THAT ORIGINATED IN INDIA

4
HINDUISM: REBIRTH AND RELEASE

With the recent rekindling of interest in the great Indian leader Mohandas K. Gandhi, many Westerners have wanted to know more about the religion that inspired such a spiritual giant. His stance of nonviolent resistance has stirred the imagination of a world poised for nuclear holocaust.

In this chapter we will be looking at the most ancient religion that we will study. Of the great religions, only Hinduism and Judaism predate the Axial Period. During its long history, Hinduism has become very unstructured in terms of its beliefs and practices—unlike Catholic Christianity, which is highly organized. For this reason alone, Hinduism challenges some of our fundamental ideas about religion.

Svetaketu's Father Explains Brahman

"Place this salt in water and come to me tomorrow morning."

Svetaketu did as he was commanded, and in the morning his father said to him: "Bring me the salt you put into the water last night."

Svetaketu looked into the water, but could not find [the salt], for it had dissolved.

His father then said: "Taste the water from this side. How is it?"

"It is salt."

"Taste it from the middle. How is it?"

"It is salt."

"Look for the salt again and come again to me."

The son did so, saying "I cannot see the salt. I only see water."

His father then said: "In the same way, O my son, you cannot see the Spirit. But in truth [It] is here."

An invisible and subtle essence is the Spirit of the whole universe. That is Reality. That is Truth. *Thou art That.*

(Upanishads)

In Western thought, God is referred to as a personal being who thinks and loves as we do. Historically, the masculine pronoun *he* has been used to refer to a personal God. In the Christian tradition, God is everywhere and keeps everything in existence yet remains distinct from creation.

Hinduism sees life in very different terms. In Hinduism, ultimate reality is absolute and unknowable — an impersonal *that* or *it*. The name that Hindus give to this remote, transcendental force is **Brahman:** the word means "ever-growing." Most Hindus believe that only Brahman is real; everything else is illusion (referred to as *maya*).

Brahman is like the ocean, and creatures are like drops of ocean spray, momentarily hovering above the water. They seem to possess independence, but actually they are only a momentary phase of the ocean's being, destined to return to oneness with it.

Thus, as illustrated in the above dialogue between father and son, human beings at their deepest core, or soul (called *atman*), are but temporary forms of the deity. Therefore, *atman* is Brahman and Brahman is *atman*. This belief is summed up in the ancient Hindu phrase *Tat tvam asi,* "Thou art That." Brahman is ultimate reality seen from a cosmic point of view; *atman* is the same reality seen from the personal angle.

The fundamental human problem, according to Hindu thinking, is that most people are blinded to Brahman by the illusions of this world and do not realize that this life is like a prison that separates us from reunion with Brahman. Even death will not end this imprisonment because life flows through countless rebirths. The hope of Hindus, then, is for release from *maya,* followed by union with Brahman. That this release is possible is attested to by **Krishna,** a very popular god among Hindus: "Whoso shall strive to win release from age and death, putting his trust in Me, will come to know That Brahman in Its wholeness . . ." (*Bhagavad Gita*).

The Eternal Religion

Known to its followers as "the Eternal Religion," Hinduism may indeed be the world's oldest religion. Developed over a period of five thousand years, Hinduism has evolved through three distinct historical stages. These three periods draw their names from two of the three most important writings of the Hindu Scriptures: the *Vedas* and the *Upanishads.* The third sacred book, known as the *Bhagavad Gita,* will be discussed later.

The Pre-Vedic Period (2500–1500 B.C.E.)

In the Indus Valley in northern India, a mother goddess was worshiped and sacrificed to. Evidently, this deity was a predecessor to the many goddesses worshiped in India today: each village might have its own goddess.

A horned, three-faced god was also worshiped and sacrificed to. Scholars believe that this god may represent an early form of the triad of major Hindu gods that were later worshiped separately. Hinduism in this pre-Vedic period may have also included renunciation rites and exercises similar to Yoga.

The Vedic Period (1500–600 B.C.E.)

In the middle of the second millennium B.C.E., the Aryans invaded northern India and imposed their gods and their elaborate system of sacrifices on the native residents. But the Aryans also adopted some of the aboriginal beliefs and practices.

The earliest Hindu Scriptures are the *Vedas,* which date from the period of the Aryan invasion. (The word *veda* is related to our word *video* and means "seeing" or "knowledge.") These scriptures contain simple but inspiring thoughts, myths, hymns, and prayers, as well as instruction on ways to reach liberation.

The Vedic traditions focus on this world: its rituals are aimed at maintaining a social order that will ensure for the individual a long and robust life. The afterlife is believed to be very much a continuation of earthly life.

The Upanishadic Period (from 600 B.C.E. to the present)

The word *upanishad* literally means "to sit down before" a teacher. Although they are actually the last books of the *Vedas,* the **Upanishads** promote a religious quest that is different from the here-and-now religion of the *Vedas.* The *Upanishads* seek liberation from the world. They are the earliest scriptures to advocate withdrawal from society and the use of meditation and techniques associated with **asceticism**—that is, severe exercises in self-denial.

The tension between fulfilling a social role and renouncing the world totally has been the focus of Hindu writings from the beginning of this period to the present day. More will be said about this tension later in this chapter.

Facing page: **The god Krishna**
Above: **A Hindu holy man**

An Umbrella Religion

Hinduism today is the religion of 85 percent of the nearly 700 million people of India. A **Hindu,** a person who practices Hinduism, is not to be confused with **Hindi,** the language most commonly spoken in northern India where the religion originated.

Rather than a single, unified religion, Hinduism is a reservoir of complex beliefs and practices gathered over five millennia. Highly individualized and lacking any ecclesiastical system, Hinduism is a sort of umbrella religion in the sense that it shelters so many different religious beliefs. As such, Hinduism tests the limitations of the model of religion that was presented in the first part of this course.

For example, this ancient religion contains widely different beliefs and practices—such as the protection of cows, demon worship, and the rejection of certain classes of people. Also, Hinduism has no founder, no fixed doctrines, and no common worship. As already suggested, most

Since pre-Aryan times, Hindus have worshiped a mother goddess in many different forms. She is often depicted as a fierce warrior who, like Vishnu, protects the world. The mother goddess is often described as an eternally wakeful mother who jealously guards the world as a mother lion guards her young.

In certain areas, the goddess is also worshiped in destructive, bloodthirsty forms—especially under the name of **Kali.** Kali is typically shown with a sunken stomach, signifying her insatiable hunger and thirst for blood. Kali reminds her devotees of the painfulness of the world and points them toward the path to liberation.

In contemporary Hinduism, Brahman is said to manifest itself in the form of three gods that together symbolize the cycle of existence.

- *Brahma,* the creator, is often portrayed with four faces, embracing the four points of the compass, and with four arms in which he holds the Vedas. Brahma is considered above and beyond worship, so there are few temples dedicated to him.

- *Vishnu* is the preserver of the world who is typically depicted as descending to earth in various forms called **avatars** to uphold order. The god Krishna is himself the eighth such avatar, *the human incarnation of a god. Interestingly, Gautama the Buddha—the founder of another religion—is considered the ninth* avatar *of Vishnu.*

- *Whereas Vishnu is attentive to worldly matters, the god* **Siva**—*the destroyer—is indifferent to them. His cosmic dance is invariably so wild that it results in the world's being burned to ashes. Siva is portrayed as wearing a necklace of skulls, his hair tangled and matted. Like Kali, Siva beckons humans out of the world to their liberation.*

Top: **The goddess Kali**

Bottom: **The god Siva**

Right: **A Hindu temple dedicated to the worship of Siva, dating from the tenth century** C.E.

Hindus subscribe to **monism:** that is, the belief that everything is a part of one deity, Brahman. Other Hindus, however, believe in **polytheism** and so worship up to 330 million Indian gods.

Pointing out this great diversity is not to say that Hinduism has no common basis of belief. The millions of sacred cows that are allowed to roam the cities and the countryside are reminders to Hindus of the sacredness of Brahman that runs through the universe. Cow protection, said Gandhi, is a symbol of the human obligation to protect the weak, the oppressed, and the handicapped. Indeed, the Hindu doctrine of non-violence (or *ahimsa*) flows from the belief that Brahman permeates the world: thus, to kill anything is to attack Brahman.

In the belief that no religion can claim to be the one true religion, Hindus accept all religions and object to efforts to convert people from one religion to another. Of this complicated yet tolerant religion, Gandhi once wrote:

> If I were to define the Hindu creed, I would simply say, a search after truth through nonviolent means. A man may not believe in God and still call himself a Hindu. Hinduism is relentless pursuit after truth. Denial of God we have known; denial of truth we have not known.

Left: **Sacred cows in the streets of Bombay**

Above: **A Hindu elephant god**

Karma and *Samsara:* **The Flow of Life**

Two of the key religious concepts at the foundation of Hindu belief are related to each other: *karma* and *samsara*. Under the law of *karma,* or "action," every person is born into a station in life that is merited by the deeds of his or her former life. According to this merit system, a person who performs good deeds, spiritual exercises, and meditation can be reborn

Top: **A spring festival ceremony in a private temple, attended by Hindus of the higher castes**

Bottom: **A lower-caste Hindu**

to a higher form in a future lifetime. This process of rebirth is known as *samsara,* that is, "transmigration."

To many Westerners this belief in transmigration, or **reincarnation,** is an intriguing or even humorous notion. We joke about wanting to "come back" as film stars or rock musicians. As a religious belief, however, *samsara* offers very little hope to the individual.

For one thing, according to the concept of *samsara,* a person must go through countless rebirths before achieving salvation. Moreover, if the sum of one's deeds is evil—demonstrating a rebellion against *karma* or a neglect of spiritual exercises—then the person is reduced to a lower caste, or even to the form of an animal, an insect, or a plant. Someone who steals grain, for example, may become a rat. A traditional story tells of a nagging, cranky person who was reborn as a hot pepper. The more evil one's life is, the greater the number of lower life forms the soul must pass through before achieving liberation. By some accounts, even the gods themselves eventually make mistakes and lose their divinity.

Cyclic Time

Samsara also refers to the Hindu notion of time. Periodically, after billions of years of existence, all of creation is dissolved and enters a state of suspended being when Brahman alone exists. At the end of each rest period, the world is created anew, society is reformed, and the scriptures are recomposed. Like waves washing on the shores, history repeats itself every billion or more years in never-ending cycles of creation and destruction.

For Hindus and many others in Eastern religions, time is a pool that never changes, except for slight ripples on the surface, which represent created forms coming into existence. The West, on the other hand, sees time as linear—leading to the climactic day of God's complete reign. Pierre Teilhard de Chardin stated the Catholic view of time when he wrote, "In spite of all the apparent improbabilities, we are inevitably approaching a new age in which the world will cast off its chains, to give itself up at last to the power . . . of universal love."

The Caste System and Duty

In the Vedic period of Hinduism, four main social divisions called **castes** developed. As described in the sacred texts, highest among the castes are the leaders and priests, called **Brahmins;** then come the chiefs and warriors; and third, the merchants, farmers, and artisans. The lowest caste is the servant class, and below the lowest caste are the outcastes, or Untouchables, now called the **Harijans.**

In modern India, where public discrimination against the lowest castes and outcastes is illegal, the caste system is still an integral and complex structure in society. Today there are more than three thousand rigidly fixed castes in India. Historians suggest that the caste system has helped India's many races and cultures to preserve their respective traditions.

However, the caste system is more than a convenient stratification of society based on circumstances of birth; the caste system also has religious significance. Whereas Hinduism allows great freedom of belief, its caste system imposes many restrictions on behavior: Each person is locked into the caste in which he or she was born. Escape is not possible until death. Fidelity to **dharma** (that is, duty) demands that a person submit willingly to the social status, occupation, eating habits, dress, and religious rituals prescribed for his or her caste.

In short, according to Hindu thinking, unless one achieves liberation or total union with Brahman, death is the occasion of the rebirth of the *atman* into another form. To achieve total union, a person must either be born into the Brahmin caste or undergo **moksha**—that is, the experience of release or liberation.

The ancient symbol of *om,* the most sacred *mantra* in the *Vedas*

The Hindu Paths to Salvation

The dreary prospect of passing through countless reincarnations led Hindus to the formulation of several ways to achieve *moksha*—in effect, to fly off the wheel of endless rebirths and become forever one with the world soul.

The Path of Knowledge

According to the *Upanishads,* liberation is gained by "enlightenment," although purely intellectual knowledge is not what is meant. Rather, salvation comes through an ecstatic flash of certitude that is experienced in the midst of deep meditation. Because this moment of truth involves the whole person, it has the power to transform the person. The content of this moment is the realization that Brahman and *atman* (the personal soul) are one, that the person is already divine—"Thou art That." Simultaneously comes the realization that everything else is *maya,* that is, illusion. Even the gods—except Brahman, of course—are caught in this grand illusion.

Many types of **Yoga** (from a word meaning "yoking," that is, joining of body, mind, and spirit) are described as ways to enter into deep meditation. Some Yogic techniques involve demanding ascetic disciplines that use physical and psychological methods to bring the mind to total concentration. These disciplines include strenuous exercises; scrupulous cleanliness; deep breathing; rigorous training in morality; extended concentration on complex designs, or **mandalas,** that focus attention; and the repetition of chants and **mantras.** A most sacred *mantra* involves repetition of the mystic syllable **om,** which signifies the presence of the living deity. Westerners have experimented with some of these techniques without realizing that, like the mastery of ballet or the other arts, Yoga requires long years of training.

The Path of Devotion

The favorite sacred book of the Hindus is the long poem ***Bhagavad Gita*** within the popular Indian epic, the ***Mahabharata.*** A relatively recent sacred book (written sometime between 200 B.C.E. and 300 C.E.), the *Bhagavad Gita* recounts the adventures of the well-loved god Krishna. In the course of the story, Krishna teaches the worship that most Hindus follow today. It is called ***bhakti,*** that is, "devotion" to a particular god. In this path to *moksha,* a person surrenders to a particular deity in ardent and hopeful devotion and performs acts of worship (called ***puja***) in a temple, at a wayside shrine, or before an altar at home.

Bhakti is salvation understood as a gift, not as the result of human striving. To the followers of this path of worship, the gods are seen as powerful forces rather than as victims of an illusion, as the path of knowledge teaches. Also, *bhakti* does not require the harsh and disciplined exercises found in Yoga. Speaking through one of his followers, Krishna declares:

> Right hard to see is this my form
> Which thou has seen;
> This is the form the gods themselves
> Forever crave to see.
>
> Not by the Vedas or grim ascetic practice,
> Not by the giving of alms or sacrifice
> Can I be seen in such a form
> As thou didst see Me.
>
> But by worship of love [*bhakti*] addressed to Me alone
> Can I be known and seen
> In such a form as I really am:
> [So can my lovers] enter into Me.
>
> *(Bhagavad Gita)*

The Path of Action

The ways of knowledge and devotion require either grim renunciation of the world or an escape from it into devotional ecstasy. Because some people cannot follow these extreme means, another model for reaching *moksha* has evolved—one harking back to the early, Vedic emphasis on ritual and on *dharma* (duty). While this path requires renunciation, it also allows for the fulfillment of what are considered life's legitimate desires, namely, pleasure, success, usefulness, and union with Brahman.

According to this plan, a person must fulfill his or her duties to society and only then pursue liberation through the ascetic disciplines. Designed to lead to rebirth into a higher caste or to final liberation, the way of action consists of four stages:

1. *Student*—ten to twenty years of study and the practice of chastity and other virtues and rituals under a **guru,** or teacher
2. *Householder*—marriage and faithful fulfillment of duties to family, caste, and community

Temple worship in Hinduism may predate Aryan times, going back five thousand years to the early rituals in the Indus Valley. Today Hindu worshipers prepare themselves to draw near to their gods through purification rites—including washing the feet, bathing, and dressing. The worshipers then perform their puja (acts of reverence), make requests, and share in a ritual meal. On occasion, a priest might add to the worship by reading the Vedas to those assembled. Temple worship, however, is more of an individual than a group ritual.

Worship rituals in the home vary according to class. Those of the Brahmin, or priestly, caste are the most complex. For puja, many such families set aside a room, often containing a shrine, to a favorite deity. "Twice-born" Hindus—those of the first three castes—perform their devotions, including prayers, offerings to the deity, and meditation.

Hinduism also celebrates major festivals that are linked to seasonal changes. The most popular of these is **Holi,** a spring festival dedicated to the god Krishna. During Holi, normally forbidden behavior is allowed, and people are encouraged to play the roles of those in castes above them. The many street celebrations and the practical joking might remind a Westerner of Mardi Gras or Halloween.

Divali is the joyous autumnal celebration that is considered the national festival of India. The name means literally "a garland of lights," and the festival marks the beginning of a new year. Thus, Divali is a time to celebrate a fresh start: people repaint their houses, and businesses begin new account books. Special devotion is paid to Lakshmi, the goddess of wealth and good fortune, who visits houses that are lighted by lamps. Fireworks and gift giving make Divali the favorite festival of children.

The sacred Ganges River is a symbol to Hindus of life without end: hundreds of thousands of Hindus flock to its banks daily to perform devotions. Once every twelve years a festival called **Kumbh Mela** brings as many as ten million people to northern India to worship at "Mother Ganges." The holy city of Varanasi on the Ganges is considered an especially appropriate place at which to die. After cremation, the ashes are cast upon the waters of the sacred river.

Top: **Children, garlanded and covered with ashes, performing their *puja* at the city of Varanasi**

Bottom: **The goddess Lakshmi**

Left: **A Holi ceremony at the city of Bharatpur, India**

HINDUISM   79

3. *Hermit*—sexual abstinence and retirement into solitude for meditation and prayer
4. *Spiritual pilgrim*—a return to society as a wandering ascetic, preparatory to final liberation and death

This path, it must be noted, is available to men of the three highest castes and only to men, not women. In fact, only a few people of the highest castes follow it—just as monastic life appeals only to a few in the West. The traditional role of Hindu women is to stay at home under the protection and control of a father, a brother, or a husband. As in Western societies, alternative roles for Hindu women are now becoming possible.

Hinduism and Christian Faith

Certain aspects of Hinduism resemble Western belief, but, as we have seen, the differences are many. For instance, the doctrines of reincarnation and *karma* are foreign to Western theology. Nor do Westerners find in Brahman anything resembling the God of the Bible, who knows and cares about us. Also, because creation is illusion (*maya*) and because the final aim of life is to renounce illusion, Hindus tend not to see themselves as participants with God in making the world a better place in which to live. Therefore, improving society for the good of others has a low priority among Hindu values. In short, while Christianity is a "world-transforming" religion, Hinduism is basically "world-denying."

Yet Hindu values are changing. In recent years Hinduism has shown a new face—it is more willing to become involved in the world. In the twentieth-century, leaders such as **Mohandas K. Gandhi** (1869–1948) and **Jawaharlal Nehru** (1889–1964) labored for national independence and for civil and human rights in India. The caste system is now illegal—although, like racial discrimination in the United States, it will take time to eradicate its effects.

The East, it seems, is learning from the West; and the West is enjoying the riches of the East, especially its traditions of meditation. The leaders of Vatican Council II declared:

> In Hinduism [people] explore the divine mystery and express it both in the limitless riches of myth and the accurately defined insights of philosophy. They seek release from the trials of the present life by ascetical practices, profound meditation, and recourse to God in confidence and love.

Offshoots of Hinduism

As might be expected of a religion as ancient and tolerant as Hinduism, it has produced many sects. Among the reform movements that sprang up from it were Buddhism, which grew to rival Hinduism in its number of adherents, and Jainism, which remains under the umbrella of Hinduism. A third religious movement, Sikhism, grew out of the clash of Hinduism with another titanic religion—Islam.

Top: **A Hindu holy man lying on thorns, in the city of Varanasi**

Bottom: **A temple dedicated to Siva in the town of Khajuraho, India**

Mahatma Gandhi

*The basic beliefs of modern Hinduism are well portrayed in the life of **Mohandas K. Gandhi,** called by his followers* Mahatma, *that is, "the great soul." Born in 1869, Gandhi spent most of his life attempting to live out the teachings of the* Bhagavad Gita—*the part of the Hindu Scriptures that he cherished above all.*

In the Bhagavad Gita, *the god Krishna teaches that renunciation of the world does not mean abandonment of it. Rather, true renunciation is the surrender of selfish actions. Acting for the good of society or God, and not oneself, allows the true self to shine forth.*

The principles of nonviolence and fearlessness characterized all of Gandhi's campaigns, which began with his defense of the civil rights of Indians who were living in South Africa.

During his years in South Africa, Gandhi also worked on behalf of the Untouchables, or Harijans. From that time until his death, Gandhi made the abolition of untouchability one of his major concerns. Gandhi involved Harijans in the communes that he established, stayed with them when traveling, and conducted campaigns to improve their situation.

Above: **Mohandas K. Gandhi**
Left: **Nehru and Gandhi in 1942**

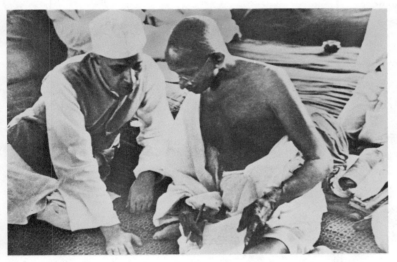

At the age of forty-five, Gandhi returned to India to help in its struggle to secure independence from British rule. However, when India finally became free in 1947, Gandhi found no respite: Hindus and Muslims could not agree to live in a united India. The two nations of India and Pakistan were created amid murderous riots that cost the lives of tens of thousands of Indians. Gandhi himself was the victim of a Hindu fanatic and died in 1948.

Gandhi summarized his life efforts in this way:

> *The immediate service of all human beings becomes a necessary part [of our endeavors] simply because the only way to find God is to see Him in His creation and be one with it. . . . If I could persuade myself that I should find Him in a Himalayan cave I would proceed there immediately. But I know that I cannot find Him apart from humanity.* (All Men Are Brothers)

Sankara and Buddhism

Since the next chapter will focus on Buddhism, not much will be said here about that religion. What is worth noting, however, is the effect that the rise of Buddhism had on Hinduism itself—as seen in the teachings of the brilliant philosopher **Sankara** (c. 700–c. 750 c.e.).

The Hindu story of the salt and water with which this chapter began is a simple summary of the teaching of Sankara—a teaching that stressed the deep-seated illusions that persist among people. Salvation, according to Sankara, is achieved only by the profound and personal recognition of the unity of Brahman (the cosmic Self) and *atman* (the personal self). Sankara's school of thought became dominant among those Hindus who taught the "path of knowledge."

Sankara's commentaries on the *Upanishads* and his public debates with proponents of different theologies—including Buddhism and Jainism—reconverted many people to Hinduism and possibly spelled the end of Buddhism within India. Interestingly, Sankara's teachings themselves include borrowings from Buddhism. For this reason, many Hindu teachers who came after Sankara felt that his teachings were not genuine, or orthodox, Hinduism.

A Jain temple in Calcutta

Jainism

Founded by **Mahavira** (c. 599–527 b.c.e.), **Jainism** arose in northern India during the Axial Period, which produced so many other spiritual and intellectual developments. Mahavira (which, literally translated, means "the great hero") claimed to be the last of twenty-four *Tirthankaras* (that is, "pathmakers"), who have planted the seeds of Jainism.

Today there are two million Jains in India. The southern sect of Jains, the "sky-clad," require their monks to go about nearly naked—as did Mahavira—to signify their renunciation of all things. Jains of the northern sect are called "white-clad" because, by the first century c.e., they had abandoned the practice of nudity. Also, the northern sect believes that it is possible for women to find salvation, while the southern sect does not.

Jains are best known for their strong opposition to the caste system and for their radical reverence for life. Some Jains, for instance, carry strainers to catch insects that may fall into what they drink. Some also examine their food carefully in order to prevent any living thing from being harmed as they eat. Other Jains carry a broom to sweep their paths so as not to step on insects. Under the mandate to "hurt no one," the Jains have such compassion for all living things that they build asylums and rest homes for aged and diseased animals. Jainism's teaching of nonviolence *(ahimsa)* was later embraced by Hinduism.

To the Jains, all things are separated into two categories: living matter possessed of soul and nonliving matter. All individual life forms were once pure souls, but they became filled with the "fine dust" of *karma*. Salvation consists in the removal of this karmic dust so that the soul with its natural lightness can float free. To accomplish this, one must acquire the Three Jewels:

- **right knowledge** — that is, knowing the Jainist creed
- **right faith** — believing this creed
- **right conduct** — following the creed, the foremost obligation being nonviolence

As you might have guessed from what has been said about their beliefs, Jains are vegetarians, and certain occupations — such as farming — are forbidden because they result in the death of living things. Ascetical practices, truthfulness, honesty, chastity, and detachment are other rules of right conduct.

Sikhism

Even many Westerners recognize the turbaned Indian as a **Sikh,** although followers of this sect number only six to eight million. **Sikhism** was founded by **Guru Nanak** (1469–1539 C.E.), a Hindu born into the ruler-warrior caste in northern India. Sikhism originated two thousand years after Jainism and about the same time as the Protestant Reformation.

In his mid-thirties, Nanak abandoned his family to absorb himself in prayer, fasting, and meditation. He was influenced by Muslims who migrated to India, but his movement — possibly an attempt to bridge Hinduism and Islam — was also a fresh start inspired by an apparition that Guru Nanak received of "The True Name." Nanak's followers believe he was charged with a redemptive mission to convert Muslims and Hindus to a more socially responsible faith.

While keeping the Hindu concepts of reincarnation and *karma*, Guru Nanak rejected the concept of nonviolence and accepted the Muslim idea of submission to one God. Hindu and Muslim ritualism was replaced by the need for obedience to the divinely directed human gurus of which Nanak was the first, followed by nine others.

The fifth Sikh guru, **Arjun** (1563–1606 C.E.), is especially important because he compiled a Sikh "Bible" of the poems, the prayers, and the wisdom of former gurus and other writers. These scriptures later became known as the *Guru Granth.*

The last five gurus gave Sikhism a military turn. The tenth and last

Top: **The Golden Temple at Amritsar, in the Indian province of Punjab, the most sacred Sikh shrine**

Bottom: **A Sikh working in the community kitchen of the Golden Temple**

Sikh guru, **Gobind Singh** (1666–1708 C.E.), instituted a military order that instantly raised men of any caste to free and fearless soldiers. After a baptism of the sword, they were pledged to worship one invisible God, to reverence the *Guru Granth,* and to perform ascetical practices. They were also charged to wear henceforth the five *k*'s:

- the *kesh*—long, uncut hair on one's head and chin
- the *kangha*—a comb
- the *kaccha*—short pants
- the *kara*—a steel bracelet
- the *kirpan*—a dagger

Although historically some Sikhs have remained more peaceful, it was with the aid of militant Sikhs that the Mogul Empire of India was overthrown in 1849. Today these "Pure of God" are still renowned as outstanding soldiers.

The high court building in Lahore, in the Pakistani province of Punjab

Despite the Sikhs' renunciation of idolatry, they worship the *Granth* as their "royal guru"—even though only learned scholars can read its difficult poetic forms, special scripts, and many archaic languages. Sikhs also observe special days and ceremonies for such events as initiations, marriages, and funerals.

At the formation of Pakistan, 2.5 million Sikhs were forced to leave their holy places, such as the birthplace of Nanak. Although they now enjoy a semblance of statehood in the Punjab, unrest among militant Sikh groups led to the 1984 assassination of Indira Gandhi, the prime minister of India.

For Review:

1. What is the Hindu concept of ultimate reality? of the world?
2. Why are cows and other living things considered sacred in India?
3. What is the law of *karma?* What is the Indian notion of reincarnation (*samsara*)?
4. Describe the caste system. How is it more than a convenient division of society?
5. What is Hindu salvation? What is the main hindrance to attaining it?
6. Explain briefly the concept of *bhakti*.
7. Name the life stages in the path of action.
8. How is Hinduism different from the Judeo-Christian tradition?
9. What is Jainism, and how has it influenced Hinduism?
10. What two religions does Sikhism attempt to bridge?

For Reflection:

1. Look back at the brief summaries of influential philosophies in chapter 2 (pages 46–47, 49). Which of these philosophies is most closely aligned with Hindu thought? Why?

2. Gandhi defined Hinduism as a search for truth through nonviolent means. How would you define Christianity?

3. In what ways do the Hindu paths to salvation resemble the religious styles outlined in the previous chapter on community?

4. What does Hinduism teach in contrast to each of the following Christian beliefs?
   a. God is one and dwells in us by the Holy Spirit.
   b. God is our Father.
   c. The Incarnation of Christ affirms the great dignity of each person.
   d. Creation is good, though flawed. We have the responsibility to heal it.
   e. We are all sinners, but Jesus has reconciled the world to God.
   f. Each person is given but one life in which to work out his or her salvation.
   g. No one can become united with God except through Christ.
   h. Christ is the clearest revelation of God to the world.
   i. Time will end with the Second Coming of Christ.

5. Reflect on how this prayer from the *Upanishads* expresses Hindu faith.

   Out of unreality
      lead us into reality.
   Out of darkness
      lead us into light.
   From death
      lead us into immortality.

6. The following story comes from the *bhakti* tradition (the path of devotion). In light of it, reflect on our Christian understanding of grace.

   In the Middle Ages, there was a long dispute between the "cat" and the "monkey" schools. The cat school thought that the relationship between the individual and God is like that of a kitten to its mother. That is, the mother transports the little one around by the scruff of the neck. In the same way, God takes the individual from here to eternity: salvation is by God's grace alone. But the monkey school saw things differently. The mother monkey carries her little one on her hip: the little one has to do something, to cling to the mother's waist. Similarly, we cling to God, and God effects our salvation.

5
BUDDHISM:
ENLIGHTENMENT AND *NIRVANA*

Just as Protestantism is an offshoot of Catholicism, so Buddhism is the most important of the thousands of offshoots of Hinduism. After Christianity and Islam, Buddhism may be the largest religion in the world, with about 500 million followers currently. And, next to Hinduism and Judaism, it is the oldest of the great religions that we will study in this course.

Buddhism was not "discovered" by Westerners until the middle of this century when the head Buddhist monk of Tibet, the Dalai Lama, was sent into exile by Chinese Communists. Later, in Vietnam, the Buddhist monks who set themselves afire to protest religious discrimination captured the attention of the Western public. More recently, the Japanese form of Buddhism called Zen has gained popularity in the West.

The Buddhist Prodigal Son

Once upon a time, a young man left home soon after reaching adulthood. He wandered about for perhaps thirty years, and the older he got, the more needy he became. Eventually he returned to his own country a beggar.

In the meantime, the man's father had changed his name, made good in business, and amassed great wealth. Yet during all those years he wanted nothing more than to bequeath his business and wealth to his long-lost son.

Now one day the son arrived, begging at his father's own gate. He saw his father—whom he did not recognize—seated on a luxurious couch, dressed in great finery. The son tried to sneak away unnoticed because he was worried that this rich lord might force him into slavery.

The father, however, recognized this beggar as his own son and sent his servants to bring him back. The servants dragged the son back to the estate. Out of sheer terror, the son fainted.

Now the father saw that he must proceed gently in this matter. So he ordered his servants to release the younger man and to give him his freedom. Naturally the son, who thought he had been enslaved, was overjoyed.

Later the father sent servants to persuade his son—without telling the son who he was—to take a job on the estate. The work was dirty—

shoveling manure and garbage. But because the wages were good, the son agreed.

Then, disguised as a supervisor in old clothes, the rich man visited his son. He told the younger man that he would adopt him as his son, giving him a new name. The son thought this was all quite wonderful, but still he saw himself as a humble hireling.

Twenty years passed, during which the son grew in confidence. Eventually he was promoted to the position of accountant in charge of the older man's affairs. In that position, he became familiar with his father's business and wealth. Yet, while the son was delighted with his new role, he still had no idea of his true identity and that all of this wealth would someday belong to him.

Finally, nearing his death, the father summoned his son and publicly announced that this was indeed his son. The son, who earlier could not have coped with such wealth, now took up his position with great skill.

The Buddha, a Chinese wooden statue dating from the seventeenth century C.E.

This story is among the most famous of Buddhist writings. Because of its similarity to the Christian parable (Luke 15:11–32), it is sometimes referred to as "the Buddhist parable of the prodigal son." Both the Christian and the Buddhist versions depict a generous and loving father who welcomed his maverick son back home. Yet beyond that, the messages of the two stories differ greatly.

For instance: The Buddhist story focuses as much on the son's confused identity as on his degradation. At different times, the son saw himself as a beggar, a slave, and a hireling—but he never knew who he really was. Like the son in the story, say Buddhists, people are confused because their minds are mired in trivial matters, referred to in the story as manure shoveling. As a result, people are in need of profound enlightenment.

Moreover, where the Christian story moves quickly to the joyous ending, the Buddhist version stresses the time and patience that the father invested in enlightening his son. This emphasis is in line with the Buddhist belief in moderation: Good fortune can be as dangerous to us as bad fortune when we are not prepared for it. For instance, we often read of bitter results when people win million-dollar lotteries or suddenly become wealthy as sports heroes or rock stars.

Finally, the two stories differ on the identity of the father. We Christians usually identify the father with the loving, forgiving God of the Bible. The father in the Buddhist version, however, is clearly the Buddha, who generously and wisely guides his followers into possession of the riches that the Buddha acquired in his lifetime.

The question remains: what are these riches that the Buddha has bequeathed to his many millions of followers? To find that out, we must begin where the Buddha himself began—that is, in India and within Hinduism.

Who Was the Buddha?

A Rich Young Man

Over 2,500 years ago, a Hindu named **Siddhartha Gautama** (c. 563–c. 483 B.C.E.) was born into the wealthy warrior caste in Nepal. His father was the chief of the Sakya people, who lived in the foothills of the Himalayas.

Tradition has it that a wise, old Brahmin at the court predicted that the child would become either a world emperor or a world savior. Gautama's father preferred the idea of his son's being an emperor. Yet he feared that if the gifted boy saw the suffering in the world, he would be moved by compassion and so would choose to save rather than to rule. Consequently, his father built for Gautama glorious palaces filled with every delight imaginable, from chariots to dancing girls.

In these circumstances, Gautama got married and raised a healthy son. Even delight has its limits, however. Inevitably the prince began taking trips into a nearby city. There, for the first time in his life, he encountered human suffering in three forms: an old man, a very sick person covered with sores, and a corpse. To his questions about these unsettling sights, Gautama's companion could only respond with infinite sadness: "Yes, master, there is no escape. Old age, sickness, death—such is the lot of all people."

A Devout Hindu Ascetic

While legends have built up around Gautama's life, it seems clear that he was tormented by the questions about life and death that have troubled many people. As a result, at the age of twenty-nine, he left his family and his inheritance to take up Yogic disciplines in search of answers to his questions.

Gautama's decision to leave his family may be somewhat shocking to us. Yet we must remember that the decision to become a hermit or holy man was supported by Hindu tradition. Also, in Jesus' own words, we Christians find a similar example of apparent heartlessness: "If any man comes to me without hating his father, mother, wife, children, brothers, sisters, yes and his own life too, he cannot be my disciple" (Luke 14:26).

For six years Gautama practiced harsh and rigorous Hindu disciplines, but without success. At the end of this time, at the very brink of death from denial of his physical needs, Gautama realized that if his goal was to gain answers to the great human questions, then he had only one instrument with which to gain those answers—namely, his mind and heart, housed in his body. How could he attain his goal, he asked himself, if he abused the only instrument that could aid him?

The Enlightened One

Gautama thus abandoned the traditional, ascetic methods and vowed to meditate until he achieved enlightenment. Sitting beneath a fig tree, Gautama finally came to a profound moral and intellectual experience. As a result, he became known as **the Buddha,** a title that means "the enlightened one."

His personal mission fulfilled, Gautama was torn between remaining in blissful meditation until his death and teaching others to escape from the chain of rebirths. Out of compassion, he stayed to instruct five companions—the first Buddhist monastic order. (While skeptical of the practice, Gautama was persuaded to admit women to his order.) Afterward, for forty-five years he traveled India, sharing his insights. When Gautama finally died at the age of eighty, legend says that his departure was accompanied by an earthquake.

The Teachings of the Buddha

What Gautama realized during his meditation under the fig tree is contained in his famous first sermon, given in the holy city of Varanasi to his five companions. This sermon is considered the clearest summary of all that Gautama taught and stood for.

Two extremes, monks, are not to be approached by him who has withdrawn from the world. Which two? One is that which is linked and connected with lust, through sensuous pleasures, because it is low, of the uncultured, of the mediocre man, ignoble and profitless. The other is that which is connected with mortification and asceticism, because it is painful, ignoble, incapable of achieving the target. Avoiding both these extremes, monks, take the Middle Path, . . . which brings insight, brings knowledge, and leads to tranquility, to full knowledge, to full enlightenment, to *Nirvana*. . . .

Now monks, this is the [First] Noble Truth as to sorrow. Birth [earthly existence] indeed is sorrowful. Disease, death, union with the unpleasing, separation from the pleasing is sorrowful; in brief, desirous transient individuality . . . is sorrowful.

Again, monks, this is the [Second] Noble Truth as to the origin of sorrow. It is the recurring greed, associated with enjoyment and desire and seeking pleasure everywhere, which is the cause of this sorrow. In other words, it is the greed for sense-pleasure, greed for individual existence. . . .

Again, monks, this is the [Third] Noble Truth as to the cessation of sorrow. . . . [It is] the complete cessation, giving up, abandoning, release and detachment from greed.

And this once more, monks, is the [Fourth] Noble Truth as to the path to the cessation of sorrow. It is indeed that Noble Eightfold Path: right understanding, right thought, right speech, right action, right livelihood, right effort, right mindfulness, right concentration. The Middle Path, monks, leads to *Nirvana.*

As soon, monks, as my knowledge and sight concerning these four Noble Truths became complete, I knew that I had attained supreme and full enlightenment. I became aware and fully convinced that my mind was liberated, that existence in its unhappy form had ended, that there would no longer be an unhappy survival. (*Vinaya Pitaka*)

The Middle Path

In his first sermon, Gautama defined a middle road to salvation between sensuality and asceticism. This stance may seem like a compromise of a sort. Actually, in setting up the **Middle Path,** Gautama immediately identified his position as a revolutionary one in the history of religion.

The revolutionary nature of Gautama's Middle Path does not come from his rejection of sensuality: there was nothing new in a religion's warning people to avoid excessive pleasure seeking. What was revolutionary was the Buddha's rejection of asceticism, which from time immemorial had been a religiously sanctioned and socially approved route to salvation. Even today the popular belief in most religions is that greater self-denial

Top: **Gautama and his disciples, a sculpture dating from the second century B.C.E.**

Bottom: **The Dhamek Stupa, a shrine just outside Varanasi that marks the site of Gautama's first sermon**

implies greater holiness. For Gautama, however, the way to salvation lay through intelligence, and both excessive pleasure and self-denial blunt the mind.

Hard on the heels of this rejection of self-denial came a rejection both of worship and of any talk about gods. Note that no deity is mentioned in the first sermon, nor is worship numbered in the Eightfold Path.

Scholars have suggested that Gautama himself did not reject the gods. Rather, his focus was the salvation of people, and any talk about gods seemed to him to distract from that endeavor. Gautama might be described as an early **humanist** — that is, someone who is concerned with human problems rather than religious questions.

When asked about the meaning of life or about the origin of the universe, Gautama usually maintained a "noble silence." Occasionally, he would offer this parable by way of a reply: A man was once hiking through a jungle. Halfway through it he was hit by a poisoned arrow. If the arrow remained in him, he would die. Yet the injured man thought, "I will not pull out this arrow until I know who shot it, whether he is tall or short, fat or lean, young or old, of a high caste or a low caste."

Besides avoiding "god talk," Gautama also rejected Hindu worship. On this point, however, Gautama was not merely indifferent. Although Gautama accepted *karma* as the law of life, he rejected the idea that a person had to pass through innumerable rebirths to reach the priestly, or Brahmin, caste before gaining salvation. Instead, Gautama taught that people could reach salvation within their lifetimes. In this regard, Buddhism has a more optimistic worldview than Hinduism.

Gautama's rejection of worship and of inevitable rebirth naturally put him at odds with the Brahmin caste, which officiated at Hindu worship rites. In the long run, a lack of support among Brahmins for Gautama's ideas contributed to the failure of Buddhism within India.

Nirvana

Perhaps the most challenging of Gautama's teachings was that the soul (*atman*) does not exist. While Hindus taught that the *atman* was really God, Gautama took the concept one logical, yet radical, step further. (You may have thought about this yourself when studying Hinduism.) Gautama taught that if the soul is purely God, then it is not a soul in an individual sense at all. Instead, it is *an-atman* or "no soul."

According to Buddhist thought, the problem is this: The "bundle" of mixed feelings, faulty perceptions, confused consciousness, and impulses that fill one's life desperately wants to claim selfhood for itself. And this desire for a false kind of selfhood is at the root of all the suffering that one encounters in life. Once people have let go of the yearning for false selfhood — along with other desires — they will achieve liberation in the form of **nirvana,** which means "extinguished" or "quenched." Paradoxically, *extinguishment* and *enlightenment* occur simultaneously.

Rephrased from Gautama's sermon, the **Four Noble Truths** that lead to this conclusion are listed here:

1. All life involves *suffering*.
2. Suffering results from desire or *greed*, especially for pleasure, prosperity, and the continued existence of a false sense of self.
3. Suffering ceases with one's *enlightenment*.
4. The cure for suffering and the way to enlightenment lies in understanding these truths and in following the *Eightfold Path*.

Is Gautama's teaching utterly pessimistic—as many people have accused it of being? The answer depends partly on one's viewpoint regarding suffering. Buddhists believe that their teachings are realistic, not pessimistic. In other words, they see suffering as the overriding truth about life. As the leaders of Vatican Council II stated approvingly: "Buddhism . . . testifies to the essential inadequacy of this changing world." Yet, by comparison, we Christians view life more hopefully—no doubt optimistically from the Buddhist viewpoint. In Christian faith, suffering and sin will ultimately be overwhelmed by the greater reality of God's grace. God's Kingdom will thus be established on earth, and our lives will end in glorified selfhood.

To be fair, however, Gautama did not merely teach that we suffer and then die—that would certainly be pessimistic. Instead, he taught a way out of suffering, and he described *nirvana* as a blissful experience. Gautama often compared *nirvana* not to a flame being blown out but to a flame (meaning, oneself) losing itself in another flame (that is, total being).

Top and bottom: **The Buddha, a gigantic statue in a shrine in Burma portraying Gautama in a very lifelike manner and in a lying position**

The Eightfold Path

Of the Four Noble Truths, the most important by far is the fourth, which contains the Eightfold Path. In it Gautama revealed the moral code that leads to *nirvana:*

1. **Right Understanding:** Life is understood as changing and painful. Also, the self as we falsely understand it—especially its desires—must be rejected.
2. **Right Thoughts:** Gautama explained these as including thoughts of renunciation, goodwill, and "nonharming."
3. **Right Speech:** Right speech necessarily follows right thought. Thus, one must avoid lies, slander, gossip, and harsh words.
4. **Right Action:** The requirements contained here are familiar to Christians and Jews, that is, refraining from killing, stealing, and harmful sexual behavior.
5. **Right Means of Livelihood:** Most religions make worship and the priesthood central to gaining salvation. For Gautama, liberation lay in dealing morally with the tasks of daily life, not in temple rituals. To be avoided are jobs having to do with the sale of weapons, the slaughter of animals, or the production of intoxicating drinks. "Earning without disserving" is the motto behind this component of the path.
6. **Right Effort:** In Gautama's teachings, impulses and false understanding of the self generate feelings of greed and violence. Thus, relentless effort is required in order to attain the "Buddha-wisdom."
7. **Right Mindfulness:** This includes attention to whatever is being done at the moment, to the ever-changing realities of life, and to one's inner impulses and motives.
8. **Right Concentration:** People who concentrate on right goals will not be distracted or preoccupied by useless details or unworthy thoughts. Meditation techniques help to calm the mind, to widen its vision, and to focus it on right goals.

Because they represent aspects of meditation—which was the key to Gautama's own enlightenment—the last three parts of the Eightfold Path are at the heart of Buddhism. As it became a religion, spread throughout Asia, and developed in new directions, meditation remained Buddhism's central path to enlightenment.

The eight-spoked wheel, the Buddhist symbol of the Eightfold Path

Buddhism's Early History

When Gautama died, the teachings that he left behind could hardly have been considered the basis for a religion. After all, he implied that the gods were irrelevant, and he denied the necessity of worship, scriptures, temples, and priests.

However, Gautama also left behind a community of monks and nuns, the first *sangha,* to carry on his message. This was no small gift in addition to the teachings that he bequeathed. Historically, Buddhism has been centered on these *sanghas*—small communities quietly dwelling in society, providing guidance to those who seek it. Buddhists believe that it is in these communities that one learns to recognize and to renounce false selfhood. Throughout its history, the *sangha* has remained the primary institution within Buddhism. Usually no national structure exists, nor does Buddhism possess an international ecclesiastical structure like that of the Catholic Church.

The first *sangha* must have been a special group of intelligent and disciplined persons. Yet, as in the case of almost every new religion, Gautama's followers were soon fighting over the meaning of his teachings. According to one tradition, the first dispute occurred the day after Gautama's death, about 483 B.C.E. Within a year, his followers were forced to call a council that attempted, unsuccessfully, to settle disputes among several factions.

In 390 B.C.E., a second council was called, during which the majority of Buddhists were declared to be heretics by a minority group. It was at this early point in its history that Buddhism divided into two major forms: the more orthodox or stricter wing known as **Theravada** (that is, "the tradition of the elders") and the larger, more liberal form known primarily as **Mahayana** ("the larger vehicle"). We will discuss these two forms of Buddhism in the next two sections.

A crucial third council was called in 253 B.C.E. by **Asoka,** the emperor of India and a patron of the Buddhists. The support of Asoka has been considered as important to Buddhism in Asia as the conversion of Constantine the Great was to Christianity in the West. Asoka may, in fact, be credited with having made Buddhism a world religion. At the council that he convened, for instance, an authoritative canon of the Buddhist Scriptures was drawn up. In addition, Asoka sent missionaries outside India to Sri Lanka, Egypt, southeastern Asia, and perhaps to Syria and Greece. In doing so, Asoka surely preserved Buddhism, for by the time that it finally disappeared from India, following the Muslim conquest of India, Buddhism was firmly established in other countries.

Theravada Buddhism: Monasteries and Meditation

As mentioned, early Buddhism developed into two main divisions, Theravada and Mahayana, the latter of which became the more successful missionary form of Buddhism. Let's look briefly at the Theravada tradition first.

Theravada Buddhism is the more conservative of these traditions and is found in the southern Asian nations, including Sri Lanka, Burma, Thailand, Kampuchea, and Laos. Sri Lanka, in particular, provides a rough model of early Buddhism, for Sri Lanka was converted to Buddhism early on and has escaped the conquests and turmoil that have plagued other Buddhist countries.

According to the Theravada model of Buddhism, people must work out their own salvations without help from gods or other divine forces. The main task of each person is acquiring wisdom through meditation,

Top: **Young Theravada Buddhist monks at a monastery in Bangkok, Thailand**

Bottom: **A Burmese Buddhist monk**

for he or she is to imitate the Buddha, who entered *nirvana* by this path. Thus, the lives of monks and nuns are considered ideal because they can spend most of their time learning to meditate. The ultimate goal is to follow the Eightfold Path and to become an **arhat**—that is, a saint who has tasted *nirvana* and who only waits for death when he or she will achieve it fully.

Note well, however, that *nirvana* remains a remote goal for most Buddhists, even for monks and nuns. The great majority of Buddhists are very likely more interested in pursuing community matters and monastic concerns than in attempting continuous meditation.

In Burma and Thailand, young men traditionally spend several months in a monastery. At a ceremonial initiation they have their heads shaved and are given new names, yellow robes, and begging bowls. This experience introduces the young men to the religious life and also serves as an initiation into manhood. A man will not marry until after he has served as a monk, and as an adult his closest friends are likely to be those with whom he had lived at the monastery. Older men often enter a monastery after their children are grown. In all, nearly one million Buddhists live as monks and nuns—although they may return to society at any time.

Lay Buddhists visit the temples for instruction, meditation, and private devotions to golden statues of the Buddha. Although the people sometimes chant when gathered together before an image of the Buddha, there is little common ritual. However, holy days and other festivals are commonly celebrated each month. Furthermore, relics of the life of the Buddha are important to Theravadins: his bones and possessions have become venerated objects. To win merit, the laypeople support the monasteries. If they cannot join the *sangha,* however, they cannot hope to become saints in their present lives.

Besides its emphasis on meditation and on monasticism, the Theravada tradition retains some of the early attitudes of Buddhism in other ways:

- The Theravadins accept as authoritative only the early Pali Scriptures, called the *Tripitaka,* or "Three Baskets." These are writings that deal with the Buddha's teachings, with monastic rules, and with spiritual instruction.
- In the Theravada tradition, the Buddha is the "thus gone"—that is, he is unavailable to his followers on earth other than through his teachings and through meditation on his image.
- While Theravada Buddhism has been tolerant of other people's deities and practices, it has not been quick to embrace them. As a result, the Theravada tradition did not become as strong a missionary force as did the Mahayana tradition.

Mahayana Buddhism: Deities and Devotions

Mahayana—northern, liberal—Buddhism is found in China, Japan, Korea, Tibet, and Vietnam. In each of these countries Buddhism has been a powerful civilizing force. In turn, each of these countries has changed Buddhism,

A young monk with his begging bowl

Buddhist Temple Art

In the early days of Buddhist art, the Buddha himself was not represented. Images of the fig tree that Gautama sat under, of his disciples, or perhaps of his footprints were to be found, but no images of the Buddha. Scholars speculate that the absence of his image was itself a way of representing his disappearance into nirvana.

Later, Buddhist artists began to depict Gautama directly and forcefully in giant statues. Many of these sculptures are reminiscent of Greek art—and for good reason. Following the conquests of Alexander the Great in northern India, Greek art made a deep impression on Indian schools of art. As a result, some of the statues of the Buddha offer a strikingly beautiful synthesis of Eastern and Western artistic qualities.

Ordinarily, the statues depict the Buddha in one of three postures, namely, a sitting position, representing his enlightenment; a standing or walking position, reminding the followers of his teaching; and a lying position, suggesting his passing over into nirvana.

In the countries of the Theravada tradition, a single statue of the Buddha or perhaps a relic is found in a stupa—that is, shrine—or temple. In Mahayana countries, on the other hand, the temples are filled with many statues of the Buddha or with statues of bodhisattvas—both male and female.

Many Westerners have been profoundly affected by the ancient stone statues of the Buddha found in Sri Lanka. Among them was Thomas Merton, who described his reaction in his Asian Journal.

> Looking at these figures I was suddenly, almost forcibly, jerked clean out of the habitual, half-tired vision of things. . . . The rock, all matter, all life, is charged with [the Buddha Truth] . . . everything is emptiness and everything is compassion. I don't know when in my life I have ever had such a sense of beauty and spiritual validity running together in one aesthetic illumination.

Top: **The Buddha, a Japanese wooden bust dating from the twelfth century** C.E.

Bottom: **The Angkor Ruins, a Buddhist place of pilgrimage in Kampuchea dating from 1100** C.E.

each developing a special, national form of the religion. Zen Buddhism, which we will look at shortly, is one of these national forms.

The Mahayana tradition first appeared about a hundred years after Gautama's death. Its earliest disputes with Theravada Buddhism centered on the following issues:

- The Mahayana Buddhists wanted to admit laypeople to meetings.
- They also wanted to reconcile Buddhism with the popular religious practices of the time.
- Lastly, the Mahayanists taught that the Buddha was himself a kind of deity or a perfectly compassionate being who came to earth to teach people about salvation. Mahayanists considered the Theravadins too self-concerned and uncompassionate.

The more open stance that lay behind these issues led the Mahayanists to develop a form of Buddhism that was more inclusive, accommodating, and universal in its appeal.

For example: The Mahayanists came to believe that, in addition to what Gautama had taught his disciples openly, he taught many other principles in secret, which had been kept hidden, awaiting a time when they would be needed. Of course, this belief opened the door to many new teachings. Eventually, it led to the creation of scriptures called *sutras,* which were written over the course of several centuries, adding up to a hundred times the bulk of our Bible. The clear mark of a Mahayanist is the acceptance of these *sutra* scriptures—rather than of any particular Buddhist teaching.

Also, according to the Mahayanists, the wisdom that the Buddha brought to earth with him was available to everyone everywhere. Thus, everyone was seen as a "Buddha-in-the-making." Any workable means of attaining the Buddha-wisdom became acceptable. Besides the meditation techniques found in Theravada Buddhism, Mahayana employed many other methods, ranging from devotional practices to chanting to folk magic.

While Gautama himself was unconcerned with gods and opposed to worship, the Mahayanists went on to develop practices centered on worshiping Gautama the Buddha—and many other Buddhas besides. Temples were built, priests were trained, and systems of worship were established. The emergence of worship and of many deities within Buddhism was crucial to its missionary efforts. Potential converts did not have to give up their old gods; these gods could be reinterpreted as Buddhas, and their cults could continue. Consequently, the Mahayana tradition was much more appealing in new countries than was the Theravada. Gods and goddesses emerged, including the mother goddess Tara, believed to be the mother of all Buddhas.

Probably the most important contribution made to Buddhism by the Mahayana tradition was its belief in *bodhisattvas.* These "enlightened beings," and not the Theravada *arhats,* became the saintly models and the key to Mahayana spirituality. The *bodhisattva* is a person who, after death, stops at the doorway to *nirvana* out of compassion for the countless beings mired in ignorance and suffering. In doing so, the *bodhisattva* shares

Top: **A Tibetan lama belonging to an order that claims to dispel any evil spirits. Tibetan Buddhism includes many magical practices.**

Facing page: **Japanese monks leave the monastery chanting Buddhist sutras and seeking donations from townspeople. This discipline is practiced by only a few Buddhist orders in Japan.**

his or her merit with all of humanity. In return, he or she receives devotions.

Thus, in the Mahayana tradition—instead of relying on a self-help approach to salvation—one could hope for helping graces from deities. Indeed, salvation in itself was redefined in some Mahayana sects. In the Chinese sect called **Pure Land Buddhism,** for example, by earnestly calling upon the name of one of the Buddhas, one could enter a paradise in which full enlightenment was easily available. In short, Buddhism in the Mahayana tradition became a *religion* in every sense of the word.

Zen Buddhism: Humor and *Haiku*

Although well known to Westerners as a Japanese religion, Zen Buddhism actually began in China as an offshoot of the Mahayana tradition. Yet Zen represents a step back from that fully religious form of Buddhism.

The founder of Zen was **Bodhidharma,** an Indian Buddhist teacher who lived in the sixth century C.E. According to legend, Bodhidharma was once called to the court of the Chinese emperor for a private interview. The emperor began telling Bodhidharma about his accomplishments—the temples he had built, the scriptures he had translated, the privileges he had granted monks and nuns. In response, Bodhidharma offered the opinion that all of the emperor's good works were useless. Furthermore, he said, the Buddha's teachings were not to be found anywhere in the scriptures. Bodhidharma then left the court and began a ten-year stint of sitting meditation.

This legend reveals much about the aims of Zen Buddhism—aims summarized in these often-quoted lines attributed to Bodhidharma:

A special tradition outside the scriptures,
No dependence on words,
A direct pointing at man,
Seeing into one's own nature and the attainment of wisdom.

At a deep level, Zen was a reform movement within Buddhism. That is, Zen harked back to some original elements of Gautama's teachings. The Zen tradition, for instance, reasserted the earlier, Theravada idea that enlightenment was to be found in individual meditation and not in communal devotions. One is admitted to wisdom through a flash of insight known as *satori* (meaning "awakening").

The emphasis on a monastic lifestyle was also restressed. Zen monks, however, were expected to work, not only beg, because it was believed that if one seriously concentrated on even the most menial job—such as scrubbing a latrine—a person might stumble upon enlightenment.

The Zen teachers, again like Gautama and his first followers, were suspicious of bulky scriptures and of wordy philosophical discourses. As the early Zen teachers saw it, enlightenment was not to be found in scholarly words: reason only contradicts itself, theories only lead to more theories, and reality cannot be reached by arguments. Instead, the Zen masters

Meditation on koans underlines the playful quality of Zen Buddhism. Indeed, the good humor in the Zen tradition makes it unique among religions. In Zen, laughter is not merely encouraged; it is insisted upon as a way of keeping the self in its proper place in the universe. That may explain why much of Zen humor is at its own expense. For example, a Zen "cartoon" shows a frog sitting with a big smile on its face. The caption reads, "If you think by sitting you can become a Buddha . . ."

Here is another example of Zen humor: A monk named Ten Yin-feng, knowing he was about to die, wanted to do so in a spectacular fashion in order to demonstrate his self-discipline. Asking around, he discovered that no one had ever heard of a monk's dying while standing on his head. So Ten promptly stood on his head and gave up the ghost. His body remained in this headstand position for so long that it became a public spectacle and then a national tourist attraction. Ten's fellow monks did not know what to do with the body, until at last Ten's sister, a Buddhist nun, arrived on the scene. She accused her late brother of being the show-off that he always was and sharply prodded Ten's body with her finger—whereupon it fell with a thud and was carted off to the burial grounds.

developed a style of meditation that was nonintellectual. Its purpose was to escape the limitations that language and theories impose on one's thinking. The stated goal was to "take as thought the thought of No-thought." Its aim was to attain Buddha-wisdom in one's own heart.

The key to this kind of meditation is the **koan,** which is a word or statement that is intended to throw the mind out of its accustomed pathways. Zen students will focus on a *koan* for days or weeks, applying their concentration and imagination. Familiar examples are unanswerable riddles, such as "What is the sound of one hand clapping?" and "Imagine your original face before your parents were born."

Zen in Japanese History

When Zen entered Japan in the twelfth century, the **samurai,** the ruling military class, were especially drawn to it because of its stress on overcoming the fear of death. Added to that was the training that Zen provided in "right mindfulness" and in martial arts, such as archery and swordsmanship. The effectiveness of Zen teachings was soon demonstrated on battlefields, and this form of instruction thus became a part of Japanese military tactics from then on.

Yet Zen contributed much more than martial arts to Japanese culture. For Zen adopted all sorts of secular activities as its disciplines, transforming them into arts. Zen activities ranged from dance to calligraphy to tea ceremonies. In the process, Zen brought about a moral and intellectual revolution in what was mainly a barbarous culture at the time.

By the 1300s, for instance, the Zen temples in Japan had become schools of art, where artists of enduring fame were trained in literature—especially in poetry. Zen teachings are clearly demonstrated in a poetic form called the *haiku*. In these very brief poems of only seventeen syllables, we can see Zen's aversion to wordiness, as well as to philosophizing and sentimentality. The aim of *haiku* is to capture the timeless yet fleeting moments in nature. Perhaps the best known *haiku* of all is the following one by the seventeenth-century Zen poet who was popularly known as **Basho:**

> An ancient pond,
> A frog jumps in—
> The sound of water.

Haiku demonstrate another element of Zen spirituality, that is, its emphasis on the lessons to be found in nature and in everyday life. Hundreds of Zen stories illustrate a concern that we today might think of as "ecological." For instance, one old story tells about two monks who traveled toward the isolated mountain retreat of a reputed sage. As they neared their destination, they were surprised to see a radish top floating down a nearby stream. Their surprise turned to dismay when they saw a second radish top float by. The monks turned back at the sight of a third radish top: they knew that they were not about to meet a wise sage, for the wise are not wasteful.

Zen's good humor and good sense have exerted a fascination on Westerners. Some corporations offer their employees exercises in modified Zen techniques as a means to healthier, happier, and more productive lives. The Japanese arts of flower arranging and ink drawing are taught in many schools. In addition, books with titles such as *Zen and the Art of Archery* and *The Inner Game of Tennis* offer very practical psychological insights. Yet authentic Japanese Zen Buddhism is as spiritual as it is practical: it is a serious endeavor to discover the Buddha-wisdom within oneself.

Top: **The Garden of Ryoanji Temple in Kyoto, Japan. Its subtle, meditative quality is typical of Zen Buddhist temples.**

Bottom: **The Great Buddha of Kamakura, Japan. This bronze statue, dating from 1252, has been out in the open since 1493, when the building that housed it was washed away by a tidal wave.**

Facing page: **The famous Heian Shrine Gardens in Kyoto**

Buddhism Today

In the last fifty years, Buddhism has had to confront Communism, which today functions as a civil religion in many of the Asian countries that were once Buddhist strongholds. Because Buddhism does not promote any competing social or political programs, some Communist governments have looked favorably on it. In Sri Lanka and in Burma, for instance, a mix of Communism and Buddhism has been attempted—supposedly on the grounds that both systems offer freedom from suffering. The differences between the two approaches to suffering are considerable, however. While Buddhism strives to eliminate human greeds, Communism claims to fulfill human needs. So it remains to be seen just how successfully these systems can function in tandem.

In other Communist countries, such as China and Tibet, the governments have almost eliminated any visible signs of Buddhism. The fact that Buddhism lacks an institutional structure beyond the *sangha* has made it vulnerable to repression: these small communities have nowhere to turn for support when a government becomes repressive. In similar circumstances in Poland, the Catholic Church has been able to survive because of the strength of its national church structure, as well as because of the international support offered by the Vatican.

In Japan, the apparent decline of Buddhism is not due to Communism but to the upheavals that followed the Second World War. In the face of Japan's defeat, the Japanese people have turned away from their older religions, generally in favor of the newer cults or sects that make more promises and paint a brighter future. Even so, many people in Japan identify themselves as members of both Buddhism and Shintoism, which is a religion that we will discuss in the next part of this course.

Curiously, as Buddhism fades somewhat in the East, it may find a foothold in the West. Interest in Buddhism began with the Christian missionaries who traveled to the Orient. In order to learn more about the Asian people, these missionaries translated the ancient Buddhist texts and thus made them available to Westerners. Buddhist "societies" were established in England and in the United States by the late 1800s. Today the U.S. schools and groups are united in the Buddhist Church of America.

More recently, the exotic and highly ethical character of Buddhism has made it appealing to young people who are weary of their own culture. Although courses on meditation and on Eastern wisdom are widely available, they frequently offer smorgasbords of concepts that have little to do with actual Buddhism. Yet elements of the Buddha's teachings and of the Buddhist way of life will doubtlessly continue to inspire people who come in contact with them. This sort of inspiration is reflected in the following prayer composed by Thomas Merton, the U.S. Trappist monk whose writings drew much attention to the virtues of Zen teachings. Merton died in Bangkok, Thailand, while attending a conference on building bridges of understanding between Eastern and Western spiritualities.

> My Lord God, I have no idea where I am going. I do not see the road ahead of me. I cannot know for certain where it will end. Nor do I really know myself, and the fact that I think I am following your will does not mean that I am actually doing so. But I believe that the desire to please you does in fact please you. And I hope I have that desire in all that I am doing. I hope that I will never do anything apart from that desire. And I know that if I do this you will lead me by the right road, though I may know nothing about it. Therefore I will trust you always though I may seem to be lost and in the shadow of death. I will not fear, for you are ever with me, and you will never leave me to face my perils alone. (*Thoughts in Solitude*)

Above: **A Buddhist monastery in San Francisco**

Facing page: **In Zen Buddhist temples, it is common to come across scenes of quiet meditation.**

For Review:

1. How does the story of the Buddhist prodigal son reflect basic Buddhist teachings?
2. Outline the three stages of Gautama's life. What experiences compelled him into each stage?
3. How is Buddhism similar to Hinduism? How do these religions differ?
4. In what way is the Middle Path revolutionary in the history of religion?
5. What are the Four Noble Truths? Which is the most important of them? Why?
6. What has remained the central pathway to enlightenment in Buddhism?
7. Why is the *sangha* important in Buddhism?
8. Name the three forms of Buddhism described in this chapter, list the places where they flourished, and describe briefly the main characteristics of each.
9. Christianity, which began as a sect within Judaism, eventually became the more popular and widespread religion. In what ways does the development of Christianity as a world-class religion parallel that of Mahayana Buddhism?
10. Which of the models of Buddhist sainthood—the *arhat* or the *bodhisattva*—is more akin to our Christian model?
11. Why did Zen Buddhism have great appeal to the Japanese *samurai?*

For Reflection:

1. Spend some time reflecting on the accounts of Siddhartha Gautama's life and on those of Jesus' life. How do their early lives compare? their ascetic periods? their teaching years? their deaths?
2. *Buddha,* the title given to Gautama, means "the enlightened one." *Christ* means "anointed" or "sent by God." And *Israel,* the name given to Jacob, probably means "let God rule." How does each of these titles reflect the central message of its religion?
3. In describing the life of the gifted writer and Trappist monk Thomas Merton, a *New York Times* columnist once commented that Merton had great promise but regrettably had denied his talents by hiding from society. What contribution to the world do contemplative nuns and monks make? Would you support the Buddhist monks, who rely on the laity for all their needs? Why, or why not?
4. Gautama has been called the first great psychologist in history because of the way he pushed people toward new modes of consciousness. This psychological element is an integral part of Buddhist thought. Reflect for a moment on the psychological sense behind this verse from the *sutra* scriptures:

   Good friends once, of a sudden they dislike you,
   You try to please them—quite in vain.

5. The *haiku* quoted on page 101 is said to summarize all of the teachings of Gautama. What can you see of Buddhist thought in this poem?

USSR

MONGOLIA

Peking ■

CHINA

Seoul ■
SOUTH
KOREA

TOKYO
JAPAN

Tibet
NEPAL
Lhasa

Shanghai ■

INDIA
Calcutta ■

Canton ■

TAIWAN

BURMA

Hong Kong

Pacific Ocean

C. GREAT RELIGIONS
OF THE FAR EAST

6
CONFUCIANISM AND TAOISM: THE TWO "WAYS" OF CHINA

When Buddhism spread into China and Japan, it encountered three major religions that were native to these countries: Confucianism and Taoism in China and Shintoism in Japan. The success of Buddhism in these countries depended on its ability to deal with these religions individually and on their shared, basic religious tenets, which are centered on a view of the world as fundamentally harmonious.

These native religions were almost unknown in the West until recent times. Yet for over two thousand years and for millions of people, these religions have been fountains of wisdom, espousing a love of nature and of the family. While the Chinese religions that we will look at in this chapter are in decline in their homeland, they still have much to teach us about developing our characters and our communities.

What Is Good or Bad?

Once upon a time a farmer's only horse ran away. His neighbor came by to console the farmer, but the farmer merely replied, "Oh, who knows what is good or bad?"

The next day the horse returned, bringing with it a herd of wild horses. This time the neighbor came over to congratulate the farmer, but again the farmer replied, "Who knows what is good or bad?"

On the third day, the farmer's son mounted one of the wild horses to break it and instead broke his leg when he was thrown. Upon hearing of the son's misfortune, the neighbor wished to share the farmer's sadness. But the farmer only replied, "Who knows what is good or bad?"

On the fourth day, some government agents came to draft the farmer's son into the army. But seeing that he had a broken leg, they deferred him. The neighbor, upon hearing the news, wanted to share in the gladness. But the farmer, in his infinite wisdom, again replied, "Who knows what is good or bad?" . . .

The above story about the farmer suggests a worldview quite different from our Western thinking. In the West we tend to see life in terms of good luck and bad luck, or good and evil, or blessings and curses.

Clearly, the farmer's luck moves from good to bad. Yet he is not quick to judge life in terms of good and bad. The farmer's response to drastic change is not to judge it or to try to take control of events. Instead, he takes a calm, balanced attitude toward his changing circumstances.

This story summarizes the worldview that is common to Oriental religions. The Chinese and Japanese religions that we will discuss all see a unity of the human, natural, and sacred levels of reality. Society is seen as a part of nature, united with woods, streams, and mountains. Even the gods dwell invisibly within this worldly realm, not separate from it. And within this unity a profound harmony exists, with gods and people working together to keep the world in balance.

Yin and Yang

In the Oriental worldview, two great, opposing forces fill the universe, and world harmony depends upon their interplay. These are the forces called yin and yang. **Yin** is associated with the natural qualities of darkness, coolness, femaleness, and dampness, as well as with dying things and the moon. **Yang** is found in the natural qualities of brightness, warmth, maleness, and dryness, as well as in growing things and the sun.

The Orientals placed no judgment upon the yin and the yang: neither was seen as the better or the worse. No one felt that one force was good and the other evil. The interaction between them was simply the way that the universe operated. Except for a few objects, such as the sun and moon, everything in life combined both forces. When these forces worked in harmony, life was what it should be.

The *t'ai chi* symbol of yin and yang, a concept fundamental to the Chinese worldview

Traditionally, the interplay of yin and yang is represented in the *t'ai chi* symbol. The symbol represents the world, composed of opposites that flow into each other and that together make up the whole. The dots signify that each force contains a little of the complementary force. In a similar vein, the story of the farmer suggests that good can be found in bad events—and vice versa.

In Chinese religions especially, a unifying force is seen as the single greatest worldly force, greater even than yin and yang. The Taoists called this force the **Tao,** meaning "nature," while the Confucianists called it **T'ien,** meaning "heaven." In both cases, this force was understood to be the root of universal harmony. Interestingly, some scholars suggest that especially in this concept of Heaven, the Chinese moved close to a belief in one God.

In the opening story, then, the farmer's calm attitude is not just a resignation in the face of fate. Rather, this calm flows from a belief in the ultimate harmony in the world and a deep trust of its forces.

The Great Beginning

The following Taoist account of creation is of special interest because it was taken over by Confucians and also incorporated into the Japanese Shintoist Scriptures.

Before heaven and earth had taken form all was vague and amorphous. Therefore it was called the Great Beginning. The Great Beginning produced emptiness and emptiness produced the universe. The universe produced material-force which had limits. That which was clear and light drifted up to become heaven, while that which was heavy and turbid solidified to become earth. It was very easy for the pure, fine material to come together but extremely difficult for the heavy, turbid material to solidify. Therefore heaven was completed first and earth assumed shape after. The combined essences of heaven and earth became the yin and yang, the concentrated essences of the yin and yang became the four seasons, and the scattered essences of the four seasons became the myriad creatures of the world. After a long time the hot force of the accumulated yang produced fire and the essence of the fire force became the sun; the cold force of the accumulated yin became water and the essence of the water force became the moon. The essence of the excess force of the sun and moon became the stars and planets. Heaven received the sun, moon, and stars while earth received water and soil.

Ancestor Worship: The Flow of Life

The veneration of elders and ancestors is a traditional trait of both the Chinese and the Japanese. This practice is closely tied to the harmonious worldview just described because a long life was seen as proof that a person was in tune with the universal forces. Consequently, older people deserved the respect and attention of younger persons.

For most Westerners, who live in a youth-oriented culture, the veneration of old age is difficult to comprehend. In Oriental societies, however, life really begins when a person reaches the age when he or she becomes respected. Parents and grandparents are revered while they are alive and worshiped after death.

Above: **The veneration of elders is closely linked to ancestor worship in the native Chinese religions.**

Right: **A Chinese man offering devotions to the spirits of his ancestors**

Facing page: **Confucius, from a bronze statue portraying him in royal garments**

This practice has roots deep in the past, going back to the first historical ruling house of China, the Shang dynasty, which held power for six hundred years beginning about 1700 B.C.E. Even at this early date, ancestor worship was practiced—at least among the royalty. Common people were not thought to have any ancestors worth recalling. The supreme deity, called **Shang-ti,** seems to have been the original ancestor of the royal house. To the Shang rulers, divine ancestors represented the great unbroken flow of life, extending back into a golden past.

The goodwill of the royal ancestors ensured the prosperity of the kingdom. One of the essential functions of the Shang kings, then, was communicating with departed ancestors, as well as sacrificing to the gods. In fact, the Shang era is famous for using **divination** for revealing messages

sent by ancestors. Divination can take many forms, such as foretelling events by "reading" the patterns in the flight of birds or in the intestines of animals. The Chinese, in particular, would seek answers by reading the cracks in tortoise shells that were heated over a fire.

Chinese divination reached its peak in the development of the *I Ching* (that is, *The Book of Changes*), which was edited by Confucius and is still in use today. Using the patterns depicted in the *I Ching,* answers or predictions are read into the random combinations that are made by casting coins or sticks.

Japan's royal history is similar to China's in the sense that the rulers also were considered divine on the basis of their lineage: according to legend, the first emperor of Japan was the grandson of the sun goddess. For many centuries, the Japanese emperors were merely figureheads, but their claim of a "divine right" to rule persisted until World War II.

Together these basic tenets—the beliefs in one, harmonious world and in ancestor worship—suggest something important about the religions that we are about to discuss. That is, while Chinese and Japanese religions are capable of worship and theological speculation, historically they have emphasized a human-centered view of the world in which religion functions primarily to enrich human life and to support civil authorities. Unlike Hindus and Buddhists, they do not seek a release from life, nor do they look forward, as we Christians do, to a heavenly existence that completes and replaces the earth as we know it. Even Maoism—the most recent brand of religion to appear in China—fulfills these same humanistic aims.

Confucianism: The Way of the Ancients

The Chou dynasty followed the Shang and ruled China for about eight hundred years, until the third century B.C.E. Early in the reign of this dynasty, the Chou rulers organized the empire into a feudal system in which the peasants provided the necessities of life for a tiny but powerful nobility. Toward its end the Chou rule degenerated into continual war and mass slaughters.

K'ung Fu-tzu (better known as **Confucius,** the Westernized form of his name) was born in 551 B.C.E., in the waning years of the Chou dynasty. He was the child of an aristocratic family that had lost its wealth in the decaying Chou feudal system. His biographers record, however, that Confucius received a complete education in the traditional subjects of that time, namely, poetry, history, music, fishing, and archery.

When he was unable to advance beyond minor administrative posts in his home province, Confucius turned to teaching as a career. He set up a school for gentlemen—a one-teacher university of sorts—and for the next twenty-five years, he taught history and good government. Later, in his fifties, Confucius and his followers wandered from place to place, hoping in vain to find a ruler to put his political teachings to use. His last years were spent teaching and compiling classical Chinese writings.

Everyone knows at least one say-ing that is attributed to Confucius. Complete any of the following say-ings that you can:

- *To go too far is as bad as to . . .*
- *People are put to shame when their words are better than their . . .*
- *The person who errs, errs again by not . . .*
- *The superior person covets the reputation of being slow in word but prompt in . . .*
- *The superior person takes as much trouble to discover what is . . . as inferior people take to discover what will pay.*

The following sayings from the Analects *may be less familiar—but no less wise. Try to put them into your own words.*

- *"He who learns but does not think, is lost. He who thinks but does not learn is in great danger."*
- *"Shall I teach you what knowledge is? When you know a thing, to recognize that you know it, and when you do not know a thing, to recognize that you do not know it. That is knowledge."*
- *"In the presence of a good man, think all the time how you may learn to equal him. In the presence of a bad man, turn your gaze within [and examine yourself]!"*

Among these writings is the ***Analects,*** which is often called "The Sayings of Confucius." The *Analects* is believed to be a record of some of the dialogues that Confucius had with his students. Confucius summed up his own career and life goals in these words:

> At fifteen, I had set my heart upon learning. At thirty, I had formed my character. At forty, I no longer suffered from perplexities. At fifty, I knew what was the mandate of Heaven. At sixty, I heard it with docile ear. At seventy, I could follow the dictates of my own heart for what I desired no longer overstepped the boundaries of right. (*Analects*)

Like some of his contemporaries—Gautama in India and the com-pilers of the Jewish Scriptures who were exiled in Babylon—Confucius observed that life was not what it should be. All around him was the decay and cruelty of the declining Chou dynasty. Yet Confucius did not despair: he believed that people could improve their lot through education. He urged the Chinese to restore society to what it had been in the golden age of the ancestors, as described in the classical texts.

After the fall of the Chou dynasty in the third century B.C.E., it ap-peared as if the ideals of Confucius might be forgotten. The Ch'in dynas-ty that followed (from which the name China comes) was established on political principles very different from those that Confucius taught. The Ch'in rulers favored strong laws and intimidation; they had no interest in education.

Fortunately for Confucianism, the Ch'in dynasty barely outlived its founder. The succeeding Han dynasty (206 B.C.E.–220 C.E.) was far more successful, lasting over four hundred years. Fundamental to the success of the Han dynasty was its decision to adopt Confucianism as a state religion. Based on writings associated with Confucius and his followers, this civil religion held that the ruler was responsible for assuring the well-being of the people and for setting an example of moral virtue. One of the results of the Han policies was that a sort of Confucian priesthood developed within China's civil service, which dedicated itself to Confucius's teachings.

At about this point in its history, Confucian thought began to be merged with Taoist insights, just as later it was combined with Buddhist ideas. In these mixtures, Confucianism survived. By the sixth century C.E., every district in China had a temple to Confucius, who was looked upon almost as a deity. In 1908, just prior to the collapse of the Chinese Em-pire, Confucius was declared a god coequal with Heaven and Earth. As we will see, however, the Communist Revolution in China attempted to wipe out Confucian practices.

The Teachings of Confucius

Confucius seems to have thought of himself as a prophet, as well as a teacher. Reportedly he said, "Heaven is the author of the virtue that is in me." Yet Confucius, like Gautama the Buddha, was much more interested in people than in gods. Confucius seems to have believed that while worship and rituals were of value, they took second place to social duties. Living in a time of political chaos, Confucius and the early Confucian writers were interested primarily in helping to reestablish a stable and prosperous social order. Education and morality, not worship, are at the heart of Confucian thought.

Note also that, unlike Buddhism, Confucianism does not concern itself with the problem of rebirth or with release from this life. Remember that the Chinese valued a long life and saw the afterlife in the most optimistic light: at death one became a revered ancestor without further ado. Neither rebirth nor salvation were concepts in the traditional Chinese worldview.

Moreover, Confucius and his later followers saw no reason to establish local churches or monasteries as small communities of faith, such as those found in the Christian and Buddhist histories. On the contrary, Confucius aimed to enhance and sanctify the institutions of the family and the local community.

While Confucius's teachings were not strongly religious, they were very traditional. In fact, the early Confucians called these teachings "The Way of the Ancients." Let's look at the major tenets of Confucianism and see how they tie into the traditional Chinese worldview.

Jen: Good-Heartedness

As suggested above, the Confucians had a bright outlook on human nature, which they saw as identical with nature itself. Adopting this traditional Chinese perspective, they saw the world as a place smiled on by Heaven and populated by gods and people who strove together for the same harmonious order.

Harmony was also a basic human trait. And as people became more in touch with harmony, they acquired the Confucian ideal of *jen*—a term that is variously translated as "good-heartedness," "humaneness," or "love." *Jen* is best understood as the largeness of the human spirit that seeks the welfare of others.

Chun-tzu: **The Superior Person**

The model of human perfection is *chun-tzu,* that is, "the superior person," who habitually acts for the good of others. Confucian writings describe the superior person this way: "His unworthiness vexes him; to live unknown does not vex him. He fears lest his name dies when life is done. He is firm, not quarrelsome; a friend, not a partisan. He is consistent, not changeless" (*Analects*).

Li: **Proper Conduct**

If *jen* is described as the commitment to seeking others' welfare, then *li* is its outward expression. *Li* refers to proper conduct, courtesy, and doing things the right way. Confucius had a keen awareness of the role of courtesies and ceremonies in maintaining the social order. In his thinking, social harmony depended on such simple gestures as a smile or a compliment, as well as on religious ceremonies.

Of course, courtesies and ceremonies can become empty formalities. But in the Confucian teachings, ideally these social gestures flow from the sincere good-heartedness and are performed with the aim of rebuilding a harmonious society. Linked with this ideal of *li* is the teaching that a powerful cosmic energy called *te* flows from good behavior. *Te* is also the power to rule by good example rather than by brute force.

Li was to be exercised in the five basic relationships within the family and in society:

1. Kindness in the *father* is met by respect in the *son.*
2. Courtesy in the *elder brother* is met by humility in the *younger.*
3. Justice in the *husband* is met by obedience in the *wife.*
4. Consideration in *elder friends* is met by deference in *juniors.*
5. Benevolence in *rulers* is met by loyalty in *subjects.*

Wen: **Education**

Learning the art of peace, as opposed to the art of war, is an essential ingredient in Confucius's system—as it was in traditional Chinese education. He believed that the nation with the highest culture would ultimately triumph. Specifically, *wen* refers to the cultivation of music, poetry, and painting.

The influence of Confucius is still visible in the character of the Chinese society that he helped to mold. Nowhere, for example, has family solidarity been stronger than in China. Confucius's emphasis on education and peace is seen also in the fact that until recently scholars ranked at the top of the social scale; soldiers, at the bottom. Finally, the Chinese, great believers in negotiation as a "middle course," are among the most peace-loving people.

Taoism: Nature as "The Way"

From its beginning, Confucianism has shared the hearts of the Chinese people with another spiritual tradition, known as **Taoism.** These two religions, in fact, developed in response to each other, and thus they represent the yin and the yang of Chinese spirituality. For instance, while Confucianism worked for the public good, Taoism was more concerned with the individual person. While the first taught gentility and sensibility, the second taught rebellion and spontaneity. While the one focused on solidarity and good government, the other focused on freedom and nature. And while Confucianism more or less ignored the gods, Taoism came to worship them enthusiastically.

While it is easy to describe Taoism in relationship to Confucianism, Taoism in itself is difficult to define. It cannot be talked about in the way we would discuss Buddhism or Christianity because little is known of its founder, its origins are almost unknown, and it has no clear set of doctrines. Moreover, some of its followers see Taoism as a *philosophy,* not as a *religion.* Still others see it as a form of *magic.* So we need to discuss Taoism in all three of these aspects.

Taoism as a Philosophy

According to tradition, the founder of Taoism is held to be a man who went by the title of **Lao-tzu** (meaning "the old master"). Born about 600 B.C.E., Lao-tzu is said to have lived most of his life as an official in the court of the Chou emperors. Bored by the routine of court life, he retired from his post and, according to legend, sat down to write the ***Tao Te Ching,*** the book from which Taoism got its name. Having completed this work, Lao-tzu disappeared into the mists of history.

Modern scholars suggest that actually the *Tao Te Ching* (often translated as *The Way and Its Power*) was not the work of one person, but was written by several persons over many centuries. In any case, this small book has been a source of Chinese wisdom for over two thousand years.

The basic messages of the *Tao Te Ching* are these:

1. **Life is to be lived in harmony with the Tao.** The Tao, meaning "the way," is best said to refer to nature in its entirety, existing prior to the forces of yin and yang. A central tenet of Taoism is the doctrine of noninterference with the harmony and power residing in nature. A Western catchphrase for this belief might be "Let go; let God." The following passage describes this attitude of noninterference in terms of the passive qualities of water:

Top: Tao, the Chinese word literally meaning "the way." It can be used as a symbol of both Confucianism and Taoism. To the Confucians, Tao came to refer to morality and education; to the Taoists it meant nature itself.

Bottom: Lao-tzu, depicted in a stone rubbing dating from the Ming dynasty (1368–1644 C.E.)

There is nothing in the world more soft and weak than water,
Yet for attacking things that are hard and strong
There is nothing that surpasses it. . . .
The soft overcomes the hard;
The weak overcomes the strong.

(Tao Te Ching)

2. **Life is to be lived simply.** Whereas Confucianism taught people how to build up the Chinese Empire, the *Tao Te Ching* suggests that the ideal community is a village of hardworking, prosperous farmers who are so content with their own village that they never get around to visiting another one nearby. One of the key ideas in the *Tao Te Ching* is that civilization interferes with the ebb and flow of nature.

There is a thing vast and perfect
That existed before Heaven and
   Earth were born.
. . . It stands alone and does not
   change.

. . . .

We can see it as the mother of
   everything under Heaven.
I don't know its name,
   so I call it . . . Tao.

          (Tao Te Ching)

3. **Human achievement is foolish.** Taoism teaches that one person's achievements only make other people envious and unhappy.

It is better not to make merit a matter of reward
Lest people conspire and contend,
Not to pile up rich belongings
Lest they rob,
Not to excite by display
Lest they covet.

As these fundamental teachings suggest, in its early form Taoism was much more a philosophy than a religion. The *Tao Te Ching* contains almost no references to gods or to heaven. As was Confucius, the early Taoists were concerned with everyday life and not with worship, celebrations, or the afterlife.

Taoism as a Religion and a Magical System

In its early, philosophical phase, Taoism appealed mainly to a small group who were discontented with the conformity in society that was promoted by the Confucians. Later, during the centuries that followed the collapse of the Han dynasty (from 221 to 618 C.E.), Confucianism was somewhat discredited. With the failure of the social order, many people turned to more personal paths to meaning, among them Buddhism and Taoism.

Yet the Taoism that people turned to was itself undergoing changes. Some Taoist teachers began to turn their attention to the search for immortality. Their interest was not the afterlife as much as the extension of present life. These Taoists thought that if a person became attuned to the Tao, long life would result. The explicit goal was to "steal the secret of Heaven and Earth"—that is, to discover the secret of life itself.

Various methods were developed in the quest for long life; other techniques were already in use from ancient times. For instance, charms were sold, drugs were experimented with, and special diets were taught. Also, breathing exercises much like Yoga were tried. Interestingly, the first deity to enter into Taoist teachings was the god of the stove, who was sacrificed to by Taoist alchemists in their attempts to work magic with metals. Behind all of these experiments lay a belief in the value and goodness of life—a belief that connects Taoism with the basic spirituality of China.

Kwan-yin, the Chinese goddess of mercy, a wood sculpture dating from the Sung dynasty (960–1280 C.E.)

At the same time that Taoism was becoming involved in magical practices, it was also becoming more religious in its character. In the second century C.E., the powerful leader **Chang Ling** was named the first "Heavenly Teacher"—a title that has been used ever since. His successors began to exercise spiritual authority over the Taoist priests in southern China. Later still, Taoists began borrowing from the practices of Mahayana Buddhism, which was becoming very popular in China. By the sixth century, the Taoists had begun monastic communities for men and women.

By the 900s, Taoism had a rich pantheon of gods, lavish temples, complex rituals, and colorful festivals. Where Confucianism offered the Chinese people common sense, Taoism as a religion made its appeal to their romantic, fanciful, and celebrating nature. This fully developed religious dimension, combined from the start with magical practices, assured Taoism of a popular following that lasted until the coming of Maoism in China.

The Impact of Maoism

The Communist Revolution of 1949 was destructive to Taoism, but in many ways it was a direct attack on Confucianism. Because it supported social traditions so strongly, Confucianism had long been criticized by both democratic and Communist liberals who supported human rights. During the fifties a civil religion emerged that worshiped the revolution's leader **Mao Tse-tung** and his writings. Especially during the Cultural Revolution in the sixties, this civil religion called **Maoism** turned many Confucian values upside down.

For example: the young heaped not just criticism but abuse on the old; the society looked to the golden future of Communism rather than to a golden past; tyranny and force replaced courtesy and good example. On the positive side, Maoism brought an end to the horrible famines that have historically plagued China. Moreover, women are now treated as the equals of men.

Rush hour in present-day Peking is dominated by bicycles and buses.

What remains to be seen is whether or not Maoism will survive its founder. Shortly after Mao's death, his successors have already begun to reevaluate Maoism and to rediscover Confucian writings. It may be that both Taoism and Confucianism will continue to influence the modern world mainly through the wisdom to be found in their philosophical writings.

For Review:

1. Explain the principle of yin and yang.
2. When in Chinese history did the practice of ancestor worship begin?
3. Explain the practice of divination.
4. Describe the political situation in China during Confucius's lifetime.
5. Why did Confucianism almost disappear during the Ch'in dynasty?
6. Why did Confucians see no need to establish churches or monasteries?
7. Why is it said that Confucianism and Taoism represent the yin and the yang of Chinese spirituality?
8. What are the three basic teachings of the *Tao Te Ching?*
9. What methods did Taoists employ in their search for immortality?
10. From where did the Taoists borrow their religious practices?
11. What is the status of Confucianism and Taoism in China today?

For Reflection:

1. Continue the story of the farmer in the same spirit. What lesson do you draw from the story?
2. Psychologists sometimes divide people into two types: type A persons who are punctual, excitable doers; and type B persons who are easygoing and unthreatened by schedules. Given their spirituality, which type do you suppose many of the Chinese might be? Which type are you?
3. Confucianism puts more stress on manners than on motivation. That is to say, you feel better because you smile; you don't smile because you feel better. Are you a Confucian in this regard?
4. Reflect on this saying from the Confucian text called *The Great Learning*:

   If there be righteousness in the heart,
     there will be beauty in the character.
   If there be beauty in the character,
     there will be harmony in the home.
   If there by harmony in the home,
     there will be order in the nation.
   If there be order in the nation,
     there will be peace in the world.

5. Confucius was once asked if there is one rule that could serve as the guide for one's whole life. He replied, "What you do not want done to yourself, do not do to others." How does this rule compare with Jesus' teaching?
6. Taoism maintains that knowledge comes from listening to the universe, not from attempting to master it. Do you agree? Why, or why not?
7. Do you see a connection between the water image of the Tao mentioned on page 116 and Jesus' teaching in the Sermon on the Mount about the meek inheriting the earth? Can you describe that connection? What virtues that we think of as Christian are reflected in Taoism?
8. Do you think that a religion that becomes unpopular is proven worthless?

7
SHINTOISM:
"THE WAY OF THE GODS"

We have seen how Confucianism and Taoism grew alongside each other in China and how they came to complement each other. Together these two religions provide a key to the character of the Chinese people. In a similar way, learning about Shintoism offers us a look at the core of the Japanese character and culture. Before beginning this chapter, reread the introductory sections of the previous chapter (pages 107–111): much of that information also relates directly to Shintoism.

Early Shintoism: The Gods of the Land

Shintoism is a loosely organized native religion of Japan about which little is known prior to the 700s C.E. Before that time there were no Shintoist Scriptures. Only when Buddhism became popular in Japan, and Shintoism was thus threatened with oblivion, did the Shintoists begin to define and structure their religion.

From what we do know about its remote history, Shintoism seems to have begun as **animism,** that is, as a belief that spirits or gods dwelled in natural objects—even in such simple objects as plants and pebbles. The number of Shintoist gods, called *kami,* was thought to be eight million. These gods were apparently divided into two classes: those of the sky and those of the soil. History was shaped by the interaction of these two classes.

Shintoism is much more than a simple animistic religion, however. At its heart is a love and worship of Japan as a land. Traditionally the Japanese have considered their homeland the center of the world. Their love of it as a whole also involves a love of its every detail. In every hill, lake, and river—and particularly in its beautiful mountains—the Japanese have encountered sacred mystery.

This perception of the divine quality of Japan as a land also extends to its people. Since its early history, Shintoism has held that the human soul becomes a *kami* after death. More important persons were naturally thought to become more important gods in the afterlife. Thus, ancestor worship and emperor worship have long had a place in Shintoism. Shintoism sees people as elements *in* nature, not separate from nature.

A dramatic application of this worldview occurred during World War II. The Allied forces could only wonder at the courage of Japanese pilots who, in planes loaded with explosives, crashed suicidally on enemy targets. These pilots were called *kamikaze* — a term combining the word for "god" with *kaze,* which means "wind." That is, the pilots saw themselves as a "divine wind" coming to the defense of their land.

Shintoist Shrines: Places of Purity and Festivity

The first Shintoist shrines were built on sites in which the more powerful gods dwelled — for example, mountains, rivers, or waterfalls. Later on, shrines took on historical and political, as well as religious, significance. While some shrines remained of purely local interest, others became nationally famous, visited by vast throngs of Japanese each year.

One of the most popular and historic shrines is the Grand Shrine of Ise, which actually includes two shrines. One of these is dedicated to the sun goddess **Amaterasu** — the chief Shintoist deity and the divine ancestor of the emperor's family. Founded in ancient times by the imperial family, Ise memorializes the unification of Japan as a country. Consequently, Ise — and many other shrines — are visited for their national, as well as religious, importance. Many U.S. citizens visit places such as the Washington Monument or Gettysburg, Pennsylvania, for somewhat similar purposes, namely, to remember the historic persons and events of U.S. history and perhaps to say a prayer for the nation.

Today Shintoist worship is based on the practices related to each shrine — practices that vary widely depending on the purpose for which the shrine was founded. Virtually every Shintoist shrine has its own traditions and rituals. Yet two themes are constant among these rites and give us clues to basic Shintoist values.

Above: **The sun is both the symbol of the Shintoist goddess Amaterasu and the national symbol of Japan.**

Facing page: **Fuji and its goddess Sengen-Sama. Fuji, an inactive volcano, is the highest mountain in Japan and a popular place of pilgrimage.**

Misogi: Cleanliness and Godliness

First, the shrines represent pure spaces in an impure world. So a visitor washes before entering a shrine. This cleansing, which is called *misogi,* is considered to be the most important ritual in Shintoism. Pollution is further swept away by a priest waving a green branch. The branch — fresh, lively, and bright — is considered pure. This concern for purity is also demonstrated by the fact that typically shrines are torn down and rebuilt with new wood every twenty years. In addition, nothing sick or dying is brought into the precincts of the shrine. Even today births and marriages are celebrated at Shintoist shrines, but funerals are performed at Buddhist temples. This sense of purity has become closely tied to Japanese culture as a whole. In the Japanese view, to be utterly clean is to be wholly natural.

Top: "The Wedded Rocks," representing the deities Izanagi and Izanami. The rocks are joined by a huge straw rope that is replaced in a ceremony every January.

Bottom: Young priestesses at a shrine at Kyoto. Many Shintoist shrines have priestesses who demonstrate ritual dances for tourists.

Right: A *matsuri* at Tokyo, with tattooed youths standing on the bars of a portable shrine that is carried on others' shoulders

The story of Amaterasu's birth suggests that purity as a religious value gained early and deep acceptance in Shintoism. This national myth tells how, in the beginning, the highest *kami* in heaven sent the male **Izanagi** and the female **Izanami** down to earth. There these deities mated, and their offspring became the islands and the gods of Japan. Eventually Izanami died, and though he tried, Izanagi could not bring her back from the underworld. When he left the underworld, Izanagi bathed in the ocean to cleanse himself of the underworld's pollution. From his washings were born several great deities, above all the sun goddess Amaterasu.

Matsuri: Celebration, Not Salvation

In contrast to the quiet, passive rites of *misogi,* the Shintoist festivals called **matsuri** demonstrate the dynamic and colorful side of Shintoist worship. Originally, it was believed that in springtime the sky gods descended to the mountains. So, in festive rituals, people climbed the mountains to welcome them and to accompany them down to the rice fields where the sky gods mated with the earth gods, thereby assuring a bountiful crop. In the autumn the gods were thanked and given send-offs in harvest festivals.

Today the annual festivals at the major shrines are exciting occasions that suggest a dramatic change of pace from ordinary life to a more divine atmosphere. Often the *kami* are borne zigzagging through the streets in a portable shrine, carried by shouting young men. The shrine grounds are usually set up like a carnival, including food booths and exhibits. Splendid parades, costume pageants, dances, horse racing, and archery may all be part of the *matsuri* at a particular shrine.

Actually, these festivals may be more important than the gods themselves to the practice of Shintoism. The name and story of a particular *kami* may mean nothing to people visiting a shrine. Yet the *matsuri* are well known and widely participated in. The reason for this indifference to their deities may lie in the fact that, like the religious Chinese, Shintoists do not seek the grace required for salvation. As long as one's family name continues, a person will live in the memories and prayers of one's descendants.

Both major themes that undergird Shintoist worship—that is, purity and festivity—flow from the Japanese peoples' traditional love of life and the land. Indeed, the changed features of Shintoism that came about in response to Chinese religions have not affected these basic values.

A Japanese cemetery, with gravestones set tightly together to make use of the limited available space

Shintoism and Chinese Religions

Chinese civilization, entering by way of Korea, began to influence Japan in the sixth century C.E. The Japanese quickly caught on to the practical skills imported by their neighbors. These skills included metalworking and woodworking, farming and gardening, silkworm culture, and road and canal building. They also adopted the entire body of Chinese written characters. Soon the first Shintoist Scriptures appeared—the **Kojiki** (which means *Chronicles of Ancient Events*) and the **Nihongi** (*Chronicles of Japan*). These writings described the historical and mythical origins of the Japanese people. Even the name of their native religion was derived from the Chinese term *Shintao,* meaning "the way of the gods."

Shintoist Worship

The ritual of worship performed in village shrines, which are usually set among trees in peaceful glens, consists of these steps:

- Passing through the torii, the gateway that keeps out evil spirits
- Washing one's hands and cleansing the mouth (misogi)
- Removing one's hat, coat, and scarf
- Performing a gasho (a profound bow) at the central shrine, clapping the hands (to get the attention of the gods), bowing again, ringing a bell under the eaves, and making a third bow
- Kneeling on the top step and bowing almost to the floor
- Leaving an offering, praying, bowing in meditation, and retiring—pausing once to turn around for a final profound bow

Past the outer shrine is a covered passageway—the inner sanctuary. This sanctuary houses a "god-body," that is, a sacred object, often of little material value, like an ancestor's sword. Because the god-body is considered symbolic of the divine and often called a "spirit substitute," it is never looked upon directly, but is wrapped in finely woven cloths and enclosed in several caskets.

Religion is also observed within many Japanese homes. A "god-shelf" holds a sacred mirror, and scrolls are inscribed with the names of ancestors and patron deities. Both Buddhist and Shintoist ceremonies are carried out daily with bits of food offered first to the gods. For special occasions or in times of crisis, candles, rice brandy, and cloth are offered while the entire family prostrates in prayer. During the yearly Girls' Day Festival, beautiful dolls are displayed in tiers on the home altar. During the Boys' Day Festival, a colorful paper carp for each boy in the family swings from a pole outside the house.

Confucian and Buddhist influences contributed mightily to this rapid cultural transformation. For its part, the strong Confucian stress on ancestral veneration turned early Shintoism into a comprehensive cult of ancestor worship. High officials began to trace their descent from deities related to Amaterasu, and the common people, from more distantly related deities. The whole Japanese people were thus related to the emperor as descendants of the gods. The Confucian ethical code also shaped the moral character of the Japanese.

With the advent of Mahayana Buddhism in Japan, the upper classes became acquainted with an exciting literature, emotionally satisfying rituals, and fresh insights into every field of human thought. The best minds were attracted by these contributions of the new faith, and they began to adopt Buddhist ways. As a result, Shintoism itself has never developed a theology, a set of doctrines, or a moral code.

Another result of this strong Buddhist influence was **Ryobu** (that is, "two-sided") **Shintoism,** which worshiped gods of both religions. The simple, primitive Shintoist shrines soon added pagodas, drum towers, large bells, assembly halls for preaching, and intricate exterior ornamentation that was characteristic of the Buddhist temples. Even the *torii,* the unadorned Shintoist gateways to the shrines, were now decorated. By the 800s, Japan could fairly be described as a Buddhist nation. By that time, the Buddhist deities were presented as the original gods, and the *kami* were only the gods' "appearances." Even the emperors, who claimed Amaterasu as their ancestor, were forced to accept the view that the sun goddess was merely an "aspect" of the Buddha. Except in the eyes of the rural Japanese, Shintoism had become a second-class religion.

Pure Shintoism as a Civil Religion

The 1600s saw **Pure Shintoism** reinstated as a separate religion. Under the rule of the *shoguns,* or warlords, Japan had became "a hermit nation," closing its ports to foreigners and rejecting foreign religions. This rejection included, by the way, the persecution of the Catholic Christian communities begun in Japan by Saint Francis Xavier and other missionaries.

Under the *shoguns,* Buddhism was the official religion, but a movement had developed that was determined to rid Japan of all foreign elements, including Buddhism. Shintoism was then reinterpreted as the parent of all religions, and so it gained ascendancy over Buddhism. Although the emperor was politically a figurehead, he remained a symbol of national unity and was worshiped as divine. **Moto-ori,** the greatest scholar in Japanese history during the 1700s, wrote:

> From the central truth that the [emperor] is the direct descendant of the gods, the tenet that Japan ranks far above all other countries is a natural consequence. No other nation is entitled to equality with her, and all are bound to do homage to the Japanese sovereign and pay tribute to him.

A "god-shelf" in a Japanese home, including both Buddhist symbols (the drums) and Shintoist symbols (a *torii* and a shrine)

The Way of the Fighting Knight

Throughout the history of Japan, individual soldiers were hired as bodyguards by nobles. During the shogun *era especially, this warrior class, called* **samurai,** *was influenced by the practices of Confucianism and Zen Buddhism, as well as by Shintoism.*

In the 1600s a warrior code called **bushido,** *or "the way of the fighting knight," became the standard of conduct. This code for Japanese feudal knights is similar to the one established for Christian knights during Europe's feudal era.* Bushido *includes the following rules:*

1. *The* samurai *must have great courage in life, in battle, and in his willingness to lay down his life for his master.*

2. *Above all, the* samurai *is to be a man of honor. He should prefer death to dishonor and is expected to take his own life rather than be dishonored. (This attitude led to the practice known as* **hara-kiri,** *a form of ritual suicide by disembowelment.)*

3. *Like a true Confucian, the* samurai *is expected to be polite to his master and to people in authority above him. (Apparently, this courtesy did not extend to every level of society. Stories are told of samurai who would test the sharpness of their swords on luckless peasants.)*

4. *In general, the* samurai *is expected to be a gentleman, to right wrongs, and to bring justice to victims.*

One hundred years later, in concluding a treaty with Commodore Matthew Perry of the U.S. Navy in 1854, the *shoguns* abruptly ended the period of isolation and paved the way for the next landmark in Japanese history. That is, the *shoguns* opened the doors of Japan to the modern world and unintentionally initiated their own extinction. As the revolutionary economic, educational, and political changes introduced by the

adoption of Western technology weakened the faith, the Shintoist priests attempted to once again revive the myth of the emperor's descent from the gods. In the new constitution of 1889, the emperor's position was strengthened, Shintoism was declared the state religion, and Buddhist images in the shrines were purged.

Heated Japanese nationalism, partially fueled by Shintoism, led to Japan's involvement in World War II. With the Japanese defeat, Shintoism as a civil religion was finished. In 1946, **Emperor Hirohito** publicly renounced his divinity in these words:

> We stand together with you our countrymen. Our gains and losses have ever been one. We desire that our woe and weal should be shared. The bonds between us and our countrymen have been tied together from first to last by mutual trust and affection. They do not originate from mere myth and legend. They do not have their basis in the fictitious ideas that the emperor is manifest god and that the Japanese people are a race superior to other races and therefore destined to rule the world. . . .

Since that historic pronouncement, indifference to religion has prevailed among the Japanese. Less than 25 percent of the population professes any religion, and although new sects periodically flare up, materialism and religious indifference seem to have infected a people who less than fifty years ago were willing to sacrifice their lives for their faith.

Top: **Costumed as a *samurai*, a Japanese participates in a reenactment of Commodore Perry's arrival in Tokyo Bay in 1853.**

Bottom: **Emperor Hirohito and the empress, at the end of the Second World War**

Right: **Commodore Perry's arrival in Japan, from a lithograph**

For Review:

1. Why are the Japanese so attached to their land?
2. What cultural value does the national myth of Japan illustrate?
3. Describe the effects of Chinese culture on Japan.
4. What is the religious situation in Japan today?

For Reflection:

1. In the last chapter we saw that Confucian teachings stressed education, not salvation. Similarly, Shintoism emphasizes celebration over salvation. What does this suggest about their common roots in the Oriental worldview?
2. Which elements of Shintoism remind you of Catholic belief or practice? How is Shintoist shrine worship similar to the Catholic Mass? How is it different?

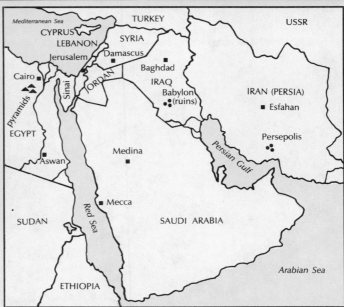

D. GREAT RELIGIONS THAT ORIGINATED IN THE NEAR EAST

8 ZOROASTRIANISM: CHOOSING THE GOD OF GOODNESS AND LIGHT

Although Zoroaster may have been the first great religious prophet, very likely you have never heard of him. Yet your images of heaven, hell, Satan, and even God are largely shaped by his genius. Indeed, Zoroaster's concept of a single deity came to replace completely the many gods of the ancient Western cultures. Although only a small sect of his followers survive today, Zoroaster influenced much of the world through the later religions—including Christianity—that adopted his ideas.

The Original Choice

Now at the beginning the twin Spirits have declared their nature, the better and the evil.

In thought and word and deed. And between the two the wise ones choose well, not so the foolish.

And when these two Spirits came together, in the beginning they established life and non-life.

And that at the last the worst existence shall be for the wicked, but for the just one the Best Mind.

Of these two Spirits, the evil one chose to do the worst things; but the most sacred spirit, clothed in the most steadfast heavens, joined himself unto Truth.

And thus did all those who delight to please the Wise Lord by honest deeds.

Between the two, the false gods did not choose rightly; for, as they deliberated, delusion overcame them so that they chose the Worst Mind.

Then did they, with one accord, rush headlong unto Wrath, that they might thereby deprave the existence of mortal man.

(*Gathas*)

135

In less democratic, less affluent societies than ours, people often have very few choices or freedoms. What they will do with their lives is usually decided for them—where they will live, how they will work, sometimes how many children they will have. A basic feature of our freedom-loving, technologically advanced society is, in fact, the number of choices that we have available to us. We have a range of choices that most other societies and all earlier societies would consider fantastic. These choices involve our education, occupations, residences, marriages, children, leisure time, diet, property, and more.

Whether in rich or in poor societies, however, people in general consider freedom of choice valuable, and in the West it is deemed almost as sacred as life itself. In an earlier chapter, we saw that the Western philosophy called individualism is built around the ultimate value of this freedom.

Yet freedom of choice is not a Johnny-come-lately among human beliefs. Well over two thousand years ago within the Persian Empire, Zoroastrians were teaching the crucial importance of this freedom. As the passage above (from their scriptures called the *Gathas*) suggests, Zoroastrians believe that the creation of the world itself was caused by spirits' choosing between good and evil. In that sense, this story takes our Christian "original choice" story about Adam and Eve one step further.

In Zoroastrianism, however, freedom of choice and the consequences of that freedom are bound together more tightly than most of us today would even care to imagine. For example, Zoroastrians believe so firmly in the freedom of people to choose good or evil that they see no way to undo a choice once it is made.

Therefore, no forgiving grace or blessing can release us from the consequences of sin. At death, a person's good deeds and bad deeds are weighed next to each other in a divine balance, and the slightest tip of the scale toward the good or bad deeds decides whether one goes to heaven or to hell. Mercy does not enter into this final judgment. Thus, in the Zoroastrian worldview, human beings are free to choose how they will live, but they are also wholly responsible for their choices. To understand this rigorous moral perspective at the heart of Zoroastrianism, we must begin with the teachings of its prophet and founder.

Zoroaster: The Prophet of the One, True God

As in the cases of the other ancient religions we have looked at, not much is known about Zoroaster's personal history. (The name **Zoroaster** is a Westernized form of **Zarathushtra**.) His date of birth, for instance, cannot be pinned down even to a particular century. The most widely accepted date is about 600 B.C.E., but some scholars have placed it as early as 1500 B.C.E. What we do know is that by the sixth century B.C.E., Zoroaster's message had gained a foothold in the region that is today western Iran.

According to tradition, Zoroaster was born into the warrior class, and as a young man he had three wives and fathered six children. Possibly

The prophet Zoroaster, from a painting based on traditional representations

he was a priest in the religion of his society, which was a branch of the same Aryan people who conquered India about 1500 B.C.E. As was mentioned in our discussion of Hinduism, the Aryans appeased their many gods by ritual actions and animal sacrifices that were presided over by priests.

After a profound religious experience at the age of thirty, Zoroaster began to teach the totally innovative concept of **monotheism**—that is, the belief in a single god who created and rules the cosmos. Zoroaster did not merely name one of the many popular gods as the leader of the rest.

Instead, he discredited all the other Aryan gods in favor of **Ahura Mazda**—that is, the "Wise Lord."

Zoroaster's preaching of monotheism presented many problems. The Aryans' belief in many gods (called **polytheism**) reflected a richness in the nature of divinity. Compared to this great diversity, the concept of one, lonely god may have seemed colorless. Yet in Zoroaster's teachings, Ahura Mazda lacked neither company nor a vivid personality. Indeed, he was revealed through six aspects called the "Holy Immortals"—three of which represented masculine qualities and three of which represented feminine qualities. The Holy Immortals represented human traits, such as love, piety, and purity, rather than natural forces, such as the sun or the sky, with which the Aryan gods were identified. In addition to the Holy Immortals, hosts of angels surrounded the throne of God and were thought to be of service to people. One of these angels appeared to Zoroaster to tell him about Ahura Mazda.

Zoroaster's teaching of one God evidently met with failure at first. His frustrations are recorded in the *Gathas*, or hymns, which are attributed to Zoroaster.

> To what land shall I flee, where bend my steps? I am thrust out from family and tribe; I have no favor from the village to which I belong, not from the wicked rulers of the country. How then, O Lord, shall I obtain thy favor?

Just how successful Zoroaster was in his life is not clear from the historical evidence. Tradition has it that after a fruitless ten years, he converted a chieftain who then established the new religion within his territory. Many years later, in an attack by a neighboring tribe, Zoroaster was killed at the age of seventy-seven while in a temple tending its sacred flame.

The Spread of Zoroastrianism

By the sixth century B.C.E.—when the historical record becomes somewhat clearer—Zoroaster's teachings had spread throughout the Persian Empire. Although they do not mention Zoroaster by name, inscriptions from that time indicate that the Persian Emperor Darius I (who reigned from 522 to 486 B.C.E.) was a devoted worshiper of Ahura Mazda.

The Persian Empire was conquered in 331 B.C.E. by Greek forces led by Alexander the Great. In Persian history, incidentally, he is known as Alexander the Vandal because during his conquest of Persia, he burned down the royal palace and killed priests. We can only assume that these events were setbacks in the growth of Zoroastrianism.

The Greek rulers of Persia were eventually replaced by a native Persian dynasty known as the **Parthians.** During this era (c. 250 B.C.E.–224 C.E.), Zoroastrianism seems to have flourished. The Parthian rulers were also tolerant of other religions: when they conquered Israel, they deposed the hated Herod and put a Jew on his throne. Unfortunately, the Romans quickly recaptured the land and restored Herod. (It is interesting

Darius I and, behind him, his successor Xerxes the Great, from a wall of the palace at Persepolis in Iran, dating from the fifth century B.C.E.

Left: The Persian king Darius III being defeated by Alexander the Great at Issus (in Asia Minor) in 333 B.C.E., a detail from a Roman mosaic

Below: The ruins of Babylon, the city in central Iraq in which Alexander the Great died in 323 B.C.E.

to speculate how different history might have been if Israel had been in the hands of the tolerant Parthians at the time of Jesus instead of under the rule of the oppressive Romans.)

The people mainly responsible for the spread of Zoroastrianism in the Parthian era were the **magi,** a priestly tribe that acted as royal chaplains and diplomats throughout the empire. When, in the Gospel of Matthew, three of these magi appear at the birth of Jesus, Matthew's readers well understood the significance: these respected foreigners were verifying Jesus' identity as the Messiah.

Zoroastrianism did not become the offical religion of the empire until the era of the Sassanid rulers of Persia (224–651 C.E.). The *Avesta*—which are the Zoroastrian Scriptures, including the *Gathas*—were compiled during this period.

One God or Two?

By the time of the Sassanid dynasty, in the third century C.E., Zoroastrianism had become a **dualistic** religion as much as a monotheistic one. That is, Zoroastrians sometimes taught that there were two gods, while at other times they taught that there was only one deity. When looked at closely, we can see that this confusion began with Zoroaster himself.

In Zoroaster's teaching, Ahura Mazda is supreme but not unopposed. From the beginning of creation, Ahura Mazda had two children—the "twin spirits" mentioned in the passage at the opening of this chapter. One of the twin spirits chose life, truth, and good; the other, evil spirit chose death, lies, and hate.

Zoroaster grappled with the question of whether the evil spirit, called **Ahriman** and later **Shaitan,** was an independent and eternal principle of evil. If so, that would make Ahriman a god. On the other hand, if Ahriman was really a child of Ahura Mazda, that meant that evil and lies could flow from God. This latter view has always been repugnant to Zoroastrians, to whom God is Truth.

Yet this second position seems to have been closer to Zoroaster's conclusions. That is, Zoroaster saw evil as introduced into the world by the free choice of the evil twin who became, not a god, but the "chief servant of the Lie." In other words, Ahura Mazda did not create evil; God only created the freedom of choice that permitted evil to occur. (Notice also that Zoroaster was defining God as a totally good being but not as a totally powerful one. God could not, for example, immediately defeat the evil spirit.)

Zoroaster's teaching on monotheism did not find full acceptance among his followers. Later Zoroastrians began to identify the good spirit with Ahura Mazda, and so the twin spirit Shaitan was naturally elevated to a god also. Eventually, Zoroastrians came to see the cosmos as a battlefield between the forces of these good and evil gods. In a sense, these gods are like the forces of yin and yang, existing independently but relating to one another. Yet in the Zoroastrian outlook, disruption, not harmony, results from their interaction. Clearly, harmony could only come about with the defeat of the evil forces. This defeat is, as we will see, the reason for which people were created.

Human Freedom and Destiny

Besides his teachings on monotheism, Zoroaster provided a new slant on one of humanity's most profound and most perplexing questions: why is there evil? Instead of attributing evil to God, he taught that it exists because freedom must include the possibility of making wrong choices. Zoroaster described human beings as being much like the twin spirits—that is, as created and therefore dependent but, at the same time, as free and therefore independent.

Zoroaster went on to define humanity in noble and dignified terms.

He taught that people were needed to play a part in the struggle against evil; every time that a person was tempted and yet chose good, evil was weakened. Ultimately, when the spirit of evil was sufficiently weakened in this way, it would be defeated and destroyed.

We can see now why freedom of choice became a crucial element in the Zoroastrian worldview. An individual's moral choices determined the outcome of the cosmic battle, as well as one's own fate in the afterlife. All in all, Zoroaster's teachings put a new stress on morality, making morality and not worship the focus of Western religion. We have seen morality stressed in other religions, but not with the terrific force of religious insight that Zoroaster brought to bear on the matter.

Regarding one's personal destiny, the Zoroastrian idea of heaven is familiar to us as a place of light, beauty, and noble souls. Zoroaster's

teachings on hell, which were recorded a thousand years after the prophet's death, are less clear. Some scriptural passages mention annihilation of the soul, while others assert that all evil will eventually be burned out of the soul in hell, ultimately purifying all souls for sharing in eternal happiness. Hell's punishment, it was believed, often fit the crime. For instance, a cruel ruler who starved his people would himself be starved in hell.

An ancient village in southeast Iran (formerly Persia)

Until a child is old enough to know the difference between right and wrong, Zoroastrians do not believe it can sin. At the age of ten, Parsi boys and girls are formally initiated into the faith by promising to strive always to choose good. They receive special undergarments that they wear during waking hours to remind them of this pledge. Each of the initiates also puts on a white shirt, a cap, and a sacred thread, symbolizing their birth to a new life and the armor they always wear in their battle against evil.

Although highly moral and philanthropic, Parsis remain aloof to outsiders. They do not accept converts, nor do they allow outsiders to gaze upon their sacred rites. Women who marry outside the faith are ostracized.

Just as their moral code centers on integrity, the Zoroastrian worship rites center on purity. Pollution is understood as contamination by evil. Since death and suffering do not come from God, these things are avoided as evils. The pollution of the four natural elements of the world— fire, water, air, and soil—is avoided at all costs. Among the striking features of the Parsi religion is the liturgical use of fire to symbolize the essence of the

Because choosing what is good is crucial, you might guess that defining precisely what is good and evil is also important. And, in fact, the Zoroastrian moral code is complex. At its core, however, are the concerns for "good thought, good word, and good deed." Zoroastrianism, with God as Goodness at its heart, is especially concerned with the good of creation and the goodness in people. Traditionally, agriculture and the raising of children in marriage are seen as religious activities. Therefore, to be celibate is to refrain from fulfilling one's religious duty. Also, since Zoroastrianism sees no evil in the human body, it teaches against ascetic practices that cause physical harm.

The Parsis

The Muslims conquered the Sassanid Empire in 651 C.E., and at first the Zoroastrians were tolerated because, like the Muslims, they had accepted the revelation of a supreme god. Persecution gradually replaced tolerance, however, so that today only about fifteen thousand followers of Zoroaster still live in Iran.

In the tenth century C.E., a small band of Zoroastrians set out to seek a new land of religious freedom. This they found in India, where today they are known as **Parsis** (simply meaning "Persians"). Living in and around Bombay, they have grown to over a hundred thousand members. Among the most highly respected communities in India, the Parsis are conspicuous for the high quality of education in their schools and for their donations to hospitals, charitable services, and orphanages. Including many industrial leaders, merchants, bankers, and civic engineers, the Parsi community exerts an economic influence in India well beyond its small numbers.

Parsis today remain faithful to the moral teachings of their founder. They conscientiously work to relieve the misery of all, regardless of creed or race. They are outstanding for their personal integrity. Like their founder, Zoroaster's followers strive to be "deliverers" through kindness to the poor, hospitality to strangers, and efforts to achieve peace and goodwill. Parsis dedicate themselves to the will of Ahura Mazda by trying sincerely to live out their concern for people and their care for animals and the land.

Zoroastrianism and the Other Great Monotheistic Religions

As we have seen, Zoroastrianism belongs in this course on its own merits—as a religion of genius—even though it has relatively few followers today. Another reason for including it, however, is because of the influence Zoroastrianism has had on the next three religions that we are about to study: Judaism, Islam, and Christianity. Scholars cannot link the beliefs of these religions directly to Zoroastrianism. Yet Zoroaster's teachings were powerful and popular in the regions in which these three great

divine nature. As long passages from the Avesta *are read, the priests who officiate at these fire ceremonies keep their mouths covered with veils to protect the fires from possible impurity.*

Parsis also have a unique way of disposing of their dead. Because death is a pollution, a corpse cannot be consigned to any of the four elements—it can be neither exposed to the air, buried, given to the sea, nor cremated. To avoid contaminating the elements with death, which is seen as the temporary victory of evil, the Parsis expose the bodies of their dead in **Towers of Silence.** *Each of these circular structures is twenty feet high and surrounds a stone courtyard where vultures devour the flesh of the dead. Later, the sun-bleached bones are thrown into a central pit.*

Pilgrims transporting their dead to burial places

religions arose. Regarding its impact on Christianity particularly, scholars suggest that we may be as indebted for our ideas and values to Zoroastrianism as we are to Judaism. (And that is a large debt indeed, as we will see in the next chapter.)

Depending on exactly when he lived, Zoroaster may be the first-known prophet of monotheism, proclaiming a god who is not just supreme among gods but is alone God. Related to that proclamation is the other radical belief that God's sovereignty is based not as much on power as on goodness and truth. These insights alone would ensure Zoroastrianism a place in our religious history, but there is more.

Zoroaster's teachings on evil in the person of Satan (another form of the name Shaitan), on heaven and hell, on angels, and on morality—all found places in the religions that succeeded his. Likewise, his view of the world as a battlefield between good and evil has been adopted by Western religions and cultures generally. For example, many people see football or soccer games as having a sort of cosmic significance—that is, as a battle between good and evil as represented by the players on the field. Perhaps that explains the terrific emotion that goes into Super Bowl Sunday in the United States and into the World Cup games in Europe.

The Last Judgment: An End to Time

Of special note to us as Christians is the Zoroastrian idea that people will be bodily resurrected. According to Zoroastrian beliefs, the physical side of one's being is judged at the time of the resurrection, just as the spiritual side is judged at death. This belief is rooted in the Zoroastrian teachings that the body is just as important and potentially good as the soul.

Very important to the thrust of this course is the Zoroastrian belief that there is a Last Judgment—that is, a time when evil will be ended and creation will be brought to perfection. In the religions we have studied so far, the universe has a cyclic, not a linear, history. For instance, Hinduism sees history repeating itself in endless cycles of creation and destruction. Similarly, the Oriental religions tend to see life as a circle within which forces seek harmony and balance. Yet the circle itself does not change or move.

In this cyclic worldview, God is situated at the hub of the wheel of time. So at any time in history, our paths to God—like spokes on the wheel—are all of the same distance; thus, all paths are equally valid. Buddhism, for instance, speaks of eighty-four thousand paths to God.

On the other hand, in Zoroastrianism—and in the other great monotheistic religions—time is understood as a line, beginning with the creation of the world and ending in the final judgment. In this linear view, a purpose flows through history, and people have a part in fulfilling that purpose. Thus, it makes a great difference whether one lives before or after Moses or Jesus or Muhammad. In these religions, God is found most truly in the future, at the end of time.

In the West, this linear view of history is most familiar in our notion

Wheels are commonly used symbols in Hindu religious art.

of "progress," which is the idea that life improves throughout time and that a civilization much like heaven awaits us in the future. Both democracy and Marxism promote this image of an earthly paradise. Zoroaster's genius, it can be said, has influenced not only the religious but also the secular worldviews into which we in the West were born.

For Review:

1. What innovative concept regarding God did Zoroaster introduce?
2. Who were the magi?
3. How does Zoroaster account for evil in the world?
4. What distinctive doctrine did Zoroaster teach about human destiny?
5. Who are the Parsis, and what are some of the striking features of their religion?
6. What religions has Zoroastrianism influenced? How has Zoroaster influenced Western thought generally?

For Reflection:

1. Spend a few moments imagining yourself at the seat of judgment after death. Do you see it as a judgment that mixes justice with compassion? Or, in your mind, is it a strictly legal matter?
2. The Parsis use fire as a liturgical symbol. How is fire similarly used in Christian liturgies? What general symbolic meanings do you attach to fire?

9
JUDAISM: TRUSTING IN THE COVENANT

The religion of the Jewish people is probably more familiar to you than the other religions we have studied so far. After all, Judaism was a parent of Christianity, and we acknowledge the Jewish Scriptures (that is, the Old Testament) as part of our own Bible.

Yet this familiarity should not blind us to the uniqueness of Judaism and to the very different historical events that have shaped this religion, especially as compared with our Christian history. Whereas Christianity rose quickly to popularity, Judaism has suffered incessant persecution. And whereas Christians were soon at home in the Roman Empire and later in Europe, the Jews have lived for much of their history in exile.

Chosen by God

"Then, in the sight of Yahweh your God, you must make this pronouncement:

'My father was a wandering Aramaean. He went down into Egypt to find refuge there, few in numbers; but there he became a nation, great, mighty, and strong. The Egyptians ill-treated us, they gave us no peace and inflicted harsh slavery on us. But we called on Yahweh the God of our fathers. Yahweh heard our voice and saw our misery, our toil and our oppression; and Yahweh brought us out of Egypt with mighty hand and outstretched arm, with great terror, and with signs and wonders. He brought us here and gave us this land, a land where milk and honey flow.' " (Deuteronomy 26:5–9)

This passage from the Bible was written at a time when the **Israelites,** the ancestors of the Jews, had established a kingdom in **Canaan**—the land of milk and honey. In this era of the famous kings David and Solomon, about 1000 B.C.E., the Israelites achieved prestige and wealth as a nation. Most especially, in this era the promises given by the Lord to the Jews seemed fulfilled.

These promises were given nearly one thousand years earlier, when the Israelites first began to see themselves in a special relationship with their God. For God had selected them to be a **Chosen People** and had offered them a special agreement, or **covenant,** by which they promised to worship only God. In turn, God promised to preserve them throughout history and to give them the land of Canaan (later known as Palestine, Israel, or Judah).

We might raise our eyebrows at a claim by members of another religion to be chosen by God. Yet the Jews were chosen for a special mission, not for a privileged position. That mission was to bring the light of God to the whole world. And that light, it seems, is the light of humility and trust. For during much of the four thousand years of their history, the Jewish people have had to trust in God's promise and to suffer while waiting for its fulfillment. Throughout their long history, at least a core of Jews has maintained this trust. For no people, as widely dispersed and as often persecuted as the Jews have been, has ever kept a faith alive for so long.

As a matter of fact, despite the hardships suffered in every generation, the Jews have exerted a positive influence wherever they have lived. Besides furthering the arts and sciences, they have radically influenced the laws and ethics of half the world. Although numbering only fifteen million people today, the Jews continue to pursue their destiny with extraordinary joy and enthusiasm.

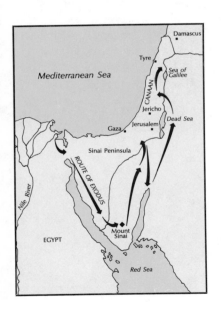

The Patriarchs and the Covenant

Central to an understanding of the Jewish covenant is the story of **Abraham,** a prosperous, wandering herdsman who answered a call from God to lead his family from Ur of the Chaldees (now in Iraq) to Canaan. This occurred around 1850 B.C.E. In the biblical rendering of the event, God appeared to Abraham and said,

> ". . . and I will make a Covenant between myself and you, and increase your numbers greatly. . . . I will make you most fruitful. I will make you into nations, and your issue shall be kings. I will establish my Covenant . . . to be your God and the God of your descendants after you." (Genesis 17:2,6–7)

According to the book of Genesis, Abraham's son **Isaac** and grandson **Jacob** (also called Israel, from whom the people took their name) inherited this covenant. So along with Abraham, Isaac and Jacob are referred to as the **patriarchs**—that is, the founders of Judaism.

Biblical narratives describe these patriarchs as nomads who followed their flocks from place to place on the fringes of the Semitic cultures of the Near East. The **Semites** originally included Jews, Arabs, Babylonians, Assyrians, Aramaeans, and Canaanites; but later the term referred specifically to the Jews. Typically the early Semitic cities contained impressive temples and powerful priesthoods dedicated to agricultural gods, like **Baal,** or to **Astarte,** the mother goddess. Consequently, the patriarchs must have come into contact with these and other Semitic deities.

The patriarchs, in fact, worshiped a god called **El,** a name used for the gods by many of the Semitic groups. In Genesis, this name is frequently used in combinations, such as El Olam ("God Everlasting"), El Elyon ("God Most High"), El Shaddai ("God of the Mountains"), or Elohim ("Gods" or "God!"). Thus, we cannot be sure that the patriarchs distinguished their God from the gods worshiped by the Semites. What does seem clear is that the patriarchs worshiped one God and saw that God as directing their destiny.

The worship of the early Israelites was not tied to a temple. Instead, they worshiped El by sacrificing animals on crude altars built of stones. In this way, El could be served wherever these poor but free people wandered.

Also dating from the time of the patriarchs is the ritual of **male circumcision,** which is the cutting off of the foreskin of the penis. In Genesis 17:10–11, God commands Abraham to circumcise all his male descendants as a sign of the covenant. Circumcision was a powerful way of initiating males into the tribe because it left permanent marks on their bodies. This practice is one of the earliest examples of the biblical laws that were to help give a special identity to the Israelite community.

Moses and Yahweh

At the close of the book of Genesis, the descendants of Abraham are about to become a great nation, but a nation without a place to call its own. In fact, as the book of Exodus opens, we find that they are slaves in the land of Egypt. We know practically nothing of the hundreds of years, commonly dated from 1700 to 1250 B.C.E., that the Israelites spent in Egypt. Yet the Exodus became the heart and soul of Judaism. These events are summarized in the scriptural passage that begins this chapter.

The Exodus story is probably familiar to you, as is **Moses**—the key character of this story and one of the great religious leaders in history. Much like the lives of other religious leaders that we have looked at, Moses' life has become legendary. Two major elements of Jewish faith, however, are part of the biblical and historical record of his time.

Above: **The Exodus, from a nineteenth-century engraving**

Facing page: **A devout Jew kisses his Bible during services in Dorchester, Massachusetts**

A New Name for the One God

First, a new name for God was given to the Israelites. Speaking through a burning bush, God revealed to Moses the name **Yahweh,** a name that may derive from an ancient Hebrew word meaning "to be." Actually it is not accurate to say that Yahweh is the name of God because the original pronunciation of the name was lost. Later Jews, out of reverence for this name, preferred not to pronounce it. Instead they used titles such as **Adonai,** meaning "lord." When writing, Jewish scribes used the letters *YHVH* to mark the name of God. Pronouncing the name as *ya*-way is a modern practice, which we will adopt for this discussion.

The events recorded in Exodus indicate that through Moses a new and deeper understanding of God was revealed. Likewise, scholars suggest that, in fact, the worship of Yahweh was unknown before Moses. The Israelites as a whole began to realize that the God of Moses was a "jealous God," who would not tolerate the worship of any other gods. Indeed, that intolerance extended not just to gods set up *in opposition* to Yahweh but also to any local gods worshiped *in addition* to Yahweh. This demand is clearly worded in the first of the Ten Commandments:

"I am Yahweh your God who brought you out of the land of Egypt, out of the house of slavery.

"You shall have no gods except me.

"You shall not make yourself a carved image or any likeness of anything in heaven or on earth beneath or in the waters under the earth; you shall not bow down to them or serve them. For I, Yahweh your God, am a jealous God. . . ." (Exodus 20:2–5)

Although the Israelites began to practice monotheism within their own group, they did not necessarily see God as ruling over all other people. Their concerns probably did not extend much beyond their own families and tribes. In other words, their understanding of the one God did not necessarily propel the Israelites to monotheism as a worldview. This global perspective came later.

A Religion of the Word

The second major element of Jewish faith associated with Moses' time is also mentioned in the above passage from Exodus. It is the prohibition against graven images of God. As with the new name of God, such a practice was unknown in Semitic cultures of that time. Its impact, not only on Jewish history but on religious history in the West, proved to be remarkable.

What this prohibition meant in practice was that images of God could be built out of *words* but not out of *things*. As a result, in Jewish faith, words became the vehicle of religious expression—especially the words found in the Jewish Scriptures. The other great religions that followed Judaism were strongly affected by this prohibition. Along with Judaism, Christianity and Islam would become known as "religions of the word" because of the central importance of sacred scriptures in their histories.

The Prophets

Moses is surely the most admired figure in Jewish history. In other religions of the Near East, such leaders have often been regarded as divine. Yet the strong push toward monotheism made such a divine status unlikely, if not impossible, in Judaism. Instead, Moses was accepted as the first in a long line of Jewish prophets. He began a tradition that gave Judaism its distinctive character.

From the Judges to the Temple

Before we talk about the prophets, let's catch up on some developments in Jewish history. Having left Egypt, the tribes that gathered under the banner of the Israelites came to the land of Canaan. Over the next centuries (c. 1250–1000 B.C.E.), the **judges** led the Israelites in their battles against the people who dwelled in Canaan.

During this time, the Israelites adapted to the agricultural way of life that was native to the region of Palestine. As they became a more settled, farming people, the idea of having a king began to appeal to the Israelites' leaders. **Saul** was the first anointed king. But Saul was soon replaced by **David,** who successfully established a political center for his people by

Sabbath Celebration

The observance of the Sabbath, which may date back to the time of the patriarchs, remains a key element of Jewish worship. It commemorates both the creation of the world and the deliverance of the people of Israel from Egypt. The Sabbath is the day when Jews let go of work and human effort to remind themselves that the world is in the hands of the Creator.

Beginning at sundown on Friday in devout households, the woman who is head of the house lights the Sabbath candles, calling on the "Lord of the Universe" to bless her family. The adults attend the synagogue, and on their return the fathers bless their children and praise their wives in the words of Proverbs. Other blessings and a Sabbath meal then follow. Traditionally, the best food of the week is served at the Friday evening meal.

Until sundown on Saturday, the family celebrates the four traits of the Sabbath: holiness, joy, honor, and rest. Thus, the Sabbath offers a taste of the age to come when the whole world enjoys the light of God.

Since no work is permitted on the Sabbath, Orthodox Jews must be employed in jobs that allow them to be home before sunset every Friday. Often this means that they will be self-employed or will work in a Jewish company.

At the close of the Sabbath, the family again gathers for a brief ceremony. Blessings are recited over a cup of wine and a box of sweet spices. The spices are intended as a reminder of the sweet moments of the Sabbath—a memory to be carried into the new week.

capturing Jerusalem in about 1000 B.C.E. David was followed by his son **Solomon,** who built the Temple in Jerusalem.

As both the political and religious capital of the Israelites, Jerusalem became a uniquely holy place. Priests were known in Jewish history as far back as the time of Moses, but they took on a special importance when the Temple in Jerusalem became the sole place of worship for the nation. Worship gained a more formal status, although its major ritual remained the animal sacrifice burned in the courtyard. In the Temple itself, prayers were offered to Yahweh.

Calling for a Return to Yahweh

Just as important to Judaism as the development of temple worship was the appearance of prophets (called *nabi,* from a word meaning "to call out"). The prophets may have begun much like the prophets in other ancient religions—that is, as small bands of people who worked themselves into highly emotional states in order to hear the voices of their gods. During the period of the monarchy, however, certain Jewish prophets became attached to the royal households. The prophet **Nathan,** for example, had direct contact with King David and even had a hand in placing Solomon on the throne.

Solomon's pools, the traditional name for a reservoir that was used to hold water for Jerusalem

Prophets played an even more important role in Jewish history after Solomon's time. During his reign (970–922 B.C.E.), Solomon had imposed heavy taxes and slave labor on his people—hardships that became even more severe over the next centuries. Solomon also established foreign alliances, sometimes through intermarriage. After Solomon's death, these policies led to the split of the nation into two kingdoms—**Israel** in the north and **Judah** in the south. (Both the terms *Jew* and *Judaism* are derived from the name of the southern kingdom.) In addition, the foreign alliances gradually evolved into government support of other religions.

Against this double threat—of injustice and of paganism—the prophets spoke out. They were not afraid to tell their kings that political success did not necessarily mean that God was pleased with them. For example, **Elijah,** whose name means "Yahweh is God," denounced King Ahab and his wife Jezebel for supporting the cults of Baal and Astarte. Elijah succeeded so well, in fact, that the term *jezebel* is still used to describe a shameless woman.

Similarly, when the Assyrian Empire defeated and dismantled the northern kingdom of Israel in 721 B.C.E., prophets in the southern kingdom called for an immediate return to the one true God:

> "Come now, let us talk this over,
> says Yahweh.
> Though your sins are like scarlet,
> they shall be as white as snow;
> though they are red as crimson,
> they shall be like wool.

> "If you are willing to obey,
> you shall eat the good things of the earth.
> But if you persist in rebellion,
> the sword shall eat you instead."
> The mouth of Yahweh has spoken.
>
> (Isaiah 1:18–20)

Isaiah, from a Bible illustration by the nineteenth-century artist Gustave Doré

In addition to urging Judah's return to Yahweh, the defeat of Israel began what is known in history as the **Jewish Dispersion,** that is, the resettling of Jews in countries outside of Palestine. Eventually this would result in the founding of Jewish settlements in various parts of the Persian Empire and later in the Greek and Roman Empires.

In 587 B.C.E., the Babylonians took control of Israel from the Assyrians, defeated the southern kingdom of Judah, and destroyed Jerusalem. The leaders of Judah were taken as captives to Babylon.

Even in Babylon the exiled Jews found in their midst powerful prophets, who taught a more universal understanding of God than they had encountered before. During this time, for example, the great prophet known only as **Second Isaiah** proclaimed a deity of all time and of all people: "I am the first and the last; there is no other God besides me" (Isaiah 44:6). Moreover, he held up other people's religious notions for ridicule:

"Assemble, come, gather together,
survivors of the nations.
They are ignorant, those who carry about
their idol of wood,
those who pray to a god
that cannot save.

. . . . . .

Turn to me and be saved,
all the ends of the earth,
for I am God unrivalled."

(Isaiah 45:20,22)

The revelation of the one true God that began with the patriarchs came to its fullest expression in the words and writings of the prophets over a thousand years later. Judaism had become a *monotheistic* religion in the fullest sense of the term.

A Message of Compassion

Yet the prophets' message went even further. They saw Yahweh as not only powerful but compassionate. In the vision of the prophet **Hosea** for example, the nation was seen as a faithless spouse whom Yahweh continued to love in spite of Israel's gross infidelity:

How can I hand you over, O Israel!

. . . .

My heart recoils within me,
my compassion grows warm and tender.
I will not execute my fierce anger,

. . . .

for I am God and not man,
the Holy One in your midst,
and I will not come to destroy.

(Hosea 11:8–9)

The Star of David, also known as the Shield of David. According to one tradition, this symbol was used on the shields of David's soldiers. Today it appears on the flag of Israel.

The Yahweh of the prophets was revealed as the God whose love is stronger than jealousy, and the covenant between God and the Chosen People was a marriage for life.

The Enduring Prophetic Vision

Apparently, the prophets were not heeded in their own time. And by the fifth century B.C.E., the line of prophets had died out. Their words were preserved by admirers, however, and the truth and beauty of these words profoundly influenced the worldview and morality of Judaism and other Western religions.

Later the prophets' common vision became focused into what was called the **Day of Yahweh,** that is, the day when Yahweh would rise up against the enemies of the Jews and bring an end to the Jews' sufferings. In the turmoil of the last two centuries B.C.E., this hope grew to include the idea that God would send a savior, the **Messiah,** who would lead Israel to a final victory.

This final victory, interestingly, was portrayed by some writers as a colossal battle between the forces of good and evil—a depiction that is very reminiscent of the Zoroastrian worldview. Also during this time, beliefs about the afterlife arose—including the promise of paradise, the bodily resurrection of the dead, and the Last Judgment.

The Scriptures and the Mosaic Law

After the destruction of Jerusalem in 587 B.C.E., the Jews were in a very difficult position. Although the Jews were eventually released from exile, Judah was no longer a politically independent nation, but merely a district within the Persian Empire and later within the Greek and Roman Empires. While Jews were sometimes granted freedom in cultural and political affairs, authority in these areas usually was divided between a high priest and a governor who were answerable to the current rulers.

As a result of these circumstances, being a Jew no longer meant being a member of a recognized nation. Also, while in Babylon, most Jews had dropped the Hebrew language for daily use in favor of Aramaic. So Hebrew had only limited use in literary writing and worship.

Yet the Jewish faith had grown stronger during this period. Their worship of the God of Moses had survived the enormous changes from nomadic to agricultural to urban life and from tribal society to monarchy. Furthermore, the community still had a history that it could be proud of—a history connecting the patriarchs, Moses, the judges, the kings, the priests, and the prophets.

Linking the present to the glorious past was accomplished in one way by the rebuilding of the Temple in Jerusalem about 515 B.C.E. The religious rites, including sacrifice and prayer, were reestablished along with the religious festivals that had helped to preserve the identity of the Jews living outside Palestine.

This link with their history was affirmed also by carefully collecting

Top: **Shepherds watching their flocks near Bethlehem**

Bottom: **Jerusalem in its glory, from a model**

and regularly reflecting on the ancestral writings. By about 400 B.C.E., the major books of what became the Jewish Scriptures were collected from writings in the Hebrew language that went as far back as 1100 B.C.E.

Certain of these books were elevated to a special status and referred to as **Torah,** which means "law" or "instruction." The Torah includes the first five books of the Jewish Scriptures and contains the laws, attributed to Moses, concerning worship and daily life.

Some of these laws are highly moral and logical. For instance, most of the laws included in the Ten Commandments provided the basis for the great legal codes that developed in the West. Other laws—about keeping holy the Sabbath, for example—are more religious in character. Still other laws deal with special customs such as circumcision and the ban on eating pork. Some of these laws may sound confusing and strange to us. Yet taken all together, the Mosaic Law wove a distinctive way of life that has helped the Jews maintain their identity down through history. The Torah remains the undisputed foundational document for members of the Jewish community.

The Rabbis and the Talmud

When the Temple in Jerusalem was destroyed by the Babylonians, temple worship was impossible. Moreover, it seems that animal sacrifice was no longer deemed appropriate in the urban centers where Jews of the Dispersion settled. So, for Jews living in cities such as Alexandria, Athens, and Rome, the **synagogues** replaced the Temple as the place of worship. The synagogues became especially important after 70 C.E., when the Romans destroyed the second and last Temple.

The word *synagogue* comes from a Greek word meaning "assembly," which suggests that the synagogue is more than just a building. In fact, even today any Jewish home can be a synagogue as long as there are ten adult Jewish males assembled and a copy of the Torah available. Synagogues are used for daily prayer and instruction, but weekly Sabbath worship is the chief reason for gathering. Although no sacrifice is offered, each synagogue recalls the Temple in its use of a perpetually burning candelabrum, called a **menorah,** representing the one that was used in Jerusalem.

Top: **The Torah in an ornamental silver case**

Bottom: **The spoils of Jerusalem, from a detail of the arch built by the Roman emperor Titus to memorialize his conquest of Palestine in 70 C.E.**

Jewish Festivals

The vivid, living faith of the Jews in God's personal concern for them has made them a celebrating people. Over thousands of years, the festivals observed in their homes and synagogues have helped to keep Jews united.

Besides the Sabbath observance, time is sanctified by the yearly festivals, which are based on the Jewish lunar calendar. In September or October of our secular calendar, the New Year, **Rosh Hashanah,** opens ten "Days of Awe" in which the Jews examine their lives in order to bring them into accord with the Mosaic Law. Celebrations begin and end the ten-day period. **Yom Kippur** ("Day of Atonement") is the closing feast of repentance and is considered the most holy day of the year. During this twenty-four-hour fast, Orthodox Jews may not work, eat, drink, engage in sexual activity, bathe, anoint the body, or wear leather shoes. Confession of sin is made corporately, not individually.

Five days after Yom Kippur, the Feast of Tabernacles (**Sukkoth**) is celebrated. This week-long autumnal feast of thanksgiving commemorates God's providence during the Israelite's sojourn in the desert. Many Jewish families build outdoor tabernacles, or booths (tents), decorate them with harvest fruits, eat their meals in the tabernacles, and sleep under the stars. A celebration called **Rejoicing in the Torah** closes Sukkoth and marks the end of the yearly reading of the first five books of the Jewish Scriptures.

Hanukkah, the Festival of Lights, is celebrated in December and commemorates the restoration of the Temple after its desecration by the Syrians in 160 B.C.E. The eight-branch candelabrum, called the menorah, is a central symbol in the eight-day celebration.

Usually in February or March, the Book of Esther is read in the synagogue. Esther is a Jewish heroine who became the queen of Persia. **Purim** celebrates Esther's success in foiling a plot to massacre all the Jews in the Persian Empire. Much buffoonery and melodrama accompany the reading of Esther as the children boo the villain and cheer the heroine.

One of the most important spring holy days is the **Pesach**—the Passover. It is observed by having special foods served at a **seder,** or ceremonial meal. Unleavened bread, blessed wine and spices, and the retelling of the story of the escape from Egypt are part of the commemoration. Fifty days later is the feast of **Pentecost,** which remembers the giving of the Law to Moses fifty days after the Passover.

Facing page, top: A Sukkoth celebration, dated about 1900

Facing page, bottom: A Hanukkah celebration

Top: Young girls celebrating Purim

Bottom: A family at a Passover meal

The Law (Torah)
Genesis
Exodus
Leviticus
Numbers
Deuteronomy

The Prophets
Joshua
Judges
First and Second Samuel
First and Second Kings
Isaiah
Jeremiah
Ezekiel
Hosea
Joel
Amos
Obadiah
Jonah
Micah
Nahum
Habakkuk
Zephaniah
Haggai
Zechariah
Malachi

The Writings
Psalms
Job
Proverbs
Ruth
Song of Songs
Ecclesiastes
Lamentations
Esther
Daniel
Ezra-Nehemiah
First and Second Chronicles

With the final destruction of the Temple, the priesthood became virtually extinct, and religious leadership passed to the **rabbis,** who led the services and instruction in the synagogues. A rabbi is more like a teacher than a priest or minister in the usual sense. With the elevation of the Torah to special importance, there was a need for some people to spend time studying the scriptures and teaching them to the community. Those persons who had the time, interest, and intelligence to study the scriptures eventually were singled out as "masters," which is what the word *rabbi* means. This stress on study and instruction, incidentally, has resulted in a level of education among Jews that is often superior to their non-Jewish neighbors.

Rabbinic Judaism, which is Judaism as we know it today, marked its debut in history at a school established in a Palestinian seacoast town soon after the final destruction of the Temple. Striving to rebuild the community on the Mosaic Law, the rabbis deliberated on the contents of the Jewish Scriptures. They agreed on which books would henceforth carry the sole scriptural authority. Actually, the books selected (which constitute much of what we Christians term the Old Testament) had been used by the rabbis for some time. What the rabbis' seal of approval did, then, was to set aside other writings that came from what Judaism considered discredited sources, including Jewish Christianity. This Jewish Bible is called the **Tanak,** which consists of three sections: the Law (Torah), the Prophets, and the Writings.

During the period from the first to the fifth centuries C.E., rabbis in Palestine and Babylonia also compiled two versions of the **Talmud,** which takes second place only to the Jewish Scriptures as the written authority governing Jewish life and faith. The Talmud (meaning "instructions") records the conclusions of learned rabbis concerning the interpretation of the scriptures and the right living of daily life. It contains marriage laws, standards for diet and hygiene, regulations for services and festivals, and a record of history, folklore, and sermons.

Although the Jewish Scriptures remained the ultimate authority, these scriptures were seen through the lens of the Talmud. Along with the Mosaic Law and the synagogue, the Talmud became an integral part of Judaism. In fact, Rabbinic Judaism is also known as **Talmudic Judaism.**

The Golden Age of the Near East

Judaism has been shamefully treated by both of its unexpected children—Christianity and Islam. When Christianity won its position as the dominant religion in the Roman Empire in the fourth century C.E., Judaism was bound to suffer. Although the Christians worshiped the same God as the Jews, most Christians wrongly blamed the Jews for killing Jesus. More to the point, as the pagan religions were suppressed, Judaism was left as the only outsider in what had become—at least in name—a Christian society. Consequently, Jews could easily be loaded with the blame for misfortunes. Worth noting, however, is the fact that the popes were generally tolerant of the Jewish community in Rome, which survived into the modern era relatively unharmed.

The religion of Islam bloomed in the Arabian desert in the seventh century C.E. By the early years of the eighth century, Jews living in Palestine, Babylonia, Egypt, North Africa, and Spain fell under the rule of Muslim conquerors. Despite sporadic persecutions and harassment, the Jews became part of the Golden Age of Islam. Especially during the period from 750 to 847, Jews in Babylonia worked side by side with Muslim scholars to advance the fields of science, philosophy, literature, government, and medicine.

The golden age of the Near East did not last long, however. Renewed persecutions and the internal strife caused by heresy drained the energies of the Jewish community. Eventually the leading Jewish thinkers were found across the Mediterranean Sea in Spain.

Scholars and Mystics

Jews were living in Spain as early as the first century C.E. In one of his Epistles, Saint Paul mentions his hopes of visiting the Jewish community there. When the Roman Empire generally converted to Christianity, Jews were given the choice of conversion or expulsion. Yet somehow Jews survived in Spain until its conquest by the Muslims in 711.

As in Babylonia, a golden age of freedom followed the Muslim conquest. Many outstanding Jewish poets, physicians, and thinkers flourished during this era. Perhaps the most famous of these is **Moses ben Maimon**

Top: **A rabbi in traditional garments**

Bottom: **The Dome of the Rock, dating from 691, the oldest surviving Muslim mosque. It was built upon the site of the Temple in Jerusalem.**

(1135–1204), better known as **Maimonides.** Although born in Spain, he was driven out by persecution and so resettled in Cairo, Egypt. Maimonides wrote important philosophical works, including a book that attempted to harmonize Jewish beliefs with Greek philosophy, particularly with Aristotle's philosophy. Maimonides' *Guide for the Perplexed* is compared with the *Summa Theologica* by Saint Thomas Aquinas, which was a very similar endeavor. In fact, Maimonides' guide was studied and often quoted by Aquinas in his work. For many Jews, Maimonides stands next to the prophet Moses as their greatest religious leader and the man whose wisdom shaped modern Judaism. "From Moses unto Moses," it is said, "there was none like Moses."

The Jewish philosopher Maimonides

Maimonides and the other scholars of his era preserved and enhanced the intellectual tradition in Judaism that is represented in modern times by such giants as Karl Marx, Sigmund Freud, and Albert Einstein. And these are just the peaks in a very high mountain range of Jewish intellectuals.

Maimonides' "Creed"

Maimonides felt that salvation was available to anyone who believed in the set of truths revealed to the Jews. So he listed what he considered the thirteen articles of faith for Judaism. Soon this list became an unofficial creed for Jews worldwide, representing a summary of the Jewish Bible, the Talmud, and ten centuries of Jewish history.

I believe with perfect faith that the Creator, praised be He, is the Creator and Guide of all creation, and that He alone has made, does make, and will make all things.

. . . is a Unity, and that there is no unity like His in any manner, and that He alone is our God, who was, is, and will be.

. . . is not a body, and that He is free from all attributes of a body, and that He has no form whatsoever.

. . . is the first and the last.

I believe with perfect faith that to the Creator, praised be He, and to Him alone is it proper to pray, and that it is not proper to pray to any besides Him.

I believe with perfect faith that all the words of the prophets are true.

I believe with perfect faith that the prophecy of Moses our great teacher, may he rest in peace, was true, and that he was the father of the prophets, both those who preceded and who followed him.

I believe with perfect faith that the entire Torah now in our possession is the same that was given to Moses our teacher, may he rest in peace.

I believe with perfect faith that this Torah will never be replaced and that there will never be another Torah from the Creator, praised be He.

I believe with perfect faith that the Creator, praised be He, knows every deed of men and all their thoughts, as it is written, "He fashions the hearts of them all and observes all their deeds" (Psalm 33:15).

I believe with perfect faith that the Creator, praised be He, rewards those who keep His commandments and punishes those that transgress His commandments.

I believe with perfect faith in the coming of the Messiah, and though he tarry I will wait daily for him.

I believe with perfect faith that there will be a revival of the dead at a time when it shall please the Creator, praised be He, and exalted be His fame for ever and ever.

The Cabala

By Maimonides' time, another philosophical system was beginning to develop in Spain. This system, however, was more visionary or mystical than scholarly in nature. In the **Cabala,** as it was called, the study of the Torah was central. But the aim was to find hidden, secret meanings in the words, letters, and numbers of the scriptures.

The mystical and magical elements in Cabalism have always been threads in Judaism generally. But Cabalism became most popular among the Jews during their very difficult times of persecution and poverty. Although the Talmud might offer rules for living in relatively normal circumstances, cabalistic literature held out the promise of a messiah and salvation to a people who had little other hope.

Persecution in Europe

Ghettos

As the persecutions in Babylonia and in Spain became more severe, Jews in large numbers began to move into Christian Europe. Frequently, Jews were invited into communities by Christian leaders to serve as moneylenders because lending money was an occupation that was forbidden to Christians. Unfortunately, only the aristocracy benefited from the moneylenders, so the European peasants added this to their prejudices against the Jews.

Commonly, European Jews were required by law to live in designated sections of cities called **ghettos.** These were often the worst parts of the cities—overcrowded, sunless places. To further set them apart from Christians, often Jews were forced to wear yellow badges or distinctive hats. Yet within the ghettos, Jews had a limited amount of political and social freedom. Thus, by the tenth century, Europe had become a major center of Jewish life.

Top: **The Jewish ghetto in Lublin, Poland, at the beginning of this century**

Bottom: **The victims of a pogrom in March 1919**

Facing page: **The destruction of the Warsaw ghetto in 1943 by German Nazis. Of the nearly half million Jews herded into this ghetto during the forties, only a handful survived the war.**

With the coming of the Crusades, however, conditions for the Jews in Europe went from bad to worse as Christian fanaticism against the Muslims spilled over to the Jews as well. On their way to the Holy Land, Crusaders ravaged Jewish ghettos all over Europe. Only a few Jews were hidden by sympathetic bishops. By 1290 the persecutions became so severe that many Jews fled to Poland or Lithuania. By the seventeenth century, more than half of all Jews lived in these two regions.

Pogroms

Yet this flight from persecution—like the many others that Jews were forced to make—brought little respite. In the late 1700s, the partition of Poland brought a million Jews under Russian rule. The next hundred years of sporadic persecution led to a series of infamous Russian slaughters called **pogroms** that occurred at hundreds of sites between 1881 and 1921. Many of the Jews who survived the pogroms immigrated to the United States along with other European Jews. Between 1870 and 1940 the Jewish population in the United States rose from 0.25 million to 4.5 million people.

The Holocaust

Persecution is madness, but in the history of the persecutions of the Jews, madness gave way to something worse when the Nazis took control of Germany in the 1930s. At this time, the Germans were a humiliated people—totally defeated in World War I and crushed by economic disaster in the Great Depression. So the moment was ripe for Hitler to take anti-Semitism—that is, hatred of the Jews—a new and horrifying step further.

Millions of Jews were trapped in Europe when Poland, Hungary, and Czechoslovakia fell into Hitler's hands. As in Germany, authorities in

Above: **A Hitler youth rally in 1935**

Right: **Corpses at the death camp at Dachau, Germany. The camp was liberated by U.S. troops in April 1945.**

these countries cooperated with Hitler's plans. Much of the rest of the world, in fact, assented by its silence to what was happening—which was nothing less than the attempted extermination of an entire race of people.

In death camps throughout eastern Europe, Jews were murdered by starvation, exhaustion, beating, mutilation, infection, gassing, and burning. Even their corpses were robbed of hair and gold teeth; and their skins, bones, and body fat were put to experimental or industrial uses. The usual estimate of the number of Jews killed during the Nazi years is six million, that is, one-third of the entire Jewish population of the world. In Poland alone, only fifty thousand Jews remained of a prewar population of over three million.

The faith of the Jews has been tested many times in history but never more than in what became known as the Holocaust. This catastrophe poses serious questions for other religions as well: How could God have allowed this to happen to believers? What did the mission to be a light to the world mean in such circumstances? Why would anyone have to suffer so much? No simple answers are possible to questions like these. We can only strive to keep the questions themselves alive by not forgetting that the Holocaust can and did happen.

The Branches of Judaism

Today Judaism has three branches—Orthodox, Reform, and Conservative—each of which professes to be truly Jewish. Yet the branches differ as much from one another as do the Catholics, the Protestants, and the Eastern Churches in Christianity.

Orthodox Judaism is the oldest and largest group within Judaism. It holds to the full tradition of Judaism, calling itself "Torah-true Judaism" because of its strict adherence to the Law of Moses. This traditional stance shapes its approach to theology, worship, morality, and festivals.

Within this Orthodox branch is an ultraconservative group known as the **Hasidim**, which developed as a reaction to the scholarly and philosophical forms of Judaism. Its founders preached that God was not to be found in researching the Jewish Scriptures or the Talmud but in simple, heartfelt faith.

Left and below: Jews who belong to the more conservative sects still wear traditional garments, including prayer shawls and phylacteries—small boxes strapped to the forehead and left arm that contain passages from the Torah.

Just before the turn of the last century, some Jewish people showed a desire to adapt to modern society, especially in the United States where they have enjoyed greater freedom and acceptance than elsewhere. This led to the rise of a liberal branch known as **Reform Judaism.** Reform Jews call their houses of worship "temples," observe the Sabbath on Sunday, and have begun to ordain women rabbis. They believe that the Mosaic Law must not be followed too literally. Yet Reform Jews still cling faithfully to the belief in one God and the need for high standards of morality.

Conservative Judaism lies between the strict Orthodox and the liberal Reform branches. Retaining the essentials of Judaism, they hold that personal conscience must be the final rule of life, and they cautiously try to apply the Jewish tradition to modern life. Frequently, Conservative Jews are involved in the professions and arts, and their rabbis are leaders in secular life, as well as in their religious congregations.

Jews Today and the State of Israel

As a response to the ghettos and persecutions, in the late 1800s a movement called **Zionism** was organized to establish a Jewish homeland. Although Palestine had been mainly Muslim for a thousand years, Jews began to settle there in the 1890s. The British, who governed the region, were persuaded to support the Zionist movement after the First World War, and additional thousands of Jews immigrated to Palestine. Tragically, it was the Holocaust that finally gained the commitment of many Jews who initially opposed the Zionist movement. By 1948 the new State of Israel had been carved out of Palestine. Since then Israel has survived continual attacks by its Arab neighbors.

For the Zionists, the creation of the State of Israel was a religious, as well as a political, feat. They saw in the Jewish state the beginning of the fulfillment of Israel's mission to bring the light of God to earth. For other Jews, especially those living outside of Israel, this achievement has become a source of pride, solidarity, and confidence.

Judaism and Christianity

In recent years the sad history of Jews and Christians has begun to improve. The documents coming from Vatican Council II reflect the Catholic Church's understanding that these two religions are deeply connected in the person of Jesus and in the Bible.

Earlier in the course, we mentioned that Jesus has been seen differently in different periods of history—that is, as the Word, as the Ransom, as the King, and so forth. Theologians today recognize that if we are to understand Jesus' ministry and mission, we must work toward a more

Facing page: Iraqi Jews register as immigrants at an Israeli airport in 1950.

Above: Egyptian patrols meet along the Gaza Strip during the fifties.

Left: A Palestinian refugee camp in Egypt in 1954. Two hundred thousand Arabs fled Israel following the First Palestine War that established Israel as a nation.

The Israeli philosopher Martin Buber

historical portrait of his life. That means learning all we can about Jesus as a Jew and as a learned and practicing member of Judaism. Worth mention also is the fact that the Apostles and many of the early disciples who first proclaimed Christianity to the world were also Jews.

The other powerful link between these two religions is the Bible—especially the Jewish Scriptures. The leaders of the Second Vatican Council summarized the common beliefs that are found in the Bible:

> The Church of Christ acknowledges that in God's plan of salvation the beginning of her faith and election is to be found in the patriarchs, Moses and the prophets. . . . Nor can she forget that she draws nourishment from the good olive tree [Judaism] onto which the wild olive branches of the Gentiles have been grafted. . . .

This biblical connection is also affirmed in the work of **Martin Buber** (1878–1965), an outstanding Jewish thinker of modern times. One of Buber's important contributions has been his hopeful thoughts on cooperation between Judaism and Christianity. Reflecting on the Bible, he wrote what can be the prayerful, closing thought on this matter:

> To you, the book is a forecourt; to us, it is the sanctuary. But in this place, we can dwell together, and together listen to the voice that speaks here. That means that we can work together to evoke the buried speech of that voice; together, we can redeem the imprisoned living word.

For Review:

1. What was the covenant that was offered to Abraham? What has the covenant meant to the Jewish religion?
2. What two new elements entered Jewish faith at the time of Moses?
3. What contributions did the prophets make to Judaism?
4. What is the undisputed foundational document for the Jewish community?
5. When did the rabbis take up the religious leadership in Judaism?
6. What was decided at the school of rabbis after the destruction of the Temple?
7. What is Maimonides' reputation in Jewish history?
8. How did European Christian communities set apart the Jews?
9. What was the aim of the Zionist movement?

For Reflection:

1. The Exodus is the story of salvation for both Jews and Christians. Describe how that story is retold in the world today or in your own life.
2. One writer refers to Rabbinic Judaism as "portable Judaism." In what ways did Judaism become portable? Do you think portability helped or hindered the growth of Judaism?
3. How does the creed proposed by Maimonides differ from the Nicene Creed? What do you disagree with in Maimonides' articles of faith?
4. What do you know about the Holocaust and its effect on the worldwide Jewish community? How do you feel about it? Do you think it could happen today?
5. Which branch of Judaism would you belong to if you were Jewish? Why?
6. Many Jews, especially those in the Orthodox branch, still await a personal messiah or a messianic era. This is a similar belief that we Christians share in our expectation of the Second Coming of Christ. In your mind, how do these beliefs differ?
7. Not all Jews were in favor of the Zionist movement. For instance, Martin Buber opposed "that Jewish nationalism which regards Israel as a nation like unto other nations, and recognizes no task for Israel save that of preserving and asserting itself." In the long run, do you think that nationhood will help or hinder the growth of Judaism?

10
ISLAM:
RELYING ON ONE GOD
AND ONE BOOK

In recent years, the followers of Islam, called Muslims, have erupted into Western consciousness. In the early 1970s, the Arabs severely restricted the flow of oil to the industrial nations to show support for their Muslim allies against Israel. Long lines for gasoline and soaring fuel prices caused Westerners to realize that they had taken the power of Islam for granted. Then, in 1979, Ayatollah Khomeini led the overthrow of the Western-oriented shah and established an Islamic republic in Iran.

But what is Islam, and who are the Muslims? The word *islam* stems from the Arabic *sallam,* meaning "peace through faith and surrender." A Muslim is a member of Islam, whose main expression of faith is total surrender to Allah—the one, true God who spoke to the people through the prophet Muhammad.

Islam is the youngest of the world religions and the second largest. The Middle East is heavily Islamic, but actually Muslims live all over the world, including three million Muslims in the United States and Canada.

Many Westerners may have negative reactions to Islam, but there must be more to this religion if it can attract such large numbers of followers. What is it about Islam that helps it attract new followers and gives them such enthusiasm for their religion?

The King Who Divined the Future

The Muslim mystic Attar of Nishapur told this story:

> A king who was also an astrologer read in his stars that on a certain day and at a particular hour a calamity would overtake him.
>
> He therefore built a house of solid rock and posted numerous guardians outside.
>
> One day, when he was within, he realized that he could still see

daylight. He found an opening which he filled up, to prevent misfortune entering. In blocking this door he made himself a prisoner with his own hands.

And because of this the king died.

This story of a king illustrates a central belief of Islam: we are all in the hands of Allah. We can try to control our destinies, but finally, we frustrate our own living when we try to deny the rule of Allah over all things.

This story is also a good starting point from which to understand the prophet of Islam, Muhammad, who never hid from what he believed to be revelations from God.

Muhammad the Messenger (c. 570–632 C.E.)

In 570 C.E. Muhammad was born into a reputable family of the Koreish tribe in Mecca (which is now in Saudi Arabia). At the age of six, Muhammad was an orphan. He was shifted around among relatives, finally becoming the ward of his uncle. Muhammad showed an early interest in religion; an aunt described him as a child of "visions." Traveling with his uncle's spice caravans to Syria and Palestine, the unlettered young camel driver camped with Christians and Jews, who shared their religious stories with him. Back in Mecca, young Muhammad listened to preachers who spoke to the crowds about one God, the Last Judgment, and the punishment of idolators in everlasting fire. By age eighteen, Muhammad was respectfully called *al-Amin*—meaning "the faithful."

The religion of Mecca included the worship of many minor gods. Some of their practices were repulsive to Muhammad. For example: Unwanted female babies were buried alive. Tremendous inequalities existed among the classes of Arabian society. Merchants in Mecca, the place of the central shrine to the pre-Islamic gods, made fortunes selling idols and sacrificial animals to poor people. The nomadic tribes, called the **Bedouin,** plundered the caravans of other Arabs. In short, Muhammad found the religion of his day corrupt and ineffectual.

Bedouins still follow a nomadic lifestyle in Arab countries in the Middle East and North Africa. The Arabic word *bedouin* means literally "desert dweller."

Muhammad began working for a rich widow, **Khadijah,** who was fifteen years his senior. Eventually she and Muhammad married and had six children. All of their children died except for one daughter, **Fatimah.** Deeply grieved by the death of his children and agitated by the thought of the Last Judgment of all peoples, Muhammad spent more and more time wandering in the hills around Mecca, meditating on death. At the age of forty while on one of his retreats, Muhammad had a revelation that would change his future and the future of the world.

The Night of Power and Excellence

Most major religions began with what is believed to be a revelation from God or with a sudden realization. Gautama the Buddha received enlightenment one day underneath the fig tree, for instance. In the Jewish Scriptures, God appeared to Abraham, telling him that he would father a new people.

About 610 c.e., Islam began with a revelation too. In a cave near Mecca, Muhammad believed that the angel Gabriel appeared to him. The angel announced that Muhammad was to be a prophet for the one God, Allah. On this night, which is called "the Night of Power and Excellence" by Muslims, Muhammad was commanded to "draw nigh to God."

Muhammad returned home stunned, wondering about his sanity. Khadijah reassured him and encouraged him to have confidence in his experience. Over the next ten years Muhammad had more revelations from Allah through the angel Gabriel. Just as the teachings of the Buddha and Confucius were written down, these revelations to Muhammad were written down in the holy book called the **Koran,** which is the source of Muslim beliefs and morality. But during the months immediately after the Night of Power and Excellence, Muhammad only gradually accepted that he was to be the mouthpiece of God, a prophet.

Muhammad began preaching against polytheism, immorality, and the class system. As expected, he made enemies of the merchants who sold idols and who lived off the pilgrims' coming to Mecca. Threats on Muhammad's life became frequent.

The Hegira: A Turning Point

Some pilgrims from Yathrib (later called the city of **Medina**) had heard Muhammad speaking when they were in Mecca. Impressed by the power of his words, they invited him to come to their city. Finally, in 622 c.e., with an assassination plot threatening him, Muhammad left Mecca. He already had sent some of his followers the 250 miles north to Medina. Thus, when Muhammad arrived in his new home, the way had been prepared. This journey to Medina is called the **Hegira,** meaning "flight." Just as Christians mark the beginning of the Christian era by Jesus' birth, the Muslims begin their lunar calendar from the year of Muhammad's journey to Medina.

In Medina, Muhammad was recognized as the *Rasul,* or Messenger, of Allah. He also assumed political and military leadership. From this time on, Muslims believed that ideally religion and state should be one, operating under the principles of the Koran.

After Muhammad's move to Medina, war with Mecca seemed inevitable. Muhammad wanted to convert Mecca from its evil ways. The authorities in Mecca wanted to crush the spread of Islam. After three major battles, Muhammad was able to ride into Mecca victoriously. He went directly to the **Kaaba,** the central shrine for the worship of idols.

The Kaaba at Mecca, during evening prayers

Muhammad believed that the Kaaba was the first structure built by humans that was consecrated to the one God. Set into one corner of the Kaaba is the **sacred Black Stone**—a meteorite that is said to have been given to Abraham by the angel Gabriel. Over the years, however, the Kaaba had been filled with the idols of many Arabic gods. Muhammad ordered the hundreds of idols destroyed but wisely stopped his troops from looting the city. From that time to the present, the Kaaba has stood empty except for the sacred Black Stone. Pilgrimages to the Kaaba later became the center of devout Muslims' lives.

People rapidly began converting to Islam. Many tribes of Bedouin fought against the forces of Muhammad, but all were eventually subdued. Jews and Christians were allowed to stay in conquered areas, but they had to pay special taxes. Muhammad believed that Christians and Jews should be tolerated because they were followers of true prophets, even though the Christians and Jews had distorted God's revelations to the prophets.

The rift between Muslims and Jews widened, however, when the Jews sided with the forces of Mecca against Muhammad. A Jewish woman tried to poison Muhammad after the Battle of Khaybar, in which he led the fight against the Jews. Although Muhammad lived, he suffered ill effects for a long time afterward.

In his private life, Muhammad remained a humble man, darning his own clothing and milking his own goat. In public, he was an inspiring prophet and an effective political and military leader. By the time of his death in 632 C.E., he had united the Arab tribes into a **theocracy,** a state governed by the will of God as interpreted by officials who are regarded as divinely inspired.

The Seal of the Prophets

The role of the prophet in Muhammad's belief is important to understand. In the Koran, twenty-five prophets are named, including Adam, David, Jonah, and Ezekiel. The five most important prophets are Abraham, Moses, Noah, Jesus, and, of course, Muhammad. Muhammad was last and most important. He is called "the Seal of the Prophets" because the revelations given to him are believed to be final and complete.

The prophets were sent by God to deliver humanity from ignorance and superstition. They were to teach about God, chiefly that there is *one* God. All these true prophets, Muhammad believed, had the same message that he did, but generations of followers had changed or corrupted the original message of the earlier prophets.

According to the Koran, none of the early prophets were God. All prophets were just human beings who had the same needs, desires, hopes, and fears as other humans. God used them as messengers, but they had no claim to godship themselves. Thus, while Jesus is greatly revered in Islam, he is not treated as divine, and neither is Muhammad. For this reason, Muslims resent being called Muhammadans, because it implies that they worship Muhammad, which they do not.

Islam Spreads

Islam spread much faster than any other major world religion. By 650 C.E., Syria, Iraq, Palestine, Egypt, and the Persian Empire fell in quick succession to Islam. Only a century after Muhammad's death, all the land between the Rock of Gibraltar in Spain and the Himalaya mountains in India was Islamic—an area larger than the Roman Empire at its height.

Preachers were sent out to convert non-Muslim peoples. Two important characteristics of Islam aided the missionaries' work:
- Islam is a universal religion. It recognizes no national barriers and no distinctions among races—all peoples are accepted as children of Allah.
- Islam is a simple religion. Unlike other religions, Islam does not require intensive study, harsh ascetic practices, or elaborate rituals.

If the missionaries were not successful, the Muslim cavalry followed swiftly to force submission. The first three **caliphs,** those recognized as both spiritual and temporal heads of Islam, were brilliant military leaders. **Abu Bakr,** who made the Hegira with Muhammad, was the first caliph. Three additional factors combined to account for their effective military expansion of Islam:
- Islam promises eternal rewards to its members who go into battle on its behalf.
- The Muslim soldiers were allowed to keep over half of the war booty.

Top: **The Alhambra, the palace of Muslim sultans in Granada, Spain, dating from 1354**

Bottom: **The Taj Mahal in India, a tomb built for the wife of a Muslim shah, dating from 1648. The Taj Mahal and the Alhambra are considered exquisite examples of Muslim architecture.**

Right: **The Great Mosque at Córdoba, Spain, showing a typical interior design of Muslim buildings**

- The early Muslims faced a confusing and corrupt world. Many Roman and Persian rulers had oppressed and abused their subjects. Therefore, the invading Muslims were often welcomed as deliverers.

As Islam spread, it influenced and was influenced by other cultures. For example, Egypt had been a center of Greek-inspired learning ever since Alexander the Great had conquered it several centuries before Christ. When Islam took Egypt, Muslim scholars were exposed to the writings of the great Greek philosophers, mathematicians, astronomers, and physicians. Indeed, one of the first universities in the world was founded by Muslim scholars in Cairo, Egypt. These scholars brought together manuscripts from all over the Muslim world. Most of the Greek philosophers were introduced to Europe only through the work of these Muslim intellectuals.

The eighth through twelfth centuries are called the Golden Age of Islam because art, literature, science, architecture, and mathematics flourished in such Islamic cities as Baghdad, Iraq; Cairo, Egypt; Damascus, Syria; Córdoba and Toledo, Spain. What helped immeasurably in the exchange of ideas and information was the common language. All Muslims learned Arabic because they could recite the Koran and their prayers only in Arabic. Muslim scholars translated numerous ancient manuscripts into Arabic from Greek and Latin. These Arabic translations were sometimes the only copies that survived when earlier versions were destroyed during the Middle Ages in Europe.

With this common language and because of the enormous size of the Islamic world, Muslims made tremendous contributions to human knowledge. For example: They kept alive the geometry of Pythagoras and the philosophy of Aristotle and Plato. In mathematics we still employ Arabic numerals. Our vocabulary is filled with words originating in Arabic: *algebra* (from *al-jabr*); *alcohol* and *alchemy; admiral* (from the name of a sea captain, Amir al Bahr); *tulip* (from *tulband*); *checkmate* (from *shah mat,* meaning "the king is dead"). Many of the maps used by Christopher Columbus and other explorers relied on the work done by Muslim map-makers and astronomers. In short, Islam in its golden period made important contributions.

But in the thirteenth century, the Islamic world began to split apart, divided by political, ethnic, and religious factions. The unity achieved in the first six centuries of its existence has never been recovered.

The Koran

The word *koran* means "that which is to be read." The final version of these Islamic Scriptures was finished by a secretary after Muhammad's death and then was approved by a committee. This passage from the Koran summarizes the attitude that all Muslims must have about their scriptures:

> This is the Book in which there is no doubt. In it is guidance to those who fear God, who believe in the unseen, are steadfast in prayer and spend out of what We [God] have provided for them, and who believe in the revelation sent to thee [Muhammad] and sent before thy time, and [in their hearts] have the assurance of the Hereafter. They are on [true] guidance from their Lord, and it is these who will prosper. (2:2–5)

While the Koran is believed to be the complete revelation of God, Muslims also believe that God was made known through a series of messengers, or prophets, as was mentioned earlier in this chapter. Only the Koran, however, was transmitted exactly as it came from God. The Torah, the Psalms, and the sayings of Jesus were divinely revealed truths that became mixed with human additions and changes. This passage from the Koran makes plain the role of earlier revelations:

The Koran, a page from a copy dating from the thirteenth century

> It was We [Allah] Who revealed the law [to Moses]. Therein was guidance and light. . . . And in their [the Prophets] footsteps We sent Jesus the son of Mary, confirming the law that had come before him [the revelation of Moses]. We sent him the *Injil* [the revelation given to Jesus]; therein was guidance and an admonition to those who fear God. . . . To thee [Muhammad] We sent the scripture [the Koran] in truth, confirming the scripture that had come before it, and guarding it in safety. . . . (5:47,49,51)

When Muslim infants are born, the first thing they hear are words from the Koran. It is the source of Muslim education and a textbook for the study of Arabic. Memorizing the entire Koran (which is four-fifths the length of the Christian Scriptures) is not uncommon for a Muslim schoolchild. Muslims recite the Koran only in Arabic, the language in which it was revealed. Those who do not know Arabic may read it in translation, but Muslims think that a reader can see the full depth of the Koran only in the Arabic original.

For guidance in applying the Koran to their daily lives, the Muslims look to the **Hadith** — much as the Jews rely on the Talmud for interpreting the Torah. The *Hadith* (sometimes translated as "traditions") contains extra-Koranic sayings and examples from the life of Muhammad and the early community.

The *shahada,* **the first pillar and the creed of Islamic faith, is expressed here in stylized Arabic.**

The Five Pillars of Islam

Certain beliefs and practices are essential for every religion. In Islam, these central obligations are called "the Five Pillars." Muslims believe that if any one of the pillars is missing, a person's religious observance is incomplete. The Five Pillars of Islam are not optional for Muslims. Like all of Islamic practice, the Five Pillars are commands contained in the Koran, the revelations from Allah as recorded by Muhammad.

1. The Creed

Central to Islam is this simple and direct phrase: *La ilaha illa Allah; Muhammadur Rasul Allah.* It means "There is no deity except Allah; Muhammad is the Messenger of Allah." This statement of belief must be recited aloud, understood, believed in the heart, professed till death, and declared without hesitation.

At the very core of Islam is the belief in Allah — meaning "the god," the one and only. This may not seem so unusual to us today because most of the people we know come from Christian or Jewish communities, which also profess belief in one God. But in Muhammad's day, the people living around him worshiped many gods and practiced many strange, sometimes brutal, rites. Thus Muhammad's revelation challenged the religions in his time.

The attributes of Allah are similar to the attributes of Yahweh as described in the Jewish Scriptures and of God in the Christian Scriptures. God knows all that has been, is, and will be. God is eternal, all-powerful, and undivided.

Angels help God administer the world. These unseen beings follow God's commands. They are always in our company, observing and noting all our actions. However, like the prophets, they are not prayed to; the angels, like Muhammad, are in God's service.

The sense that God's timeless knowledge controls all events in life is comforting to Muslims. What is beyond a person's capacity is in the hands of Allah. Everything takes place according to God's plan. Consequently, the unexplainable is accepted just as it is. Whereas Western minds might worry over an explanation of a mysterious phenomenon, Muslims would feel satisfied by simply saying, "It must be the will of Allah." Far from being pessimistic, this belief allows Muslims to rest secure in the knowledge that Allah is in control of all affairs.

The second part of the creed is nearly as important as the first part: "Muhammad is the Messenger of Allah." Muhammad is not a god. Muslims do not worship Muhammad; he is the Messenger of Allah. Islam maintains that there will be no more revelations; what Allah proclaimed through Muhammad was the complete truth necessary for salvation.

To be considered a Muslim, one must recite and believe this creed. Devout Muslims, in addition, follow the prescribed practices from the Koran, especially the remaining four pillars.

2. Prayer

At dawn, in the early and late afternoon, just after sunset, and again when night has fallen, *muezzins* (that is, "criers") call all Muslims to prayer. Five times each day they chant:

God is Most Great; God is Most Great; God is Most Great;
God is Most Great.
I bear witness that there is no deity but God;
I bear witness that there is no deity but God.
I bear witness that Muhammad is a messenger of God;
I bear witness that Muhammad is a messenger of God.
Come to prayer; come to prayer.
Come to your good; come to your good.
God is Most Great; God is Most Great.
There is no deity but God.

The *muezzins* call from special tall towers called minarets, which are part of every **mosque** (the Muslim house of worship). God does not need the prayers, but they are necessary for humans. Muslims demonstrate their submission to Allah by praying five times each day.

Five elements are required for making proper prayers. First, Muslims wash the exposed parts of their bodies—faces, hands, and feet—as an act of purification. Next, they are properly dressed. Men must be covered from their navels to their knees at least, while women are covered from head to foot. Shoes are never worn during Muslim prayers. Third, prayer is performed in a place that is clean. Usually Muslims spread small rugs to kneel on. In place of rugs, mats or even handkerchiefs are used. These first three elements symbolize the desire on the part of the worshipers to come before Allah with pure hearts, in sincerity and humility. Fourth, Muslims always pray facing Mecca, the center of Islam. Finally, when the first four steps are completed, devout Muslims recite the ritual prayers, accompanied by four positions—standing, bowing, prostrating (with foreheads touching the floor), and sitting.

Top: A *muezzin* calls Muslims to prayer from a minaret.

Bottom: A mosque in Cairo, seen in silhouette at sunset

Islam has no priests. Every Muslim must take responsibility for his or her own prayers. On Fridays, Muslim men are expected to gather at

Top: **A noon prayer meeting at Tehran University in Iran**

Bottom: **A devout Muslim stopping on his journey to pray**

Right: **A *muezzin* calls the faithful to prayer, temporarily closing all streets in Mali, a western African nation.**

mosques (meaning "places of prostration") to pray together. Whenever a group of Muslims gather for prayer, a leader (called an ***imam***) is selected from the men. The *imam* stands at the front of the group, and the worshipers follow his movements. Sometimes instruction will be given by an *imam* who is a lay Islamic scholar.

Mosques contain no altars, benches, candles, flowers, and certainly no statues. Muslims believe that statues, and even paintings of people or animals, become idols, which are forbidden in the Koran. The mosques are completely empty but for the prayer rugs that cover the floors. However, many mosques are beautifully decorated with geometric designs, brightly colored tiles, and eye-pleasing pools, which are used for the ritual washing. Standard to all mosques is a niche in one wall that indicates the direction of Mecca.

3. Fasting

During the ninth month, called **Ramadan,** Muslims abstain from all food, drink, and sexual intercourse from sunup until sundown each day. During the day, devout Muslims carry on only essential business and, when not working, meditate on passages from the Koran.

Fasting is meant to develop a true sense of obedience to God, as well as to express reliance on God. Just as in Hindu, Buddhist, Christian, and other religious traditions, fasting is practiced to free people from the slavery of their passions. In addition, the pangs of hunger and thirst remind Muslims of the suffering of the poor. Indeed, during Ramadan, Muslims are directed to aid the needy.

The penalties for breaking the fast during Ramadan are severe. If a Muslim drinks or eats anything at all during the times for fast, he or she must do one of the following: (*a*) feed sixty people a meal, (*b*) give sixty people sufficient money so that each could buy a meal, or (*c*) fast for sixty more days.

At the end of the month of fasting, Muslims celebrate much like Christians do at Christmas. Families gather for special feasting, and sometimes gifts are exchanged.

4. Poor-due

Muslims have a popular saying that, roughly translated, says, "Pray to overcome pride; fast to conquer the appetites, and give the poor-due to overcome greed." Each year Muslims are supposed to give about 2.5 percent of their income to the poor and needy. *Zakat* means "purity," and the poor-due is called *zakat* because Muslims think that helping the poor purifies their remaining property. Giving is a duty required by God, and it is a form of worship.

Muslims celebrate Ramadan at a mosque in Delhi, India

To Muslims, our situation in the world is a test from God. If one is rich, she or he must learn to be humble and generous. If a person is poor, she or he must be patient, suppress envy, and work hard. Thus, the rich prove their generosity by giving. The poor increase their humility by receiving. So important is the practice of poor-due that the first caliph, Abu Bakr, declared war on tribes who refused to pay it, even though they were faithful in the other Islamic practices.

5. The Pilgrimage

At least once in the lifetime of every Muslim, he or she tries to make a pilgrimage (called *hajj*) to Mecca, the most sacred city of Islam. Non-Muslims are not allowed to make the pilgrimage or even to enter Mecca. Chartered planes annually carry a million Muslims to Mecca from all over Islam.

The *hajj* must be made during a specified time of the year, and most of its observances are concentrated over a three-day period. When the pilgrims arrive in Mecca, they put on plain white robes that are reminders of everyone's equality before Allah. This equality at *hajj* demonstrates the ideal of brotherhood and sisterhood that will be realized on the Day of Judgment. On that day no one will be better than anyone else.

Several rituals are required of all pilgrims. First, the pilgrims enter the courtyard that surrounds the Kaaba, a simple stone structure that Muslims believe was built by Abraham and Ishmael as a place to worship the one God. They walk around the Kaaba seven times—each time kissing the sacred Black Stone or, if the crowds are too large, at least touching it.

Then the pilgrims walk to two nearby hills. Muslims believe that Abraham's wife **Hagar** ran between these two hills desperately searching for water for her suffering child, **Ishmael** (as described in Genesis chapters 16 and 21). According to legend, when she returned, Hagar found a spring bubbling up underneath Ishmael's heels. The water saved the lives of Hagar and Ishmael, from whom the Muslims trace their lineage. Pilgrims drink from the Well of Zamzam after climbing each of the hills seven times to commemorate Hagar's search.

Next, at sunrise on the ninth day of the month, those on *hajj* walk thirteen miles to Mount Arafat. Here, in the great barren plain, several hundred thousand pilgrims all rise together at high noon and remain standing, praying to Allah, until sunset. This assembly of the faithful commemorates the place where Muhammad gave his last sermon and symbolizes the gathering of all peoples on the Day of Judgment.

The last two rituals are usually added after the day at Arafat. In the small village of Mina, the pilgrims throw stones at three columns that represent the devil. The stoning recalls Ishmael's driving off the devil who tempted him and likewise symbolizes the pilgrims' rejection of evil. The final act of the *hajj* is performed not only by the pilgrims but by every Muslim throughout the world on the same day. This last rite is the sacrifice of a sheep, a goat, or a camel, which commemorates Abraham's sacrifice. Then the pilgrims celebrate with three days of feasting, climaxed by one last procession around the Kaaba.

Islamic Morality

The code of behavior mandated by God in the Koran has a familiar sound to it. When reading the following passages, a Christian will think them very Christian; a Hindu will think them Hindu; and a Buddhist, Buddhist. Central to Islamic morality is charity.

> He is pious who believeth in God, and the last day, and the angels, and the Scriptures, and the prophets; who for the love of God disburseth his wealth to his kindred, and to the orphans, and the needy, and the wayfarer, and those who ask, and for ransoming; who observeth prayer, and payeth the legal alms, and who is of those who are faithful to their engagements when they have engaged in them, and patient under ills and hardships, and in time of trouble: these are they who are just, and these are they who fear the Lord. (Koran 2:172–173)

> Woe to those who pray,
> But in their prayer are careless;
> Who make a show of devotion,
> But refuse help to the needy.
> (Koran 107:4–7)

> The Prophet [Muhammad], on being asked how many times one ought to forgive his servant's mistakes, said: "Seventy times a day."

Hagar and Ishmael in the wilderness, from a Bible illustration by Gustave Doré. "And the angel of God called to Hagar from heaven. . . .'Come, pick up the boy and hold him safe, for I will make him into a great nation' " (Genesis 21:17–18).

Then he added: "If you cannot bear your servant's weaknesses, release him from your service." (*Hadith*)

Do not come near to illicit sexual relations; surely it is an indecency and an evil way. (Koran 17:32)

O you who believe! Intoxicants and games of chance and idolatrous practices and the divining of the future are but a loathsome evil of Satan's doing: shun it, then, so that you might be graced with good everlasting. By means of intoxicants and games of chance Satan seeks only to sow enmity and hatred among you and to turn you away from the remembrance of God and from prayer. (Koran 5:93–94)

Finally, one last quotation summarizes many of the elements of Islamic morality. Muhammad said:

My Sustainer has given me nine commands: to remain conscious of God, whether in private or in public; to speak justly, whether angry or pleased; to show moderation both when poor and when rich; to reunite friendship with those who have broken it off with me; to give to him who refuses me; to forgive him who has wronged me; that my silence should be occupied with thought; that my looking should be an admonition; and that I should command what is right. (*Hadith*)

Considering the earlier discussion about the Five Pillars of Islam, these moral commands support and expand on the duties of prayer, fasting, and the poor-due.

Jihad

One moral imperative of Islam that is often discussed is the concept of *jihad.* Some Westerners think of *jihad* only as "holy war." Actually, *jihad* comes from the Arabic phrase *jihad fi sabee Allah,* meaning "striving in God's cause." Thus, teaching, preaching about Islam, and fighting corruption or poverty can be considered *jihad.*

If a force tries to eliminate Islam, then Muslims consider it their duty to resist, even by using arms. While the Koran forbids Muslims to engage in unprovoked aggression, interpretations vary as to what constitutes a threat to Islam, which it is their duty to protect. Let's look at two recent examples: In the 1970s, the Shia Muslims believed that the Western customs coming into Iran were corrupting influences, oppressive of true Islam. Since the shah of Iran allowed these anti-Islamic corruptions, the Shia Muslims felt it necessary to fight the shah and Americanism. In the second case, Muslim antagonism to Israel has its source in the defeat of the Muslim Palestinians by Jewish settlers. Since Islam was oppressed, in their view, true Muslims were called to make *jihad* against Israel. To replace an Islamic state with a Jewish state was considered an act of war on all of Islam. Therefore, Muslims felt a religious obligation to fight Israel.

Muslims do not generally separate religion and government. The ideal Islamic society is a theocracy, that is, a state governed by Islamic law based on the teachings of the Koran. Thus, in an Islamic country, alcoholic beverages, prostitution, nonmedicinal drugs, gambling, and dancing between men and women would all be prohibited. Islamic religious education would be free and compulsory for all Muslims. Women would have separate sections in public transportation systems, schools, hospitals, and sports facilities. Women would also have to follow an Islamic dress code.

In an Islamic state, non-Muslims would be granted freedom of religious practice, but they would have to follow Islamic law. The Koran says, "Let there be no compulsion in Religion" (2:257).

When a society is predominantly Muslim, Muslims see it as their duty to God to keep it an Islamic state. Lest we think this merging of Church and state a strange notion, it must be remembered that up until the French Revolution, France was a Catholic country, and other religions were not allowed. In fifteenth-century Spain, Jews were expelled or forcibly converted to Catholicism under King Ferdinand II and Queen Isabella. Catholics were persecuted in Calvinistic Switzerland and in England, where Catholicism was outlawed. Sri Lanka and Thailand are officially Buddhist, although they tolerate other religions.

Life After Death

As is common in many major religions, Muslims believe in an afterlife. The Koran teaches that there will be a final day of judgment. On that day all people will be sent to heaven or hell. These two states are described vividly in the Koran. The rewards of heaven are pictured in very human ways:

> These are they who shall be brought nigh to God,
> In gardens of delight; . . .
> On inwrought couches
> Reclining on them face to face:
> Aye-blooming youths go round about to them
> With goblets and ewers and a cup of flowing wine;
> Their brows ache not from it, nor fails the sense:
> And with such fruits as shall please them best,
> And with flesh of such birds, as they shall long for:
> And theirs shall be the Houris, with large dark eyes,
>   like pearls hidden in their shells,
> In recompense of their labours past.
> No vain discourse shall they hear therein,
>   nor charge of sin,
> But only the cry, "Peace! Peace!"
> . . . oh! how happy shall be the people of the right hand!
> Amid thornless sidrahs
> And [banana] trees clad with fruit,
> And in extended shade,
> And by flowing waters,
> And with abundant fruits. . . .   (Koran 56:11–31)

It is well to remember that to an Arab living in a desert land, paradise would include flowing water, fruit, and shade. Clearly the picture of heaven is painted for men because it includes women (called the *houris*) of marvelous beauty. A picture of heaven for women is less clear in the Koran.

The images of hell are familiar; they come from the literature of other major religions. Hell is

. . . a place of snares,
The home of transgressors,
To abide therein ages;
No coolness shall they taste therein nor any drink,
Save boiling water and running sores.

(Koran 78:21–25)

Everyday Life

In addition to the ways already mentioned, the everyday life of Muslims is shaped by Islamic beliefs.

Family Life: Marriage and close family ties are considered religious duties, moral safeguards, and social commitments for Muslims. Because marriage is seen as permanent, the prospective husband and wife must meet certain prescribed conditions—including the proper age, free consent, and honorable intentions. A Muslim wife retains ownership of any money or property that she acquired before marriage. But it is the husband who is responsible for the economic security of the family.

Although the Koran exhorts marriage partners to treat each other with kindness and equity, love and compassion, it also recognizes that some marriages will not work. Therefore, Islamic law sets down procedures for divorce. It is easier for men to divorce their wives, but wives may initiate divorces too.

Women: Although in modern, Western eyes Muslim women seem oppressed, the Koran actually protected women better than previous practices. For instance, unwanted female babies were frequently buried alive by the Bedouin. Islam also opposed unlimited polygamy as practiced by Arabs in Muhammad's time. Muhammad said, "Of other women who seem good in your eyes, marry but two, or three, or four; and if ye still fear that ye shall not act equitably, then only one" (Koran 4:3).

The dress restrictions for Muslim women reflect the attitude that women should not provide temptation for men. Thus, outside the home, women are supposed to be covered in loose-fitting garments from head to foot. Today most Islamic countries allow women's faces and hands to be exposed, although veiled women are still a common sight. In Islam, women should appear beautiful only to their husbands.

Food: Many of the Islamic dietary restrictions are similar to those in Judaism. For example, Muslims may not eat pork, animals that have died without being slaughtered, birds of prey, rodents, reptiles, blood, or offerings to other gods.

Work and Money: Since work is considered a way of supporting the family and Islam, it is thought to be worship of God. Muslims aim to treat talents, money, and everything that they have as gifts from God. Thus, Islamic law forbids giving or taking interest on loans. Muslims generally are discouraged from amassing large amounts of money. They consider it a duty to keep money in circulation so that all of society benefits.

The Islamic concept of wealth is closely related to the obligatory poor-due. The ideal Islamic society has a just and humane distribution of wealth. While wealth is not bad in itself, it must not be gained by exploiting others. In addition, riches can seduce one away from submission to the will of Allah.

Divisions in Islam

Another aspect of Islam that is shared with other major religions is that it split into factions. The most important division was between the Sunnis, the largest Islamic group, and the Shias. Another sect, called Sufis, has very few members but exercised a profound influence on Islam. In the United States, Islam was spread by a group called the Black Muslims.

Sunnism and Shiism

The Shia Muslims broke with the Sunni Muslims over the issue of the leadership of Islam. The **Sunnis** believe that the caliph, the spiritual and secular successor to Muhammad, must be a member of Muhammad's tribe, the Koreish. The Sunnis elect the caliph.

On the other hand, the **Shias** (sometimes called Shiites) believe that Muhammad intended to establish a hereditary line of religious leaders, called *Imams,* to teach and guide the faithful. **Ali,** the husband of Fatimah, is identified as the first *Imam.* (This word *Imam* is often written with a capital *I* to distinguish it from the *imams* who are the local religious leaders of the Sunnis.) Shias hold that the *Imam* is a God-given post that is open only to a descendant of Muhammad through Ali. In addition, Shias believe that **Husayn,** Ali's younger son, atoned for the sins of Muslims by dying in battle. Thus the passion of Husayn is reenacted as a solemn feast by Shias.

Because the current version of the Koran does not mention the name of Ali, the Shias reason that the Koran must have been tampered with by Ali's enemies. Therefore, the Shias are suspicious of traditional readings and interpretations of the Koran, searching instead for hidden meanings in its words. The worldview of the Shias has been heavily colored by their deep distrust of the present world order. Thus, they look to the future when a promised messiah will bring justice to the oppressed.

The majority of Muslims are Sunnis. But the Shias are the dominant sect in Iran, Iraq, Pakistan, and Lebanon. Conflicts between Sunnis and

Shias have intensified recently. For instance, Sunnis and Shias have clashed in Lebanon, and a militant group of Shia Muslims even attacked the sacred Kaaba in an attempt to wrest the control of Mecca from the Sunnis.

One of the finest and largest mosques in the Islamic world, in Esfahan, Iran

Sufism

The word *sufi* means "wool-wearers." And indeed, one of the trademarks of Sufis is the type of simple wool robe they wear as a sign of their poverty. Much like Catholic and Buddhist monks or Hindu yogis, Sufis join special brotherhoods that seek direct illumination from God by practices such as meditation and prolonged fasts. There are many different fraternities of Sufis. For example, many Westerners have heard of the whirling dervishes. These are Sufis who do a special whirling dance, all the while chanting praise to Allah. As they spin, many dervishes go into a trancelike state in which they have a direct experience of the goodness of Allah. Another type of Sufi is the *fakir* who, like the Hindu yogi, is a poor beggar depending completely on the providence of Allah.

Perhaps the most famous Sufi of all was **Abu Hamid al-Ghazali,** who lived from 1058 to 1111. Al-Ghazali became dissatisfied with his scholarly pursuits because he did not feel that he was drawing closer to Allah. He left his home and teaching position to spend several years meditating and studying the Koran in a small room at the top of a minaret. Eventually he returned home a changed man. He developed a theology of love as the root of all mystical relationships with Allah. Such important Western writers as Dante, Thomas Aquinas, and the famous Jewish scholar Maimonides refer to al-Ghazali's works.

The Nation of Islam, or Black Muslims

In 1930, the Nation of Islam (later called the Black Muslims) was founded by Wallace Fard Muhammad in Chicago. His successor, Elijah Muhammad (1897–1975) claimed to be Allah's messenger to American blacks. Under his instruction and inspiration, Black Muslims learned about

The Wisdom of the Sufi Ibn 'Ata' Illah

Ibn 'Ata' Illah was born in Alexandria, Egypt, in the middle of the 1200s. Eventually becoming part of a Sufi brotherhood, he rose to become one of the most influential mystics in Islam. The following verses are from his work The Book of Wisdom.

If He opens a door for you, thereby making Himself known,
pay no heed if your deeds do not measure up to this.
For, in truth, He has not opened it for you
but out of a desire to make Himself known to you.
Do you not know that He is the one
who presented the knowledge of Himself to you,
whereas you are the one
who presented Him with deeds?
What difference between
what He brings to you and what you present to Him! . . .

How can the heart be illumined
while the forms of creatures are reflected in its mirror?
Or how can it journey to God
while shackled by its passions?
Or how can it desire to enter the Presence of God
while it has not yet purified itself
of the stain of forgetfulness?
Or how can it understand the subtle points of mysteries
while it has not yet repented of its offenses? . . .

Let no sin reach such proportions in your eyes
that it cuts you off from having a good opinion of God,
for, indeed, whoever knows his Lord
considers his sin as paltry next to His generosity. . . .

Deprivation hurts you
only because of your incomprehension of God in it.

Sometimes He opens the door of obedience for you,
but not the door of acceptance;
or sometimes He condemns you to sin,
and it turns out to be a cause for union with God.

Islam. They followed the religious practices outlined in the Koran. However, in two significant ways, the Nation of Islam was different from orthodox Islam.

First, Elijah Muhammad insisted that all black people separate themselves from the oppressive and doomed white race. Second, he believed that it was the destiny of black people to inherit the earth. Orthodox Muslims disagreed with Black Muslims on these points because the Koran teaches brotherhood under Allah for all people. However, Elijah Muhammad's response to their objection was this:

> My brothers in the East were never subjected to the conditions of slavery and systematic brainwashing by the Slavemasters for as long a period as my people here were subjected. I cannot, therefore, blame them if they differ with me in certain interpretations of the message of Islam.

To counteract the oppressive forces of racism in society, the Black Muslims insisted on high standards of honesty, cleanliness, sexual morality, and diet. Effective drug and alcohol treatment centers were set up, and Muslims were helped in finding work. As a consequence, the Nation of Islam gave a sense of self-worth and independence to its members.

Perhaps the most famous Black Muslim was **Malcolm X** (originally Malcolm Little, 1925–1965). His encounter with Islam converted him from a dope-addicted, streetwise ex-convict into an articulate, powerful spokesperson for black aspirations. He organized many of the Black Muslim mosques in the United States. During his *hajj* to Mecca, Malcolm X saw Muslims of all races and ethnic groups assemble as equals before Allah. In his famous autobiography, he describes his experience of the *hajj:*

> The *brotherhood!* The people of all races, colors, from all over the world coming together as *one!* It has proved to me the power of the One God. . . . The true Islam has shown me that a blanket indictment of all white people is as wrong as when whites make blanket indictments against blacks.

As a result of such statements, Malcolm X was expelled from the Nation of Islam and began the Organization for Afro-American Unity. Tragically, only eleven months after his break with the Black Muslims, radical black nationalists assassinated him.

Today the Black Muslim movement has become more open to other racial groups and has changed its name to the World Community of Islam in the West.

Islam Today

Without doubt Islam is experiencing a resurgence today. Some examples have already been cited: Iran's revolution back to Islamic fundamentalism and the united Islamic front against Israel. But other examples can be given too. Both Pakistan and Malaysia are changing from British-style to Islamic legal systems.

Part of the reason for Islam's emerging as a powerful world influence is that great sums of money are available from its major natural resource, oil. Islamic countries have exerted their power by manipulating oil prices and the supply of oil and through *jihads* funded with oil money. These economic influences, combined with the duty to protect and spread Islam, guarantee that Muslims will continue to play an important role in world affairs.

Islam is also being strengthened today through its missionaries, who are sponsored by both rich and poor countries. Large numbers of Muslim converts have been made in Africa in particular. One appeal of Islam is that it is seen as a native faith, unlike the religion of the white colonizers, Christianity. Islam stresses the equality of all Muslims. While Jesus preached and exemplified love and justice, the European colonizers frequently were anything but loving and just. Thus, Islam has had a strong appeal to many Africans. In its early years, Islam owed some of its success to the fact that it is a simple, clear, universal religion. Today, these same characteristics continue to attract new followers.

For Review:

1. What was the key event that initiated the founding of Islam?
2. Describe the early life of Muhammad. What conditions caused him to be disillusioned with Arab religion in his early years?
3. How was the Koran developed? What role does it play in the life of Muslims?
4. What are the Five Pillars of Islam? Describe the meaning of and practices connected with each pillar.
5. What is the central creed of Islam? How is this creed used by Muslims even today?
6. In what ways does Islamic morality parallel Christian morality?
7. What is *jihad?* What are some examples of *jihad?*
8. How are the heaven and the hell of Islam similar to and different from the concepts of afterlife you have studied thus far?
9. Why might Westerners criticize the status of women in Islam?
10. What are the main differences between the Sunnis, Shias, Sufis, and Black Muslims?
11. What signs of a resurgence of Islam have there been in this century?

For Reflection:

1. Explore your personal reactions to Islam. List all the aspects that you find attractive about Islam. Then list the elements that are objectionable to you. Recall any stories and news reports that you have seen on television about Muslims. How much of your own attitude toward Islam is based on what you have seen on television? Describe any changes in your view of Islam.
2. Now that you have completed this overview of Islam, reread the discussion of Sikhism on pages 83–84. Sikhism has been described as an attempt to merge Islam and Hinduism. What aspects of Islam did Sikhism retain?

11
CHRISTIANITY:
HEALING THE ONE BODY OF CHRIST

Christianity is the largest religion in the world. Nearly one billion people around the globe believe that Jesus is their savior. Jesus is God made flesh, who lived among humankind and who conquered death and sin by sacrificing himself for us and by rising from the tomb. Rooted in Judaism, Christians believe that Jesus is the fulfillment of the promises made in the Jewish Scriptures.

Christian communities were at first persecuted for following this carpenter's son, who died like a criminal. But the blood of the martyrs watered the seeds of this new religion until, by the fourth century, Christianity was the dominant religion in Europe, the Middle East, and northern Africa. Like all the other religions studied in this book, tragic divisions split the Christian Church, separating Eastern Orthodoxy, Roman Catholicism, Protestantism, and Anglicanism. Today, the ecumenical movement is trying to heal these divisions, binding up the wounds in the one Body of Christ.

Who Is My Neighbor?

Jesus replied, "A man was once on his way down from Jerusalem to Jericho and fell into the hands of brigands; they took all he had, beat him and then made off, leaving him half dead. Now a priest happened to be travelling down the same road, but when he saw the man, he passed by on the other side. In the same way a Levite who came to the place saw him, and passed by on the other side. But a Samaritan traveller who came upon him was moved with compassion when he saw him. He went up and bandaged his wounds, pouring oil and wine on them. He then lifted him on to his own mount, carried him to the inn and looked after him. Next day, he took out two denarii and handed them to the innkeeper. 'Look after him,' he said 'and on my way back I will make good any extra expense you have.'" (Luke 10:30–35)

The parable of the good Samaritan is one of the most familiar stories that we know as Christians. Yet our familiarity with this story can breed indifference to its profound message. In order to recover some of the original flavor of the story and to reveal some of its deeper meanings, let's recast it into modern terms.

For example: In the Catholic section of Belfast, a woman was walking to work when she was set upon by a gang who mugged her, stole her purse, and left her lying in the gutter. A priest passed her by without much more than a glance. So did a Catholic nun. Yet a Protestant worker stopped to help her. He hailed a cab and accompanied her to the hospital. When the hospital clerk refused to admit the woman because she had no identification or money, the man paid the required minimum in cash.

Another version: An East German refugee severely injured himself on barbed wire fencing in a desperate attempt to cross the border to West Germany. It was clear that the refugee would soon die from loss of blood unless he got medical attention. A West German ambulance was called to the scene, but the attendants would not approach the man for fear of being shot by the East German border guards in a nearby watchtower. The U.S. soldiers who called the ambulance also refused to help. Finally, an East German soldier happened by, sized up the situation, disentangled the refugee from the barbed wire, and carried him across the border to the ambulance. The soldier then recrossed the border to be arrested immediately by a waiting patrol.

These modern versions of the Samaritan story may seem unlikely to you. If so, then they can help us to remember that the original story was meant to sound impossible and even shocking to those who heard it from Jesus.

Right: **A Christian missionary working with the Chinese prior to the Communist Revolution**

Facing page: **The *Pietà* in Saint Peter's Basilica, Rome, by Michelangelo, dated 1499**

On its literal level, the parable of the good Samaritan offers a reasonable reply to the question that was asked of Jesus: who is my neighbor? The answer is simply that a neighbor is someone who responds when help is needed.

That answer may seem obvious, but the parable also suggests that loving one's neighbor, as the Jewish Scriptures command, can be a terrific challenge. In Jesus' view, we must treat *everyone* as a neighbor—even a hated Samaritan, a stranger, or an enemy. In other words, a neighbor is *not* limited in terms of nationality, religion, or race.

Challenges of this sort kindle Christian faith, which has at its heart the challenging revelation of the Resurrection. This event compelled the first Christians to proclaim that the Lord of the Universe had lived among them as a teacher and as a carpenter's son. The vision of the crucified and resurrected God would continue to challenge Christians throughout the centuries.

Victory over Death

Little is known about Jesus' life from the time of his birth until he was about thirty years old. But, in the next three short years, Jesus caused such public turmoil in Palestine that in the year 30 C.E., people demanded his death as a traitor and a blasphemer. His preaching challenged the religious power structure of his day. Some factions of influential Jews thought that he was disloyal to the Law of Moses and that he blasphemed by allowing himself to be called Lord. Nationalistic Jews were disappointed that he was not leading the people to a military victory over the Romans. The Romans, like any colonizers, were worried about Jesus because of his power to influence people's lives.

If Jesus had simply been a prophet or a religious fanatic—depending on a person's point of view at the time—his teachings and deeds would probably have been quickly forgotten after his humiliating death by crucifixion. But, something happened that was completely unique and that showed to those who believed in Jesus that indeed he was the Messiah, the Son of God, the Word made flesh.

The followers of Jesus recount his Resurrection:

After the sabbath, and towards dawn on the first day of the week, Mary of Magdala and the other Mary went to visit the sepulchre. And all at once there was a violent earthquake, for the angel of the Lord, descending from heaven, came and rolled away the stone and sat on it. His face was like lightning, his robe white as snow. The guards were so shaken, so frightened of him, that they were like dead men. But the angel spoke; and he said to the women, "There is no need for you to be afraid. I know you are looking for Jesus, who was crucified. He is not here, for he has risen, as he said he would. Come and see the place where he lay, then go quickly and tell his disciples. . . ." Filled with awe and great joy the women came quickly away from the tomb and ran to tell the disciples. (Matthew 28:1–8)

In the nativity story, the angel promised the shepherds a great "joy to be shared by the whole people" (Luke 2:10). Here in Matthew's story of the Resurrection we see that promise fulfilled.

Jesus had conquered death. From this moment, the Resurrection of Jesus became the cornerstone of Christian belief. Paul, who was converted from his persecution of the Christians to become a great apostle, points out how central the Resurrection is.

> . . . I taught you what I had been taught myself, namely that Christ died for our sins, in accordance with the scriptures; that he was buried; and that he was raised to life on the third day . . . ; that he appeared first to Cephas [Peter] and secondly to the Twelve. Next he appeared to more than five hundred of the brothers at the same time, most of whom are still alive, though some have died; . . . and last of all he appeared to me too; it was as though I was born when no one expected it. . . .
>
> Now if Christ raised from the dead is what has been preached, how can some of you be saying that there is no resurrection of the dead? If there is no resurrection of the dead, Christ himself cannot have been raised, and if Christ has not been raised then our preaching is useless and your believing it is useless; indeed, we are shown up as witnesses who have committed perjury before God, because we swore in evidence before God that he raised Christ to life. For if the dead are not raised, Christ has not been raised, and if Christ has not been raised, you are still in your sins. And what is more serious, all who have died in Christ have perished. If our hope in Christ has been for this life only, we are the most unfortunate of all people. (1 Corinthians 15:3–8,12–19)

As is true in the religions studied thus far, most religions have central persons who teach ways of escaping the endless cycle of life, suffering, and death. In the case of Christianity, the central person is Jesus, who, through his sacrificial death and Resurrection, brought humankind to the possibility of eternal joy, if they only follow in his way.

Jesus the Person

Who was this person Jesus? If you want to get to know someone, you look at what she or he does and says, and what others say about her or him.

What did Jesus really do in his lifetime? His birth, death, and Resurrection are central events, but they have their import because of what he did between these events.

First, Jesus was baptized by John the Baptist. At this point John recognized Jesus as the Christ. Then, like the Buddha and Muhammad, Jesus began a life of wandering. Initially, he went into the wilderness to pray. After this, he walked throughout Palestine healing, working other miracles, and preaching. And what he preached, he practiced.

Above: John baptizing Jesus

Facing page: The *Chi-Rho*, a symbol formed from the first two letters (*x* and *p*) of the Greek word for Christ. This symbol was adopted by Constantine as his imperial standard.

Love into Action

The writings about Jesus are filled with stories that describe his acts of healing: the lepers were cleansed, the blind saw, paralyzed people walked, devils were cast out. Jesus calmed the storm on the sea, and the people said, "Even the winds and the sea obey him" (Matthew 8:27). When the people were hungry, he fed them from a few loaves and fish. All these acts showed the power of God—but power in the form of love. By becoming human, God showed humans how to love and thus how to be godlike.

Jesus also challenged people to think in new ways about their relationships to God and to other human beings. He was condemned for curing on the Sabbath by those who placed strict observance of the written laws of Moses above the law of love. As this story demonstrates, Jesus showed what sort of life God wanted:

> While he was at dinner in the house it happened that a number of tax collectors and sinners came to sit at the table with Jesus and his disciples. When the Pharisees saw this, they said to his disciples, "Why does your master eat with tax collectors and sinners?" When he heard this he replied, "It is not the healthy that need the doctor, but the sick. Go and learn the meaning of the words: *What I want is mercy, not sacrifice.* And indeed I did not come to call the virtuous, but sinners." (Matthew 9:10–13)

Repeating the theme from the angel's proclamation at his birth, Jesus made it clear that God was a loving God for "the whole people"—not just for the rich, the powerful, and the law-abiding.

Jesus loved in personal ways. For instance, Jesus received a message from Martha and Mary saying, "Lord, the man [Lazarus] you love is ill" (John 11:3). When Jesus arrived, Lazarus had been in the tomb for four days.

> Mary went to Jesus, and as soon as she saw him she threw herself at his feet, saying, "Lord, if you had been here, my brother would not have died." At the sight of her tears, and those of the Jews who followed her, Jesus said in great distress, with a sigh that came straight from the heart, "Where have you put him?" They said, "Lord, come and see." Jesus wept; and the Jews said, "See how much he loved him!" (John 11:32–36)

Then Jesus brought Lazarus back from the dead. This was an act of love and was considered proof that Jesus was sent by God.

The Law of Love: A Moral Code

The law that Jesus followed and taught was contained in the Jewish Scriptures: "Jesus said, *'You must love the Lord your God with all your heart, with all your soul,* and with all your mind [Deuteronomy 6:5]. . . . *You must love your neighbour as yourself* [Leviticus 19:18]. On these two commandments hang the whole Law, and the Prophets also' " (Matthew 22:37–40). Jesus' acts showed the people how to put love into action.

Of special concern to Jesus were the poor, the sick, sinners, and children. He knew that they acknowledged their dependence on God and relied on God more than the rich, the healthy, and the righteous. In fact, Jesus gave his sternest warnings to the rich and the hypocrites. The rich often depend on their money and power instead of on God's gifts. In addition, Jesus' ideal of loving others requires that the wealthy share with the needy.

Hypocrisy received Jesus' harshest words:

> "Alas for you, scribes and Pharisees, you hypocrites! You who pay your tithe of mint and dill and cummin and have neglected the weightier matters of the Law—justice, mercy, good faith! These you should have practised, without neglecting the others. You blind guides! Straining out gnats and swallowing camels!" (Matthew 23:23–24)

Jesus taught that love was much more demanding than doggedly keeping only dietary laws and ritual observances.

The moral teachings of Jesus have distinct parallels in the other great religions. Compassion, respect for life, and purity of heart are consistently espoused in, for example, Islam, Confucianism, and Buddhism. None of these religions went as far as Jesus did, however, when he taught us to love even our enemies.

The Christian Name for God

In the chapter on Judaism it was mentioned that Moses' vision of God as supreme was signaled by the use of the new name Yahweh. Likewise, Jesus' understanding of God also required a new name. The name that Jesus used was **Abba,** a name that must have shocked Jews who heard him utter it. Any name for God was upsetting to devout Jews, but a word that suggested such great personal intimacy was entirely foreign to their faith. For *abba*—which means "papa" or "dada"—is the term that was used by infants for their fathers.

Theologians place great weight on Jesus' use of this name because it suggests that Jesus was well aware of his special relationship to God. By calling God "Papa," Jesus implied that in his teachings and deeds, God was present in an obvious and immediate sense. This relationship was made clear in the Resurrection, after which Christians understood that the Father and Son, along with the Holy Spirit, were a single and indivisible deity. Jesus was not only the Christ or the Messiah; he was also the Lord.

As if Jesus' use of God's new name were not challenging enough, in the Our Father, Jesus taught his followers to address God using the same name. In effect, Jesus offered them a share in his sonship and invited them to approach God in the same familiar, trusting way that he did.

Although Jesus urged us to do so, we Christians have never become

The Beatitudes

Jesus summarized his moral teaching in the Beatitudes, which were given in what is now called the Sermon on the Mount. These short statements reflect the law of love and the need for reliance on God's love for humankind:

> *"How happy are the poor in spirit;*
> *theirs is the kingdom of heaven.*
> *Happy the gentle:*
> *they shall have the earth for their heritage.*
> *Happy those who mourn:*
> *they shall be comforted.*
> *Happy those who hunger and thirst for what is right:*
> *they shall be satisfied.*
> *Happy the merciful:*
> *they shall have mercy shown them.*
> *Happy the pure in heart:*
> *they shall see God.*
> *Happy those who are persecuted in the cause of right:*
> *theirs is the kingdom of heaven.*
>
> *"Happy are you when people abuse you and persecute you and speak all kinds of calumny against you on my account. Rejoice and be glad, for your reward will be great in heaven; this is how they persecuted the prophets before you." (Matthew 5:3–12)*

comfortable using the name *Abba*. In the early Christian Church, the Our Father was not commonly prayed. When they did use the name *Abba*, early Christians would preface it by saying, "we presume to say" or "we dare to say." Later, the name Papa was replaced with Father, a distinctly more formal title. In much the same way that the Jews refused to use God's name as given to them by Moses, Christians have also been reluctant to call God by the familiar names Papa or even Father. Normally we use the name God.

The name *Abba*, it seems, suggests things about God and about ourselves that we find difficult to accept. How can God be so loving and close? Is it possible that we are as dear as children to God? Perhaps that is why Saint Paul said that one sure sign of a person's conversion is the bold use of God's new name: "When we cry 'Abba! Father!' it is the Spirit himself bearing witness with our spirit that we are children of God, . . . heirs with Christ . . ." (Romans 8:15–17).

The Early Christians

After the Resurrection and the Apostles' experience of the coming of the Holy Spirit, the Christian community in Jerusalem grew in strength. As Jews from around the Roman Empire came to the Temple in Jerusalem, they met the Apostles and followers of Jesus. There were many converts. Soon these new Christians were converting others to a belief in "the Way," as Christianity was referred to in those times. Despite persecutions, new members continued to join.

One of the most important converts was **Paul.** He had been sent on a mission to persecute the Christians in Damascus, Syria. As described in the Acts of the Apostles (9:3–6), Paul had a vision of Jesus. This powerful experience turned Paul into the zealous apostle who crisscrossed the Mediterranean countries preaching and setting up Christian communities, who was shipwrecked, thrown into jail, and finally killed for his faith.

Under the leadership of Peter, the first apostle, the Christian community grew, including Jews and non-Jews. Since Christians refused to worship Roman gods, the sect was considered traitorous to Rome—a Rome that was beginning to crumble. Consequently, Christians were blamed for the disunity that wracked the Roman Empire. Finally, widespread executions of Christians were carried out.

Ironically, rather than being wiped out by persecutions, Christianity continued to grow and spread. Christian communities became better organized under local bishops, or supervisors, and deacons assisted the bishops by looking after the temporal needs of the communities.

Worship

Forms of Christian worship became more regularized too. Christians met on Sunday, the day of the Resurrection. Each community shared prayers and hymns, readings from the Letters of Paul or of one of the

Top: **The martyrdom of Saint Peter, depicted by the sixteenth-century artist Caravaggio**

Bottom: **Early Christians in a catacomb praying for the dead**

other Apostles, and the celebration of the Last Supper, or the Breaking of the Bread. Often the Lord's Supper was followed by a fellowship meal in which the community strengthened its bonds of love and faith.

To become part of the Christian community, candidates had to go through an extensive training period—from one to two years in duration. This lengthy initiation was needed to help the candidates fully appreciate the Way, to weed out possible Roman spies, and to ensure that the candidates were fully willing to be part of a community that was always subject to persecution. At the end of their training period, the candidates were baptized. Their previous lives were washed away; they put on a new way of life and were welcomed into the community.

Gradually Christians began to set aside certain days for celebrating the most important events of Jesus' life: the Crucifixion, the Resurrection, and Pentecost. Much later a date was set to remember Jesus' birth. Local communities established other special days to honor the memories of martyrs or members of their communities who had died.

The Word of God Recorded

Like the believers of all great religions, the followers of Jesus collected writings by or about the founder of their religion. The earliest of the writings about Jesus that form the Christian Scriptures were letters by the Apostle Paul to various communities that he had started.

In approximately 51 C.E., Paul wrote to the Christians in Thessalonika, instructing them not to expect an immediate Second Coming of Christ. A few weeks later, Paul had to write to them again. Eventually, his letters to other communities were collected along with these first ones. The letters were copied and distributed throughout the congregations of believers in the Way. Paul's letters were read on Sundays as part of the liturgy.

Eventually, the Christian Scriptures were completed when the four **Gospels**—literally meaning "good news"—were added to the Letters, or **Epistles,** of Paul, Peter, John, and James.

The First Gospel was written by **Mark,** who organized various scraps of written accounts with the stories he had heard. Most likely, Mark completed his Gospel in the mid-sixties. **Matthew,** writing in the early seventies, took many of the same stories Mark used, but Matthew wrote his Gospel with a more Jewish audience in mind. Then **Luke,** a companion of Paul in the later years, wrote the Third Gospel, which was clearly intended to help the Gentiles, or non-Jews, understand that Jesus had come to save everyone, regardless of race.

The last of the Gospels is attributed to the Apostle **John.** Since it was finished in about 100 C.E., the Fourth Gospel is possibly the work of John's followers, who put together his writings and stories sometime after his death. John's Gospel puts stress on the mystery of Jesus' being God made flesh.

Luke, as depicted by the nineteenth-century artist Alexander Bida

In common with the Jewish and Muslim traditions, Christians believe that their scriptures are the words directly revealed by God. Consequently, the study of the Gospels and the Epistles is essential in the Christian tradition.

The Christian Church and the Roman Empire

The fate of the Christian Church was bound to the fate of the Roman Empire for many centuries. At first the persecution of Christians was common practice for Roman emperors. All this ended in 313 C.E. when **Constantine the Great** took over the reign of the empire. Constantine believed that his most important victory in battle was due to Jesus. Consequently,

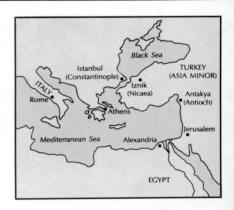

he legalized Christianity. When he built his "New Rome" in the eastern part of the empire, he placed Christians in important positions of power. His successors made Christianity the official religion of the Roman Empire. These emperors gave the Christian Church lands for buildings and money for its support.

When disputes within the Christian Church arose, the emperors frequently interfered, calling councils to settle issues. Constantine had established the pattern for this when he called the First Ecumenical Council of Nicaea, which condemned the teachings of Arius. At this council, the bishops wrote perhaps the most important statement of Christian belief: the **Nicene Creed** is recognized even today by most Christians.

As the centuries wore on, the structure of the Christian Church became much more definite, and missionaries spread belief in Jesus throughout Europe and northern Africa, and into Russia and even China. Dioceses were established, headed by bishops. Besides deacons, who still took care of temporal affairs, priests were ordained to carry out sacramental functions. In addition, just as Hinduism had wandering ascetics and Buddhism had orders of monks who spent their lives in meditation, so, too, Christianity had hermits who lived in the deserts, praying and fasting. Christian monasteries were founded with well-defined rules of life that focused their members' attention on God.

During its first ten centuries, the most critical challenge to Christianity came with the spread of Islam throughout the Middle East, northern Africa, and Spain, and into eastern Europe. Indeed, the Christian Church in the East lost huge territories and a large share of its membership. The Roman Empire, which had for centuries been divided into eastern and western parts, really ceased to exist. While there were still emperors of the East and the West, their power was challenged on all sides.

In addition to the divisions between the Eastern and the Western empires and the losses in the East to Islam, tensions grew between the Christian Church in the East and in the West. These tensions climaxed in the first major division of the Christian Church.

The Nicene Creed

I believe in one God.
The Father almighty, maker of heaven and earth,
and of all things visible and invisible.
And I believe in one Lord, Jesus Christ,
the only-begotten Son of God.
Born of the Father before all ages.
God of God, Light of Light, true God of true God.
Begotten, not made,
of one substance with the Father.
By whom all things were made.
Who for us . . . and for our salvation came down from heaven.

Jesus, from a Byzantine icon

And he became flesh by the Holy Spirit of the Virgin Mary:
and was made man.
He was also crucified for us,
suffered under Pontius Pilate, and was buried.
And on the third day he rose again, according to the Scriptures.
He ascended into heaven and sits at the right hand of the Father.
He will come again in glory to judge the living and the dead.
And of his kingdom there will be no end.
And I believe in the Holy Spirit, the Lord and Giver of life,
who proceeds from the Father and the Son.
Who together with the Father and the Son is adored and glorified,
and who spoke through the prophets.
And one holy, Catholic, and Apostolic Church.
I confess one baptism for the forgiveness of sins.
And I await the resurrection of the dead.
And the life of the world to come. Amen.

The Christian Church: East and West

In 1054 C.E., Cardinal Humbert, representing Pope Leo IX, excommunicated Michael Cerularius, the patriarch of Constantinople. In turn, Patriarch Michael called a synod at which Cardinal Humbert's actions were repudiated. The patriarch of Constantinople was recognized by the synod as having precedence over the Eastern Church. The patriarchs of Antioch, Alexandria, and Jerusalem joined in solidarity with the patriarch of Constantinople. From that time until the present, the Roman (or Western) Church and the Eastern Church have remained divided.

Although this split occurred more than one thousand years after the birth of Jesus, the roots of the division began with the separation of the Roman Empire into the Eastern empire and Western empire. For administrative purposes, the empire had been divided this way. Communications were slow throughout such a vast empire, and the languages were different. Latin was used in the West and mainly Greek in the East. In short, the empire was easier to administer from two centers: Rome in the West and Constantinople in the East. Since the time of Constantine the Great, the emperor had resided in Constantinople.

The empire in the East flourished under generally capable emperors, but they had little control over events in the West. The West was being overrun by barbarian tribes; the East, however, was protected by the well-paid troops of the emperor. When the Goths under King Alaric sacked Rome in 410 C.E., the only effective leaders in the West were the popes, who were growing in power and prestige.

Because the emperors lived in the East, so far away from the Western empire, the popes assumed much of the political and administrative leadership of the West. The patriarchs of Jerusalem, Antioch, Alexandria, and Constantinople acknowledged that the bishop of Rome followed in the footsteps of Peter, who died in Rome, but the patriarchs had traditionally been autonomous authorities in their own regions. The ecumenical council of 381 C.E. recognized that the bishop of Rome was first in honor and authority in the West, but that the patriarch of Constantinople was second in honor in the Christian Church and first in authority in his area of responsibility. Thus, when Patriarch Michael refused to submit to Cardinal Humbert, he was asserting what had been the traditional Eastern understanding of his power as patriarch of Constantinople.

For many centuries, the Eastern Church had been much larger and more sophisticated than the Western Church. Monasticism had its roots in the East. Antony of Egypt and Basil of Cappadocia (which is now part of Turkey) had composed rules for monks. The monastic life flourished throughout northern Africa, the Middle East, and Greece. Many of the great early theologians were from the East. More importantly, the very first Christian communities were in Jerusalem, Egypt, Greece, and what are now Turkey and Syria. Consequently, the Church in the East could rightly claim its roots in ancient Christian tradition.

Eventually, Constantinople and the Christian Church in the East lost

A wooden "stave church" in Norway, more than a thousand years old

vast areas of land and whole nations to Islam. Since its foundation in the seventh century, the armies of Islam had taken over more and more of the Eastern empire and the Eastern Church. Rome had become continually more independent of the emperor in the East, who was powerless to prevent the invasions of northern tribes, which swept through Europe. Consequently, when the pope crowned Charlemagne as the holy Roman emperor in 800 C.E., the pope exercised far more extensive power than any pope up to his time and far more power than that of the patriarch of Constantinople, who acted always under the eye of the Eastern emperor.

The Crusades

After 1054 C.E., reconciliation between the Eastern and Western Churches was attempted. After all, other than the arguments about authority and differences in language, there were no disputes over essential beliefs and practices. Nevertheless, whatever progress was made toward reunification was destroyed during the period of the Crusades. For example, during the **First Crusade,** the Holy Land was retaken by the Christian forces. Since these forces were primarily from the Western Church, the Crusaders replaced Eastern patriarchs with Latin bishops. At one point, the patriarch of Antioch was removed. In his place a Western bishop was installed by the Crusaders. Naturally the people of the Eastern Church resisted this crude interference in their ancient congregations, which date from the time of the Apostles themselves.

Above: **Pope Urban II proclaiming the First Crusade**

Right: **Leaders of the First Crusade**

In 1204 c.e., the Eastern empire and the Eastern Church suffered the ultimate humiliation at the hands of the West. The troops of the **Fourth Crusade,** instead of coming as allies to a Christian neighbor, destroyed Constantinople, stripping it of its great treasures and even desecrating its magnificent churches. A Latin bishop was put in power in Constantinople. Although this tragedy was done over the strenuous protests of the pope, people of the East have never forgotten this betrayal.

Two hundred years later, when the forces of Islam stood at the gates of Constantinople itself, once more reunification was called for. In 1439 c.e., a decree of union between the two Churches was signed, but the people of the Eastern Church, remembering the ruin of Constantinople, resisted the declaration. Even so, the West did not come to the aid of Constantinople, and in 1453 c.e. it fell to the Muslim Turks.

The Eastern Orthodox Church

The Christian Church in the East became known as the **Eastern Orthodox Church.** Actually this is an umbrella term for the Greek, Serbian, Russian, and other Orthodox Churches. Church governance in the East is in the hands of local patriarchs and bishops. The patriarch of Constantinople is looked to by most of the Orthodox Churches as having primacy of honor, but not actual authority. The Russian Orthodox Church eventually grew to be larger and more powerful than the Greek Church, which suffered under Islamic rule.

Approximately 200 million people are now members of the Orthodox Churches. The Orthodox are a minority in many areas, including Turkey, Syria, and Egypt. In other countries, such as Russia and Bulgaria, Orthodox Christians must live under avowedly antireligious regimes. Nevertheless, the Orthodox Churches continue to develop within their ancient traditions.

The Differences

The Christian Church split into the Orthodox Church (which is also called the Eastern Orthodox Church or the Eastern Church) and the Roman Catholic Church (also called the Western Church). After the division, each Church took on its distinctive customs, practices, and emphases. Essentially, little divided them doctrinally. However, one issue became and remains a stumbling block to unity—the role of the papacy in church authority.

In the Western Church, the popes, by tradition, have been recognized as the successors of Saint Peter, the apostle in whose hands Jesus placed "the keys"—the symbols of authority. Peter moved to Rome because it was the center of the Roman Empire and, thus, was essential to the growth of Christianity. Since Peter died there, Rome quite naturally became the most important center for the Western Church. The bishops of Rome, the successors of Saint Peter, were believed to be preeminent in the Christian Church.

The Orthodox Liturgy and Church Decoration

The Eucharist, often referred to as the "Divine Liturgy," is the central, public liturgical act of the Eastern Orthodox Church, just as it is in the Roman Catholic Church. The Eastern Orthodox also believe that the bread and wine are transformed into the body and blood of Christ. The Eastern celebration of the liturgy is more elaborate than the Roman Catholic rite: it often lasts for several hours. The liturgy proceeds in three main parts: (1) the Morning Service that commemorates the Incarnation and birth of Christ, (2) the processions that symbolize Jesus' coming to his people to teach and heal them, and (3) the Communion that signifies Christ's saving union with his people.

*Eastern Orthodox churches have domed roofs that are centered over a cross-shaped interior. The eastern arm of the cross is separated from the rest of the church by a large screen that is richly decorated with **icons,** or sacred pictures. The "mysteries," or sacraments, are enacted on a special altar behind this screen, which enhances the sense of mystery surrounding the Divine Liturgy.*

Instead of statues, Eastern communities employ icons in their worship, which are painted on wood or executed in mosaic with gold leaf. In Orthodox Christianity, earthly things are seen as already participating in the mysterious transformation that God is working in creation. An icon is not simply a painting of a saint; an icon is the reflection of the saint's transfiguration in heaven. Therefore, icons are seen as sacramental signs of a world transformed and as demonstrations of the human power to redeem creation through beauty and art.

Church vestments in both the Orthodox and Eastern Catholic Churches are splendid works of art. Most prominent and significant is the stole that signifies the power and service of the priesthood. Special veils and altar clothes are also often richly ornamented.

The purpose of the rich images used in Eastern worship is not sensual pleasure, but a stimulation of the imagination to get past the images to spiritual reality. Orthodox worshipers strive to empty themselves of sense and self by observing strict fasts and other disciplines in order to make room for the direct vision of God.

Eastern Orthodoxy encourages us to look at God's creation as a window to sacred mystery. The solemn reverence of their worship reminds us of God's mystery and of the long and holy tradition that is part of our own Christian heritage.

Facing page: **An Orthodox church in Moscow**

Left: **Church dignitaries of the Serbian Orthodox Church at a meeting in Belgrade, Yugoslavia**

Below: **A Russian icon of Mary and Jesus**

The Eastern Orthodox Church held to the practice of the early Christian communities in which the bishops were selected by their local communities and in which each local bishop was considered equal to all other bishops in authority. Eventually, patriarchs in major cities assumed more leadership and prestige, but they were not considered to have authority over the local bishops. This different understanding of church organization is still a matter to be resolved between the Eastern Orthodox and the Roman Catholic communities.

Other differences are apparent, although not real, obstacles to unity. Until Vatican Council II, the Western Church, in every part of the world, used only Latin in its rites, which is why it was also called the Latin Church. The Orthodox Churches, however, used whatever language the local people spoke. Thus, the Orthodox Churches are known more specifically as the Greek Church, the Serbian Church, the Russian Church, and so on. In Roman Catholicism, priests are required to be celibate; Orthodox priests are not. The Roman and Orthodox Churches use somewhat different calendars of religious feasts. Orthodox Churches use leavened bread; the Catholic Church does not. Liturgical art and celebrations are different, but the essentials are shared.

In virtually every country where Orthodox Churches exist, there are also **Eastern Catholic Churches.** In regard to ritual, the Eastern Catholic Churches are more akin to the Orthodox tradition, but they have retained their official ties with Rome. Including Churches in Egypt, India, Ethiopia, Albania, Greece, and Rumania, these Eastern Catholics represent the voice of the East in the Catholic Church.

The Lutheran Reformation

The Call for Reforms

An account of Martin Luther's early life would certainly not suggest that as an adult he would turn out to be one of the most influential people of all time. In the West, only Jesus has been written about more. Luther was born in Germany in 1483, graduated from the University of Erfurt, and began to study law. But after an experience of God in which Luther narrowly escaped death, he joined the Augustinian order in 1505. Two years later, at the age of twenty-four, he was ordained and sent to the new University of Wittenberg to teach moral theology. In 1510 the devout monk was sent to Rome for a year on business for the Augustinians. By 1512 Luther had completed his doctorate in theology and was made professor of biblical studies at Wittenberg.

It seems that Luther's virtues are what caused him to become known as a rebel by Roman Catholic authorities. He took seriously his religious commitment, and he studied the Bible. Looking at the way in which Catholicism was practiced around him, Luther became convinced that reforms were necessary if the Catholic Church was to be the Church founded by Jesus.

Luther was repelled by the custom of buying indulgences. An **indulgence,** usually granted through papal authority, was a pardon for sins committed. The common belief was that if a person had enough indulgences, she or he would not have to suffer the purifying fires of purgatory. Too often, people thought they could, in effect, *buy* their way into heaven. Even worse, in Luther's mind, these same people forgot that it is through God's grace that Christians are saved—not through their own efforts.

In addition, Luther believed that the Catholic Church had turned away from the Christian Scriptures and had relied too heavily on theologians and traditions to direct the practice of the Church. Consequently, while it was possible to use reason to defend some of the then common religious practices, to justify those practices from the Bible was more difficult. For instance, the veneration of relics was, to Luther's mind, indefensible from the scriptures. Thus, he reasoned, this practice should be abandoned.

The event that began the Reformation was the posting of Luther's **Ninety-five Theses** on the door of the Wittenberg Cathedral on 31 October 1517. What Luther intended to do was to start discussion and debate about certain theological issues. Soon his theses had been circulated throughout Europe. Many church officials in Rome strenuously opposed Luther and his theses. Debates took place between Luther and church representatives, most of whom saw Luther's theses as heretical. Further meetings failed to bring any reconciliation. Finally, in 1521, Luther was excommunicated. Later that year, he was outlawed by the Holy Roman Emperor Charles V. Nevertheless, Luther had many powerful allies, most of whom wanted sincere reforms in the Catholic Church and some of whom wanted to exert political independence.

Facing page: **Westminster Abbey, in England, an example of Gothic architecture**

Left: **Martin Luther, from a painting by Lucas Cranach the Elder**

Above: **Luther posting his Ninety-five Theses**

Reform Becomes Division

After his excommunication, Luther continued to develop his reform theology. He translated the Bible into German so that any literate German could read it. He wrote many books and articles that were addressed to ordinary Germans. Soon, his reforms had taken root in many German states. Indeed, Germany was split into states that accepted Luther's reforms and those that allied themselves with Rome. In the year 1529, Emperor Charles V called a meeting and tried to force the German princes to reject Luther. When they raised strong objections, Luther's supporters became known as **Protestants;** the name has been used ever since.

In 1530, **Philipp Melanchthon,** a friend of Luther's and later his successor, published the **Augsburg Confession** with Luther's approval and collaboration. In this document, we can see many points of agreement between the Reformers and the Catholics. However, three areas of Protestant thought were and are in disagreement with the Catholic position.

1. **The Absolute Authority of the Bible.** The Protestant Reformers taught that God's Word in the Bible is the final authority that must be followed by Christians. If a practice or teaching cannot be supported from the Bible directly, it is simply a human teaching and can be taken less seriously. Each Christian must read and study the Bible and make her or his own decisions based on the scriptures.

Roman Catholicism also taught that the Bible is the Word of God, but that the only true interpreter of the Bible is the Church. The creeds and traditions of the Catholic Church are interpretations of the Word of God and, therefore, must be observed.

2. **Justification by Faith Alone.** Luther, and Reformers after him, held that only by grace are we saved. We cannot work our way into grace; God gives grace freely to undeserving humans. Once we are saved, the Reformers concluded, our loving acts are the fruits of the action of the Holy Spirit in our lives.

Roman Catholics also believe that we are saved by the grace of God; however, they believe that good works are a necessary response to grace and are signs of their faith in Jesus. As James puts it, "faith by itself, if it has no works, is dead" (2:17).

3. **The Priesthood of All Believers.** Finally, Luther maintained that all believers share in priesthood. Priests are not mediators between God and humankind. All humans have the same status before God and the same responsibilities to study the Bible and to transform the world into the Kingdom of God. Although there were priests in Luther's Reformed Church, they were not special mediators.

Roman Catholicism taught that the priest was a mediator between God and humankind — taking the place of Jesus. The position was based on the apostolic succession of Peter. Jesus chose Peter to open or close the

Only Through Faith

On the morning of the nineteenth Sunday after Pentecost, 19 October 1522, Dr. Martin Luther was finishing his sermon at the Castle of Weimar in Germany. The people in the congregation were spellbound by this learned and inspiring man, and they listened in rapt attention as he concluded:

The Spirit does not come through fasting, praying, pilgrimages, running to and fro around the country; no, only through faith. So Christ bestows his gifts upon you without any merit whatsoever and what he did for him [Paul], he does for you also. Here, of course, you must guard against thinking that you are capable of faith; God must give it to you.

Therefore, this is what we say about the law; this is what it is and nothing else: The law kills; your God saves you. And he who does not believe is condemned. In short: Help us, O God, to this faith. Amen. Therefore, guard yourselves against the fool preachers who say: Yes, good works will do it. No, first faith must be present in a man. So he who does not follow Christ and also does not love him is condemned.

Hearing these forthright convictions, Luther's hearers probably understood more clearly why he had run into trouble with Roman Catholic authorities and had been excommunicated two years earlier.

"gates of heaven"; Peter, in turn, passed on this duty to bishops and priests.

Despite his disagreements with Rome, Luther never intended to break away from the Catholic Church. In fact, many beliefs are shared between Lutherans and Catholics. Lutheran liturgical celebrations are very similar to those of the Catholic Church. Luther believed in the sacraments of Baptism and the Eucharist. In fact, in a sermon delivered in 1528, Luther took to task some Reformers who denied the real presence of Jesus in the Eucharist:

> Thus the sacrament is bread and body, wine and blood, as the words say and to which they are connected. If, therefore, God speaks these words, then don't search any higher, but take off your hat; and if a hundred thousand devils, learned men, and spirits were to come and say, How can this be? you answer that one single word of God is worth more than all of these. A hundred thousand learned men are not as wise as one little hair of our God. In the first place, therefore, learn that the sacrament is not simply bread and wine, but the body and blood of Christ, as the words say.

Luther and his followers undertook some of the most important research done on the meaning of the Bible. Much recent Roman Catholic scholarship on the scriptures is based on earlier work by Lutherans.

The congregations that aligned with Luther's reforms spread throughout Germany and into Scandinavia. The Reformation was established by Swedish law in 1527. In the 1530s and 1540s, Denmark and Norway adopted the Augsburg Confession and became Lutheran. When Martin Luther died in 1546, he must have been amazed at the immensity of the changes in the religious landscape of Europe that had begun with the call for debate of his Ninety-five Theses.

Today, Lutherans are the largest Protestant body in the world, with seventy million members worldwide and about eight million members in the United States. Most Lutherans in the United States belong to one of three denominations: the Lutheran Church in America, the Lutheran Church Missouri Synod, and the American Lutheran Church. The Lutheran Church in America and the American Lutheran Church plan to unite by 1988.

John Calvin

Luther began a movement for change in the Christian Church that certainly did not end with his death. One of the Reformers who moved the Reformation along new paths was the brilliant French-born scholar **John Calvin** (1509–1564). Calvin studied law and theology at the University of Paris. Gradually, especially under the influence of Luther's thought, Calvin broke with Roman Catholicism and escaped from his native France, where the persecution of Reformers had begun. From his new home in Switzerland, he wrote *The Institutes of the Christian Religion*

Top: The cover of Luther's celebrated work *Address to the Christian Nobility of the German Nation,* dated 1520

Bottom: The King James Version of the Bible, a copy of the first edition, dated 1611

(1536), in which he defended the reform beliefs in general but took issue with Luther on several key topics.

One of Calvin's central beliefs was **predestination,** which is the idea that God has preplanned everything that happens—especially the salvation of individuals. Calvin taught that people were predestined for salvation or damnation: "For all are not created in equal condition; rather, eternal life is foreordained for some, eternal damnation for others."

Lutherans, Orthodox Christians, Catholics, and later Calvinist communities (such as most Presbyterians) objected to predestination as taught by Calvin. Part of their reasoning was that God gave humankind free will to accept Jesus or not. If humankind was predestined, such free will would be denied. Nevertheless, predestination and Calvin's other teachings had great influence.

Calvin, like Luther, believed in justification by faith alone, the absolute authority of the Bible, and the priesthood of all believers. In addition, Calvin simplified worship by focusing on scriptural readings and extensive preaching. He accepted only Baptism and the Eucharist as valid sacraments but did not believe in the real presence of Jesus in the bread and wine. Churches should be simple places, not cluttered with statues and paintings, which Calvin considered almost idolatrous.

Finally, Calvin thought that the Church should direct the state. Cities and governments should follow Christian teachings. When he moved to Geneva, Switzerland, in 1541, Calvin began establishing what he considered a godly state. If the predestined followed God's law and worked hard, they would prosper; this prosperity, in turn, would surely be a sign that they were predestined. We see Calvin's practical side in this statement to his people:

> Whoever, in the first place, will devote himself to fear God and will study to know what His will is, will strive above all to practise what Scripture teaches us, then, secondly, will apply his mind to whatever his calling is, or at least to things good and useful, and he will not have the leisure time to indulge in flights into the air in order to hover amongst the clouds without touching either heaven or earth.

Followers of Calvin

One of Calvin's more ardent pupils was **John Knox** (1513–1572), a Scotsman. Knox studied the reforms made by Calvin in Geneva. When he returned to his native land, he attacked the papacy and the type of Catholicism practiced by Mary, Queen of Scots.

Knox wrote many books and tracts to spread his ideas. His liturgical celebrations reflected the simplicity and the focus on the Bible that was taught by Calvin. Eventually, Knox restructured the Church of Scotland, forming **Presbyterianism.** The church government was in the hands of regional groups of ministers and lay elders called presbyteries.

French Calvinists, called Huguenots, grew gradually in numbers

The Reformer John Calvin

despite centuries of intense persecution. In Holland, Calvinism became connected to the nationalistic efforts of the Dutch people to overthrow the oppressive rule by Catholic Spain. In 1579 the northern counties of Holland confederated under William the Silent and eventually gained their freedom. The Dutch Reformed Church flourished in the tradition of Calvin.

Except for the Presbyterians in Scotland and later the Dutch Reformed Church in independent Holland, Calvinist Reformers generally suffered for their beliefs. Consequently, the majority of the early immigrants to America were Calvinists, most notably the **Puritans.**

One lasting legacy of Calvin is what is called the **Protestant work ethic,** a moral code that has deeply influenced Western societies. This code arose from the belief that, although good works could not help one to achieve salvation, work itself (and the prosperity that it earned) was proof that one was in God's grace. We can see these Calvinist views still strongly in effect today in the commonly held notions that wealth is a mark of virtue and that poverty is proof of one's moral unworthiness.

Today's Presbyterian and other Calvinist Churches have toned down Calvin's harsh doctrine of predestination. Presbyterians hold that no one is hindered from accepting God's grace and salvation, nor is anyone condemned at birth.

The Church of England

The **Anglicans,** or **Episcopalians** as they are known in the United States, were formed when the Church of England broke from Rome in 1536. King Henry VIII initially had no sympathy for the Reformers, although England had chafed under Roman interference for hundreds of years. Indeed, Henry had been named "Defender of the Faith" by one of the popes for his opposition to the Protestants.

Henry faced a serious problem, however: he had no son to succeed him on the English throne. Establishing the line of succession was crucial because wars broke out whenever it was unclear just who would become king. So Henry asked the pope for permission to divorce his wife Catherine, with whom he had a daughter but no son. When forbidden to marry again while his wife was still living, the king rejected papal authority and named himself and his successors the head of the Church of England. This remains the situation in England today.

Ironically, the statements of faith and practice approved by Henry for the English Church were very Catholic. He rejected Lutheran teachings and never considered himself a Protestant. The key issue in the separation from Rome was the matter of authority over the national Church in England. As the Anglican Church has spread around the globe, dioceses have been established and have formed into national synods. The archbishop of Canterbury is considered "first among equal" bishops. About sixty-five million people are now members of the Church of England.

Top: **The Saint Bartholomew's Day Massacre of Huguenots in Paris in 1572. Thirteen thousand French Protestants were slaughtered by French Catholics.**

Bottom: **King Henry VIII, founder of the Church of England**

Methodism: An Anglican Reformation

Just as Luther never wanted to depart from the Roman Catholic Church, the founders of Methodism considered themselves loyal members of the Church of England. **John Wesley** (1703–1791) and **Charles Wesley** (1707–1788) sincerely wanted to bring fervor of belief back into the Church of England, which they thought had gone soft and apathetic. Both men were ordained Anglican priests and sons of an Anglican minister.

The Wesleys began by preaching especially to the working classes, those who most suffered from the brutal conditions of industrial England. Their message was simple: there is a warm and loving God who wants to save everyone from sin and hell. As John Wesley said, "Justifying faith implies, not only a divine evidence or conviction that 'God was in Christ . . . ,' but a sure trust and confidence that Christ died for *my* sins, that he loved *me* and gave himself for *me*."

Reading the Bible was encouraged, and many of the first schools for the working classes of England were begun by Methodists. Their rationale was simple: if people are to have faith, they must read the Word of God; therefore, they must first be able to read. The Wesleys also preached social justice and charity for the needy.

Although Methodism originated in the Church of England, it placed more emphasis on the revelation of the Holy Spirit to each individual than the Anglican Church did. The role of the scriptures, justification by faith, and the beliefs in Baptism and the Lord's Supper are elements of Protestantism that are shared by Methodists. Although some later Methodists accepted predestination, John Wesley dismissed it because the "whole argument stands not only on an unscriptural, but on an absurd, impossible supposition."

To spread the Word of God, John Wesley traveled about 250,000 miles on foot or on horseback in the United States and in England. He preached forty thousand sermons—about fifteen each week. The ministers who followed him were called circuit riders. Charles Wesley is renowned as a hymn writer; his hymns can still be heard in congregations all over the world.

Worldwide, sixty-four autonomous Methodist-Wesleyan Churches presently have a total membership of about twenty-five million people. The Methodist Churches are governed by synods or conferences, which belong to the World Methodist Council. Bishops appoint ministers to local congregations.

The Baptists

At the beginning of the seventeenth century, small groups of English reformers sought to create communities of believers modeled on the first Christian communities of apostolic times. Infant Baptism was rejected by these reformers. Since only adults could freely assent to faith in Jesus, these early Baptists believed in adult Baptism by complete immersion.

Like many early Christians, the majority of early Baptists thought that the end of the world was coming soon.

Today, local congregations of Baptists are completely independent of other congregations. However, associations or "conventions" of Baptists join together to support evangelism and other joint ventures. A strong missionary thrust is common in most Baptist congregations. In many matters of belief, Baptists generally are aligned with the Calvinist tradition.

The first American Baptist congregation was founded in 1639 in Providence, Rhode Island. About twenty-nine million of the total thirty-three million Baptists worldwide live in the United States.

Facing page: **John Wesley. John and his brother, Charles, were the founders of Methodism.**

Left: **The First Congregational Church in New Milford, Connecticut, an example of Protestant architecture**

Below: **A mass Baptism in 1951 of nearly two thousand converts to the U.S. sect called Jehovah's Witnesses**

Pentecostalism

Although what is referred to as modern-day Pentecostalism did not surface until the beginning of the nineteenth century, it is probably the fastest growing of all Christian branches. As the name implies, essential to Pentecostals is the belief in a baptism of the Holy Spirit—a personal, powerful experience of the presence of the Holy Spirit, sometimes accompanied by the phenomenon of speaking in tongues. Pentecostals accept the need for Baptism by water and the celebration of the Lord's Supper. Many other beliefs are similar to those of Calvinists.

Pentecostal worship is characterized by readings from the Bible, but importance is given to spontaneous, shared revelations of the Spirit, sometimes through speaking in tongues or experiencing healing. Being missionary in spirit, Pentecostals generally believe that humankind will accept Jesus as the Savior and that then Jesus will come to establish the Kingdom of God. Although Pentecostal congregations usually have ministers, each individual is the direct recipient of the power of the Holy Spirit. Thus, very little governance comes from outside a congregation.

Because of their stress on individual revelation and action under the power of the Holy Spirit, Pentecostals have traditionally not been involved in issues of social justice and peace. However, the Pentecostals in South America seem to be making a change toward more involvement.

Top: A "tent" revival meeting in Florida

Bottom: A revival meeting in New York

Facing page: Pope John Paul II standing in prayer with newly named cardinals

Some of the congregational groupings considered Pentecostal are the Assemblies of God, the Church of God in Christ, the Church of God, and the Pentecostal Holiness Church. Pentecostalism has a strong appeal in Latin America, Asia, Africa, and even Russia. This attraction may be due to its stress on the individual's relationship with God (and its lack of emphasis on the social dimension of Christianity), the simplicity of its teachings, the personal interest taken in others within the small congregations, and the emotional fulfillment that some members find in Pentecostalism.

Estimating the number of Pentecostals is difficult because of the nature of the sect. Some Pentecostals retain membership in, for example, Methodist or Baptist Churches. One estimate is twenty-eight million Pentecostals worldwide, with seven million belonging to any one of sixteen bodies in the United States. The largest U.S. Pentecostal Church, the Assemblies of God, has about 1.7 million members.

Catholic Christianity: A Key Difference

Perhaps the greatest benefit of the Reformation was that it revealed the rich possibilities in Christianity and the many faces of Christ. Over the centuries since the Reformation, and especially due to the work of Vatican

Council II, the Roman Catholic Church and other Christian denominations have reached mutual understandings about many matters that once divided the People of God. Yet if someone were to ask you how the Catholic Church can be distinguished from Protestant and Orthodox denominations, what would you reply?

First, it is important to understand that non-Catholic Christians do not belong to a different religion. Non-Catholic Christians have different traditions and belong to different denominations. Anyone who accepts Jesus as the Christ, the Word of God in the Bible, and the Christian Scriptures as the basis for his or her life is a Christian. Thus, Catholics and non-Catholic Christians share the same essential faith. Some of the differences between the Catholic Church and other Christian denominations have been outlined above, as have many of the similarities.

A key difference between the Catholic Church and other Christian denominations is in their understanding of apostolic succession and authority, especially of the role of the pope.

Catholics believe that Jesus sent out the Apostles to spread the Good News, just as he had been sent by God. The successors of the Apostles, the bishops, led the early Church with the authority given by Jesus to the Apostles. Further, as the *Dogmatic Constitution on the Church* from Vatican Council II says, "In order that the episcopate [college of bishops] itself, however, might be one and undivided, he [Jesus] put Peter at the head of the other apostles, and in him he set up a lasting and visible source and foundation of the unity both of faith and of communion." Thus, the pope is the successor of Peter. The pope's main function is to be a source of unity in the worldwide community of Christians.

The college of bishops with the pope at its head, acting under the guidance of the Holy Spirit, is the final authority in the Catholic Church. One practical consequence flows from this authority. When Catholics are trying to make moral decisions or to understand the scriptures, they always give serious weight to the teachings given by the pope and bishops. These teachings represent two thousand years of the collected wisdom and traditions of the Catholic Church.

So, if one was asked what distinguished the Catholic Church from other non-Catholic Christian denominations, he or she would need to explain the belief in the unifying spirit and leadership of the pope and college of bishops, who are the successors of the Apostles.

The Call to Unity: Ecumenism

Since the beginning of the twentieth century, calls for Christian unity have increased. **Ecumenism** means those activities that are intended to foster unity among Christians. In 1910, the Edinburgh International Missionary Conference was one of the first meetings of non-Catholic Christian Churches. At the conference, the various denominations discussed ways in which they could work more closely in mission lands, and they established a council to coordinate and reconcile Christian missionary efforts. But this meeting was to yield even more fruits.

In the 1920s, two international councils were organized. The Faith and Order Conference began the long task of discussing issues of belief and church governance, and the Life and Work Conference was formed to unite Christian Churches in service to the world. Eventually, these two organizations joined forces to initiate the **World Council of Churches (WCC)**.

Below: **Delegates of the World Council of Churches voting on recommendations and reports at the Sixth Assembly at Vancouver, British Columbia**

Facing page: **Pope Paul VI and Athenagoras I, the ecumenical patriarch of Constantinople, embracing at their meeting in 1967. The two church leaders met three times to set aside the anathemas pronounced in 1054.**

In 1948, the World Council of Churches held its first assembly in Amsterdam. Almost three hundred Protestant Churches, representing memberships of 450 million Christians, form the WCC. The WCC meets every six or seven years in different places in the world to worship, discuss common concerns, and work toward unity. The Roman Catholic Church does not belong to the WCC, but it has sent observers to the last three world assemblies and has participants in various committees of the WCC.

Roman Catholic ecumenical efforts began in earnest as a result of **Vatican Council II.** Pope John XXIII and his successors have encouraged, for example, shared prayer, ecumenical dialogue, and common Bible translations. One of the key documents written by the Second Vatican Council participants is the ***Decree on Ecumenism,*** which begins:

> The restoration of unity among all Christians is one of the principal concerns of the Second Vatican Council. . . . such division openly contradicts the will of Christ, scandalizes the world, and damages that most holy cause, the preaching of the Gospel to every creature.

One of the ways that this desire for unity was implemented was through the establishment of the Vatican's Secretariat for Promoting Christian Unity.

The *Decree on Ecumenism* goes further in indicating that *all* Catholics must be concerned with promoting Christian unity. First, it declares that Catholics should avoid judgments or actions that misrepresent non-Catholics. Furthermore, "we must become familiar with the outlook of our separated brethren. Study is absolutely required for this, and it should be pursued in fidelity to the truth and with a spirit of good will." Also, dialogues by competent experts should promote common understandings among Catholic, Orthodox, and Protestant Churches. Third, Catholics and Catholic agencies should cooperate with other Christians in service to humankind.

Finally, the decree makes it clear that Catholics need to renew their faith through study, prayer, discussion of the Word of God, and participation in the sacraments. In other words, Catholics need to partake of their own tradition so that they are clear in their own religious commitments.

Catholic schools have a duty to foster ecumenism too. The *Directory Concerning Ecumenical Matters* says: "The authorities of Catholic schools and institutions should take care to offer to ministers of other communions every facility for giving spiritual and sacramental ministration to their own communicants who attend Catholic institutions." This directory, like many others in regard to ecumenism, may sometimes be forgotten, but it illustrates the importance that recent popes and the Second Vatican Council have placed on promoting Christian unity.

Unity with Eastern Orthodoxy

Pope Paul VI met three times with **Athenagoras I,** patriarch of Constantinople. These meetings signaled significant steps toward reconciling Roman Catholicism and Eastern Orthodoxy, two of the largest and closest

Christian communities. Concerning the mutual excommunications of their predecessors in 1054, Pope Paul VI and Patriarch Athenagoras I declared on 7 December 1965 that "they . . . regret and wish to erase from the memory and midst of the Church the sentences of excommunication."

Continual, fruitful dialogues are going on between Catholic and Orthodox ecumenists. Such dialogues reflect these declarations from Vatican Council II, in the *Decree on Ecumenism:*

> These [Orthodox] Churches, although separated from us, yet possess true sacraments, above all — by apostolic succession — the priesthood and the Eucharist, whereby they are still joined to us in closest intimacy. . . .
>
> . . . this holy synod solemnly declares that the Churches of the East . . . have the power to govern themselves according to their own disciplines, since these are better suited to the character of their faithful. . . .

These two statements indicate the esteem in which the Roman Catholic Church holds the Churches of the East and the hopes of union.

The Hopes of Unity with Protestants

Scores of meetings or dialogues have been held between Catholics and Lutherans, Methodists, Presbyterians, and representatives of other Protestant denominations. As may be obvious from the above discussion about the reasons for divisions, dialogue between Catholics and Lutherans, and between Catholics and Anglicans have perhaps covered the most distance toward unity because more fundamental beliefs are held in common.

Among the many significant points of agreement among Catholics, Lutherans, and Anglicans are belief in the saving power of Jesus, the necessity of Baptism and the Eucharist, the centrality of the Word of God, the Apostles' Creed, and the Nicene Creed. Other areas of belief and practice pose problems, for instance, the meaning of the sacraments and apostolic succession, the role of tradition, and the ordination of women. These problems cannot be slighted, but sincere and serious work is going on to clear the way to unity.

Other signs of progress are many. In 1982, the Anglican–Roman Catholic International Commission of theologians released its official final report on twelve years of dialogues. It said:

> Controversy between our two communions has centered on the Eucharist, on the meaning and function of ordained ministry, and on the nature and exercise of authority in the Church. Although we are not yet in full communion, what the commission has done has convinced us that substantial agreement on these divisive issues is now possible.

Pope John Paul II and Archbishop of Canterbury Robert Runcie kneel in the Martyrdom Chapel of Canterbury Cathedral where Saint Thomas Becket was murdered in 1170. A joint religious service was held as part of the pope's six-day tour of Britain in 1982.

In January 1982 in Lima, Peru, the Commission on Faith and Order of the World Council of Churches unanimously adopted a statement on Baptism, the Eucharist, and ministry. This statement is now to be studied by all participating Churches. Documents like this indicate that non-Catholic Christian Churches are striving for unity too.

What is the future of Christian unity? No one knows for sure. However, Pope John Paul II perhaps summarized the hopes that most Christians have:

"The second millennium witnessed our progressive separation. The opposite movement has begun everywhere. It is necessary, and I beseech the 'Father of lights' from whom every perfect gift comes down, to grant that the dawn of the third millennium shall rise on our full refound communion."

For Review:

1. What does the story of the Good Samaritan tell us about the challenge of Christianity?
2. What is the central event in the story of Jesus? Why is this the key event?
3. As a person, what were some of the chief characteristics of Jesus? Give examples.
4. Every religion studied thus far contains a code of morality. Describe the code of morality that Jesus taught. How did he demonstrate this code in his own life?
5. What are the Beatitudes? How are they similar to the teachings of the Buddha and Muhammad? Are the Beatitudes different from their teachings?
6. When Jesus referred to God as *Abba,* the Jews were shocked. Why?
7. Describe the life of the early Christian Church.
8. How did the early Christians worship?
9. Like Judaism and Islam, Christianity is a religion of a book. How were the Christian Scriptures developed?
10. In what ways were the fates of the Christian Church and the Roman Empire connected?
11. What is a creed? Why is the Nicene Creed still important?
12. What factors led to the split of the Church in the East from the Church in the West?
13. Over the centuries the similarities and differences between the Roman Catholic and Orthodox Churches have become more clear. What are these similarities and differences?
14. What key belief led Martin Luther to break from Roman Catholic Christianity?
15. Why did Roman Catholicism need reform?
16. Explain the three major reform principles that Luther taught.
17. What Catholic teachings and practices did Luther support?
18. What is predestination?
19. How did Calvinism differ from Lutheranism?
20. Describe the spread of Calvin's reforms.
21. Why did the Church of England split from Roman Catholicism? What are the similarities and differences between the two denominations?
22. Methodism was a reform of Anglicanism. How so?
23. Who are the Baptists, and how are their beliefs different from other Protestant denominations?
24. Pentecostalism is one of the newest branches in the Christian Church. What are their key beliefs, and why would Pentecostalism be so attractive to some people?
25. How do non-Catholic Christians and Roman Catholics differ on their understanding of apostolic succession and authority in the Church? Why is this difference so important?

26. What is ecumenism, and how did it grow into a movement?
27. What is the present status of ecumenism in Roman Catholicism? Why is ecumenism so important to the Christian Church?
28. What signs of hope are there for Christian unity?

For Reflection:

1. Write a letter to Jesus answering his question to Peter, "But you, . . . who do you say I am?" (Mark 8:29).
2. Every day there seem to be stories of conflicts between Christians. Find an example of these conflicts in a newspaper, in a magazine, or through an interview with someone. Write down your reflections on this conflict.
3. Write a prayer for unity among Christians. In order to help you do this, think of some recent events that illustrate the need for healing among Christian Churches.

EPILOGUE: CULTS AND YOUR RELIGIOUS JOURNEY

The great religions of the world have flourished over centuries and continue to nurture the religious lives of their followers today. But in every epoch, religious cults have existed too. In fact, it is estimated that within the last 150 years, from fifteen hundred to four thousand cults, with some twenty million followers, have sprung up in the United States alone. However, most cults spring up suddenly, have their day in the sun, and then pass away. For instance, very few people today have even heard of cults like Father Divine's Peace Mission, Psychiana, or the Shakers.

Not all cults are the same. Some are friendly places that give temporary shelter. Others strip members of their individuality and enslave them. Nonetheless, cults have been detours for a small percentage of people who are sincerely searching for authentic meaning in their lives. Most of us, in fact, could be tempted to join a cult at certain times in our lives. Unfortunately, the detour often is unnecessary and causes damage to the searcher. Thus, some knowledge about cults can be helpful so that our religious journeys may be fruitful and not be sidetracked.

Cults Are Real

In 1978, Jonestown, Guyana, was the home of more than nine hundred members of a cult called the People's Temple. A U.S. congressman and others in his party were on their way to Jonestown to find out what was going on there when they were gunned down by members of the People's Temple. A few days later, under the direction of their leader, Rev. Jim Jones, the nine hundred cult members (276 of them children) committed suicide by swallowing poisoned Kool-Aid.

In Atlantic City, New Jersey, throngs of followers of the adolescent Guru Maharaj Ji lined up to kiss his feet. Many of the devout cried and nearly fainted from the experience of seeing and touching their leader. After his marriage in 1974, his mother attempted to depose him from his leadership of the Divine Light Mission cult.

Almost all of the small town of Antelope, Oregon, was purchased by the followers of Bhagwan Shree Rajneesh, the "Enlightened Master" and founder of the Rajneesh Meditation Centers. Under armed guard, riding in one of his several dozen Rolls-Royces, Rajneesh had to be protected from the smothering adoration of his cult. Most of the residents of the town who were not cult members had moved to different cities. The city of Antelope was renamed Rajneeshpuram. During the 1984 state elections, hundreds of homeless people from all over the West were bussed into the city of Rajneeshpuram so that they could register to vote and elect state legislators who would follow the "Enlightened Master."

Above: **Bhagwan Shree Rajneesh, being led away from the federal courthouse in Charlotte, North Carolina. Rajneesh and several of his followers were arrested temporarily while fleeing the United States to India.**

Right: **Rajneesh driving past a group of his followers in the city of Rajneeshpuram**

Sam was in his last year of medicine when cult recruiters approached him. He had been studying so hard for finals that he neglected everything else, even regular meals. As he left the school counselor's office one afternoon, he was lured by the cultists to a meeting about free medical aid for the poor. The sincerity and warmth of the young people and their plans to start a hospital encouraged Sam to return for an in-depth workshop given by the group. Eventually, he stopped work on his medical degree in order to raise money on the streets for the hospital. The cultists had convinced Sam that the hospital was more important than his own degree. Some time later, Sam discovered that there was to be no hospital. In fact, all along, the money was intended to support the expensive tastes of the group's master and the frugal lifestyle of its members.

The examples cited here are not fictions—they are facts. Speaking to young people in West Germany in 1980, Pope John Paul II warned, "Withdrawing into oneself can also lead to pseudo-religious sects which abuse your idealism and your enthusiasm and deprive you of freedom of thought and conscience."

Whether cults are any larger today than in the past is difficult to determine. What is obvious, however, is that today's cults use media and marketing techniques very well. As a result, the realities of cults can be covered up until tragedies like the Jonestown mass suicide occur or until public attention is drawn by such events as the arrest and conviction of Reverend Moon, "Father" of the Unification Church, on charges of tax evasion.

Defining Cults

Before defining cults, it is necessary to make a distinction between a *sect* and a *cult*. A **sect** is a religious group that separates from the parent religion (*sectare* means "to cut") but that keeps the same worldview and acknowledges the same sources of revelation. A sect emphasizes one particular aspect of the parent religion. For example: The Shia Muslims and other Islamic sects accept everything in Islam except Sunni leadership of Islam. The Amish hold to key elements of Christianity but emphasize separation from the world. Pure Land Buddhism and Zen Buddhism are sects of Buddhism. Hinduism, it is estimated, has had more than two thousand offshoots, and Protestantism, in its 450-year history, has had an average of one new sect a year.

Religious groups can be classified into three categories: (1) mainline religions; (2) sects, or offshoots of these mainline religions; and, finally, (3) **cults.** What are cults? How do they differ from mainline religions and sects? Many definitions for cults are used. For instance, one analyst defined a cult as "a religious perversion . . . which calls for devotion to a religious view or leader centered on false doctrine . . . an organized heresy." Another writer identified the main focus of the cultist as a search for raised consciousness. The first of these two definitions is obviously negative. The second fits just about anyone who seeks holiness or wisdom.

The bodies of members of the People's Temple at Jonestown, Guyana, with the vat of poisoned drink in the foreground

Although written almost forty years ago, perhaps the most useful definition of a cult is this: "A cult is any religious group which differs significantly in some one or more respects as to belief or practices from those religious groups which are regarded as the normative [standard] expressions of religion in our total culture." Thus, in North America, this definition would include groups practicing something irreconcilable with Christianity, Judaism, or Islam. For instance, the National Council of Churches of Christ in the United States refused membership to Reverend Moon's Unification Church because the Unification Church believes that Jesus failed to bring salvation.

Spotting a Cult

Many studies have been done about cults. Consistently, analysts have picked out five characteristics that usually apply to cults.

1. The Authority of the Leader

Cults have leaders who claim divinity or special relationships with God through revelations given to the leaders alone. Most leaders act as the sole judges of every member's actions or faith. Frequently, the leaders refer to themselves as "Master," "Father," "Enlightened One," or some other name or title implying supremacy. They are absolutely sure of the equally absolute answers that they give for all problems. Their followers generally overlook the failings of these gurus who often, but not always, live luxuriously.

Some brief examples might clarify the role of leaders in cults:

- John Robert Stevens, leader of the Church of the Living Word, claims that in 1954 a revelation similar to Saint Paul's showed him that the Bible was "outdated" and that his authority was equal to the Apostles'.
- Charles and Myrtle Fillmore were the organizers of the Unity School of Christianity. Charles claimed to be a reincarnation of the Apostle Paul and declared the Bible to be only one of several sacred books.
- Paul Twitchell, the originator of Eckankar, claims to be the living manifestation of God and preaches that soul travel is the secret path to God.

Finally, let's look at the self-ordained Rev. Sun Myung Moon, who demonstrates all of the qualities of a cult leader. Moon is the founder and "Father" of the Holy Spirit Association for the Unification of World Christianity, called the Unification Church. Moon's followers are better known as the Moonies. Born in 1920 in what is now North Korea, Moon was a Presbyterian for several years. Then at the age of sixteen, he declared that he had received a divine revelation. The totality of this revelation was later put into a long book called *Divine Principle*. In 1948, he was excommunicated from the Presbyterian Church. Why? Because Moon preached that Korea would be the birthplace of a new messiah.

Three Adams were disclosed in Moon's revelation. The first Adam fell into sin, and thus the world was lost. Jesus was the second Adam, but he was not God. Jesus failed to save the physical world, although he did provide spiritual answers. Finally, a third Adam would be born in Korea between 1917 and 1930 who would marry in 1960 and live in America. Despite Moon's claims to the contrary, all these characteristics apply to him. Thus, most of Moon's followers believe him to be the third Adam—the fulfillment, the savior, the messiah, and the "Father."

Reverend Moon exercises extensive control over his followers in the United States, even though he does not speak English. Recently, for instance, he married two thousand couples in New York. All the marriages were arranged by Moon and his staff. Few of the husbands and wives even knew each other before the marriages.

2. Total Control of Its Members

The governance of cult members' lives is usually complete. For example:

- Besides having their marriages arranged for them, Moonies follow a rigid schedule that is set by their group leaders. This schedule regularly requires twelve hours a day, seven days each week of fund-raising on the streets.
- Members of the Hare Krishna movement have every minute of the day prescribed for them, from waking at 3:30 a.m. to finally sleeping at 10:00 p.m. All tasks are assigned—chanting on the streets, hustling for donations, cleaning the temple, and so on.

This giving up of personal choice is frequently desired by members of cults. Life is easier and more comfortable when people do not have to make decisions. The leaders of cults are willing to take over personal decision-making. Indeed, many psychologists who have studied cults have concluded that some people join cults precisely in order to avoid growing up. Parents typically begin pushing adolescents to assume more and more responsibilities. In an attempt to delay the decisions required of adults, some young people choose cults that will program their lives for them.

3. Emotional Dependence on the Cult

Cults typically create an aura of exclusivity and isolation for their members. Thus, cultists develop a deep emotional dependence on their leaders especially.

Frequently, cult members are isolated from outside influences by living in communes.

- The Hare Krishna movement has a secluded temple complex in the mountains of West Virginia.
- The Unification Church owns a huge training center in Barrytown, New York.

Besides communal living, which reinforces emotional dependence, followers are seldom if ever given time alone.

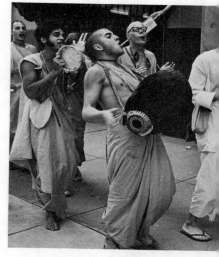

Facing page, top: **Rev. Sun Myung Moon arriving at federal court to face charges of tax evasion, for which he was convicted and sentenced to prison**

Facing page, bottom: **Reverand Moon officiating at the largest mass wedding in history, including 2,200 couples, at Madison Square Garden in 1982**

Above: **Followers of the Hare Krishna sect, on the streets of Evanston, Illinois**

Most cults have developed special vocabularies—sometimes even secret words—that give them a feeling of exclusivity. For example: L. Ron Hubbard, who abandoned science-fiction writing to found Dianetics and Scientology, called the results of unpleasant experiences "engrams." Hubbard claimed that these engrams are erasable by reenacting or confessing the negative effects in "auditing" sessions (in effect, counseling). Once a person is cleansed of engrams, they are called "clears."

Some cults require their members to wear special clothes to set them apart. In the Hare Krishna movement, celibate male devotees are identified by their saffron robes and shaven heads—except for topknots. All the female devotees wear the traditional Indian sari, part their hair in the center, and usually braid it.

Commonly, cults teach their members that the outside world is evil, corrupt, and even satanic. Only the group itself is pure and good. Thus, the cult promises to protect its members from all the forces that will lead them to hell. As a consequence, new cult members often try to convert their parents and friends; then, if they are not successful, they shun families and old contacts as lost souls.

Top: **L. Ron Hubbard, the founder of Dianetics and Scientology**

Facing page: **Maharishi Mahesh Yogi, a promoter of the transcedental meditation movement, at a university established in his name in Iowa**

4. Prohibiting Independent Thinking

Cults prohibit their members from using critical analysis and independent thinking. This aspect of cults is clearly related to characteristics 1, 2, and 3 listed above. But some cults go even further and try to destroy the egos or individual personalities of members by using mind-controlling techniques.

In some instances, cults isolate their members for long "retreats," which are really indoctrination sessions. The leaders seem overwhelmingly friendly, warm, and totally committed to the cult. The candidates are kept awake virtually all the time and are fed very low-protein foods. They listen to speeches and sing for long stretches—and are never left alone. Eventually, their resistance to what they hear breaks down. Of course, many of the candidates are looking for the sense of happiness and community that the cults promise. They know that if they want to be like the leaders, they have to give up their questions and doubts—which are usually answered by other members with the advice "Believe in Father [Master or Guru], and all your problems and doubts will disappear."

Once a member is in a cult, the tight schedule and ritual practices tend to reinforce conformity and suppress independent thinking. Rituals commonly consist of chanting certain phrases from the guru over and over. If a member does get out of line, reports indicate that a frequent punishment is shunning; that is, other members of the cult refuse to talk to the shunned member, and he or she is excluded from the group. Naturally, if the member came to the cult seeking security and unquestioning acceptance, shunning is an effective punishment.

5. Money for the Leader

Ironically, many leaders of cults preach against the corruption of the whole world but live nicely (sometimes even extravagantly) on the funds raised by their followers. Some cults require that new members turn over all of their wages and savings to the group. Often members are given tasks that neither use their talents nor contribute to the larger society. Sam, from the introductory story, could have served humankind better by being a doctor than by selling incense on the streets.

One cult practices what it calls "heavenly deception." Saying that the moneys will go to a home for the retarded or for drug addicts, the cultists sell flowers or just ask for donations; however, there is no such home. Many people have had the experience of having their ways barred by cultists in airports. Most travelers find it easier to make a contribution than to stand around and argue with the cultists. While fund-raising is common to all religious groups, cults regularly use deception to make money, and the money is frequently channeled to a guru, not to service in the larger society.

Who Joins a Cult?

Individuals who join cults are seldom atheists, junkies, unintelligent, or mentally ill. Quite the opposite. Most come from mainline religions—25 percent are Catholics, 35 percent Protestants, and 10 percent Jewish. But cultists do look upon their cults as ways of solving some of the problems of growing up. Here is a profile of the typical new cult member that was drawn by researchers at the University of California at Berkeley. People who become involved in cults can be described as follows:

- They are between eighteen and twenty-eight years old. People in this age-group have few pressing responsibilities and so have time to drop out.
- They are middle-class Caucasians.
- They are lonely, drifting, and searching for authority figures and/or groups that will give them security.
- They possess low self-esteem and little self-confidence at the time of their first encounters with the cults.
- They are under heavy pressure (from studies, work, or peers) or in a state of transition.
- They are intelligent, but naive, and highly idealistic, that is, they want to follow absolute ideals.
- They have been recently hurt or disoriented because of personal crises.
- They have little knowledge of the theology of major religions and are therefore susceptible to cultic teachings.

Why Do They Join?

Cults are appealing for many reasons. They help some people become independent from their families. At the same time, they promise the security that is found in a caring community. And, finally, for the idealists who are disappointed by the imperfections they see around them, the leaders of cults seem to have absolute answers.

People want to be independent. They want to have a sense of their own identities. Maybe the most difficult part of growing up is establishing one's own personhood—separate from parents and family. Being independent means taking action on our own and being held responsible. This can be scary. For instance, when young people begin their studies at colleges or universities, they are suddenly burdened with many more choices than they have ever made before. Who will their friends be? What careers should they pursue? How much should they spend on recreation? Will the persons they are going out with be good marriage partners? Does religion have any place in their lives? At age eighteen, as legal adults, people are treated like adults by the courts and in contractual arrangements. No longer are persons sheltered by juvenile status. In short, growing into adulthood is filled with the joys of more freedom but also the agonies of more obligations.

Being independent also requires that people give up some of their sources of security. Let's say that Sarah decides to be a social worker but her parents want her to be an accountant. If Sarah decides to pursue social work anyway, she cannot expect unconditional acceptance on the part of her parents. Stepping out on one's own frequently means encountering conflict with other people. Independence, in effect, is standing on one's own two feet, which sometimes is a lonely position to be in.

Parents are in a tough position too. They want their daughters and sons to be independent. But they do not want their children to make bad decisions and to have to suffer the consequences. They expect that their children will go out on their own, but parents wish that they could protect them.

Some young adults find it particularly hard to establish their independence. They want to be free, but they are very dependent on the love and support of their families. This is a real dilemma. And this is where cults can fit in. Joining a cult may seem to be an easy way to gain distance from the influence of one's family. After all, by doing something as objectionable as joining a cult, a person demonstrates her or his independence. At the same time, cults seem to promise unconditional acceptance. The first cult members that a young adult meets are warm, friendly, enthusiastic, and seem genuinely happy. Usually, cultists live in a community, which replaces the family. Thus, by joining the cult, a young adult seeks to gain two objectives at once: independence and security.

People who are attracted by cults are almost always highly idealistic and want everything and everyone to be perfect. Building a better world is a noble goal. Such young adults expect that their parents and other adults should have the same idealism about changing the world as they do. When they see that the enthusiasm of most adults has been tempered by experience, they become disillusioned. Consequently, they seek someone who will provide infallible answers to the world's problems. Cult leaders promise these answers. For an idealistic person, this assurance is another appealing aspect of cults.

Cult Recruiting

One of the most highly criticized features of cults is their methods of recruiting new members. Clearly there must be some readiness on the part of the recruits in order for the cults' efforts to be successful. Nevertheless, the cults' methods are usually slick, and sometimes they are dishonest.

A recent march by members of Scientology protesting a court decision that awarded thirty-nine million dollars to a former member

People are often recruited because they are lonely and need friends. In many cases, they just do not know how to say no. Almost always, the cultists deceive them and systematically entrap them. Such vulnerable people do not know what the cultic groups are or believe in, why the groups want them, or what the groups want from them. Usually, all that the potential recruit does know is that an extremely friendly, warm person, who is often of the opposite sex, is interested in him or her. This is how recruiting begins.

At an initial meeting, the recruiter may simply start talking with the young adult on selected topics such as love, loneliness, and injustice. Rapport develops. The person is not told anything about the cult. Then, the recruiter may offer an invitation to an evening with the group—"some friends of mine who you will like." The individual may think that the recruiter is just inviting her or him to a dinner at home. When the person comes to the dinner or the meeting, the food, the music, the singing, and the friendly people make him or her—who is often lonely and searching—feel accepted. He or she feels wanted. Some ex-cult members have said that this experience was nearly like falling in love.

If the newcomer is still interested, she or he will be invited to a "retreat" in an isolated, beautiful setting. More good group feeling is reinforced; there are talks, prayers, and rituals—always with the group. The message of the cult is preached directly, forcibly, and with the conviction that it is the absolute answer to all problems. The combination of companionship, natural beauty, constant group reinforcement, and simple, absolute answers, often turns inquirers into members.

Cults are frequently accused of deception in recruiting because of several practices. "Front" organizations, which disguise the true nature

of the cult, are sometimes employed. For example, the Unification Church uses the names One World Crusade, Creative Community Project, and, to recruit college students, the Collegiate Association for the Research of Principles (CARP). Moonies know that if they approached people directly they would have less luck in recruiting. Even the Korean Folk Ballet and the Little Angels of Korea are projects funded by the Moonies to create a more acceptable image.

Leaving a Cult: The Consequences

Leaving a cult may be very difficult. Members may have cut themselves off from their families and friends. Devoted group members exert tremendous pressure to stay. In some instances, those thinking of leaving have been isolated by their cults. Nevertheless, 90 percent of all people who join cults leave them and return to their former lifestyles in about two years. Why do they leave? Motivations vary.

1. Some members leave their cults because they become disillusioned with the leaders. For instance, an exodus of members from Scientology occurred when the founder and his son fought over control of the cult and when nine of its administrators were convicted of conspiracy to steal U.S. government documents.
2. Other members leave because they grow discontented with the mindless passivity and the shallowness of the lives they have accepted.
3. Some group members realize that they have, in fact, made the necessary separation from their parents and do not need the cults any more.
4. Members who have maintained contact with their parents and friends may want to reestablish those relationships.

Occasionally, members of cults have been kidnapped by their parents and "deprogrammed"—an attempt to reverse the conditioning done by the cults to their members. This is a federal crime.

Once members do leave, quite naturally consequences follow. A University of California study showed that at times ex-cult members have lost their abilities to think critically. Also, they may feel rage toward the cults and sorrow or fear for friends who are still in the cults. Furthermore, if ex-cult members return home, they may experience guilt at the pain they have caused their families and friends. These natural responses may make them feel isolated and different. In other words, they may face the same problems that made them vulnerable to the cults in the first place.

Those individuals who escape from cults require time and the care of close friends and families in order to regain the strength to adjust. Most of all, they need to be listened to seriously.

Religious Growth Without Cults

The study of cults, and indeed of all the religions of the world, should point out the need that people have for meaning in their lives—for some purpose for their existence that is larger than themselves. This purpose is often found in a relationship with God (or the Sacred or Allah or the Buddha or Krishna) and with other people. The search for authentic religious expression requires effort.

First, we must know about religion. This requires serious study. It is no wonder that we find Catholic schools, Hindu ashrams, Buddhist monasteries, and Muslim mosque academies all providing religious education. The wisdom of great religions is not so shallow that a person can just consume it like a fast-food meal. Religion engages our intelligence, not just our emotions. Ignorance and uncertainty make people easy victims of those who are determined to spread even the oddest beliefs. For Catholics, it is essential to know the scriptures and church history and traditions well. This background gives us a sense of religious identity and perspective.

If faith is to be authentic, a person must be free in mind and heart to accept or reject religious beliefs and practices. Faith that is forced or the product of manipulation is not faith at all. Knowledge of one's religious tradition aids in building freedom, but a person needs to have self-knowledge too. Those who become trapped by cults seldom have an accurate notion of what they really need. In addition, a growing person needs to see the world as it is—not only as they wish or want it to be.

Religious development is fostered by a caring, helpful community of people. People join cults in large part because they find community there. Mainline religions also must remember that community building is important. Naturally, if one expects community, one must help build it. Increasingly, parishes are seeking help from young people, and the opportunities to serve others through the Catholic Church are multiplying. For example:

- The **Jesuit Volunteer Corps** was established to organize men and women volunteers for service to the poor and oppressed throughout the United States. Volunteers live a simple lifestyle in communities.
- The **Lay Mission-Helpers Association** has trained and supported over six hundred people who have worked overseas.
- The **Maryknoll Missionaries** also sponsor overseas lay groups.
- The **Catholic Worker Movement,** founded in 1933, has over sixty communities of laypersons who operate Houses of Hospitality to feed, clothe, and house the very poor.

These are just four examples of ways in which young adults can serve others and live in community in the Catholic Church.

Very important, too, is the openness that church members should have for one another as people. Isolated, lonely, hurt people are often recruited by cults. Most of us have felt this way at one time or another. If we are not caring for others, they may try to find in cults the caring that they are missing.

All people in all epochs of history have developed religion in their lives in order to answer the ultimate concerns they have. Each of the religions and the cults studied in this course tries to answer these ultimate

Dorothy Day (1897–1980), the cofounder, with Peter Maurin, of the *Catholic Worker* **monthly newspaper and the Catholic Worker Movement**

questions. While those of us who are Catholic might find the practices, ideas, and beliefs of others strange or even wrong, we owe it to ourselves and to non-Catholics to look at these beliefs and practices seriously and respectfully. Finally, we owe it to ourselves to search the depths of our own religion.

For Review:

1. What are the differences between a sect and a cult?
2. Leaders are very important to cults. What are typical cult leaders like?
3. Describe the sort of control that cults have over their members.
4. Why do cults develop exclusivity and isolation among their members?
5. In what ways are critical analysis and independent thinking a threat to cults?
6. What is the role of fund-raising in cults? How would you evaluate the methods used?
7. Who are most vulnerable to cults?
8. Why do people join cults?
9. Describe a typical recruiting method that is used by cults.
10. Most people leave cults after a short time. Why? What are some of the effects of membership in a cult?
11. How can people grow in their religious lives so that they do not feel compelled to join cults?

For Reflection:

Review the characteristics of someone who is vulnerable to cult recruiters (see page 234). How vulnerable are you? Make a list of those characteristics that fit you. Make another list of ways in which you are developing your own identity, independence, and religious life. Think of people who support you and who will help you establish your own identity, independence, and religious beliefs; write these persons' names in a list. Then write a short prayer for each person describing precisely how they are helping you grow. Finally, outline some ways in which you need to foster your own religious development.

INDEX

Missionaries: Christian, 203; Islamic, 177, 192; Mahayanist, 98

Moderation: Buddhist emphasis on, 89

Mohammed. *See* Muhammad

Moksha ('mōk-shä), 77, 78. *See also* Liberation

Monasticism: Buddhist, 90; Christian, 203, 205; Jain, 82–83; and role of religious in religions, 64; Sufi, 189; Taoist, 117; Theravada Buddhist, 96; Zen Buddhist, 99

Moneylenders, 164

Monism, 75

Monotheism: Judaism and, 149, 151, 155; Zoroastrianism and, 137–138, 144. *See also* God, the one

Moon, Sun Myung, 230–231

Moonies. *See* Unification Church

Morality: Buddhist, 94; Christian, 197, 199–200; Confucian, 113; as element of great religions, 14, 57–58; Islamic, 184–186; in Jainism, 83; Jewish, 157; Parsi, 142; and Protestant work ethic, 215; of *samurai,* 129; unity and, 58; Zoroastrian, 136, 140–142

Mosaic Law, 157

Moses, 150–151, 162, 177

Mosque, 181, 182

Mother goddess: early Semitic, 148; Hindu, 74; Mahayanist, 98; in prehistoric religions, 27, 28; in pre-Vedic India, 58, 72

Moto-ori (mō-tō-ō-rē), 128

Muezzins (mü-'ez-ns), 181

Muhammad (mō-'ham-əd), 45, 57, 174–177, 180–181

Muhammad, Elijah, 189, 191

Muslims: in Africa, 192; and Christians, 176; conquests of, 177–178, 203, 205–206, 207; and Hindus conflict, 81; and Jews, 176; Koran and, 179–180; lifestyle of, 187–188; as scholars, 161, 178–179; and Sikhism, 83; Sunni, 188; in United States and Canada, 173; Zoroastrianism and, 142. *See also* Islam

Mystery cults, 44

Mysticism, 164

Mystics: Muslim, 190; role of, in religions, 64

Myths and mythmaking, 39–40, 41, 42–44, 50, 124. *See also* Creation stories

Nabi (nä-'bē), 153

Narcissus, 43

Nathan, 153

Nationalism: Japanese, 130; Jewish, 168

Nation of Islam. *See* Black Muslims

Nature, 27, 101, 121

Nazis, 165–166

Neanderthal tribes, 26, 27

Nehru, Jawaharlal ('ner-ü, jə-'wä-hər-läl), 80

Nicaea (nī-'cē-ə), First Ecumenical Council of, 203

Nicene Creed, 50, 203, 204

Night of Power and Excellence, 175

Nihongi, 125

Ninety-five Theses, 211

Nirvana (nir-'vän-ə), 92–93, 94

Noble Truths. *See* Four Noble Truths

Noninterference, doctrine of, 115–116

Nonviolence: Gandhi and, 71, 81. *See also* Ahimsa

Obedience: in Islam, 58, 182; to Sikh guru, 83

Om, 77

Orthodox Church. *See* Eastern Orthodox Church

Orthodox Judaism, 167

Osiris (ō-'sī-rəs), 40

Pakistan, 84, 188, 191

Pali Scriptures, 96

Papacy. *See* Popes

Parable of the good Samaritan, 195–197

Parable of the prodigal son, 87–89

Parsis ('pär-sēs), 142–143

Parthians, 138–139

Passover, 57, 159

Patriarchs, 206, 207, 210; Athenagoras I, 221–222; Michael Cerularius, 205

Paul, Saint, 198, 201, 202

Paul VI, 221–222

Pentecost, 159

Pentecostalism, 217–218

Perry, Commodore Matthew, 130

Persecution: of Calvinists, 215; of Christians, 201; of Jews, 161, 164–166; of Zoroastrians, 142

Persia, 138–139, 141

Personality types, 62–63

Pesach ('pā-säk), 159

Peter, Saint, 201, 205, 207, 212–213, 219

Pharisees, 57

Philosophers' stone, 30

Philosophy, 46–47, 49; compared to religion, 52; Greek, 43; myths of, 50; Taoism as, 115–117

Phlegmatic (fleg-'mat-ik) personality, 62

Pilgrimages, 176, 183–184. *See also* Hajj

Plato, 46, 48

Pogroms ('pō-grəms), 165

Poland, 165

Polytheism, 58, 75, 138

Poor-due, 183

Popes, 206, 207, 219–220; John Paul II, 223, 228; Leo IX, 205; Paul VI, 221–222

Prayer: Muslim, 181–182; Native American, 29

Prayer leaders. *See* Imams

Predestination, 214, 215

Presbyterianism, 214–215

Preserver, the, 74

Pre-Vedic religion, 72–73

Priests and priesthood: Babylonian, 43; Christian, 203; Confucian, 112; early Semitic, 148; in Eastern Church, 210; Egyptian, 42; in Judaism, 153, 160; Luther on, 212; as mediators between God and humankind, 212; role of, in religions, 64; Zoroastrian, 139

Acknowledgments *(continued)*

Among the many people to whom I owe gratitude in the writing of *Great Religions of the World,* my deepest thanks are due to my religious community of Chardon, the Sisters of Notre Dame, especially Sr. Mary Raphaelita Boeckmann, SND, superior general, Rome; Sr. Rita Mary Harwood, SND, provincial superior of the Sisters of Notre Dame of Chardon, Ohio; and Sr. Margaret Mary McGovern, SND, assistant superintendent of the Cleveland Diocesan School System—all of whom offered personal encouragement. By affording me the time, the training, and the staff for this project, they share its purpose, which is, in some small way, to reveal the presence of God's Word—the Logos—everywhere.

Deep thanks to Sr. Mary Dolores Stanko, SND, for endless patience in processing the many drafts of the manuscript and for invaluable editorial suggestions. Special gratitude to Sr. Mary Kathleen Glavich, SND, for her research and initial draft of the chapter on the cults. I am grateful to Sr. Louise Marie Prochaska, SND, and Sr. Patricia Rickard, SND, for their discerning editorial critiques and generous contributions of content.

My thanks to Mr. Thomas More Scott, who contributed his library on the cults, and to Sr. Marie Clarice Bates, SND, mission procurator of the province, who allowed me full access to her excellent mission library.

Thanks to Ms. Charlaine Yomant for typing and art services. Thanks, also, to the classroom teachers who tested the first versions of various chapters in their classes and who made helpful suggestions.

Unless noted otherwise below, all of the scriptural quotations used in this text are from the Jerusalem Bible, published and copyrighted © 1966, 1967, and 1968 by Darton, Longman & Todd, Ltd., London, and by Doubleday & Company, Inc., New York.

Introduction

The extract on page 9 is from *I Am Eagle!* by Gherman S. Titov and Martin Caidan (New York: Bobbs-Merrill, 1962).

The extract on page 10 is from *Declaration on the Relation of the Church to Non-Christian Religions,* 28 October 1965, nos. 1 and 2; in *Vatican Council II: The Conciliar and Post Conciliar Documents,* edited by Austin Flannery (Northport, NY: Costello Publishing Co., 1975).

Chapter 1

The extract in the sidebar on page 23 is from *The Immense Journey,* by Loren Eiseley (New York: Random House, 1946, 1957), pages 208 and 210.

The extract on page 24 is adapted from *Zorba the Greek,* by Nikos Kazantzakis (New York: Ballantine Books, 1952), pages 322 and 324.

The sidebar on page 34 is from *Markings,* by Dag Hammarskjöld, translated by Leif Sjöberg and W. H. Auden (New York: Alfred A. Knopf, 1964), page 205.

The extract on page 35 is from *God and the New Physics,* by Paul Davies (New York: Simon and Schuster, 1983), page 207.

Chapter 2

The quotation on page 37 is from *The Little Prince,* by Antoine de Saint Exupéry, translated by Katherine Woods (New York: Scholastic Book Services, 1943, 1971), page 87.

The extract on page 38 is from "Sucker," by Carson McCullers, in her *The Mortgaged Heart,* edited by Margarita G. Smith (Boston: Houghton Mifflin Co., 1971), pages 18–19.

The extracts in the sidebars on pages 40, 48, and 51 are from *Sacred Texts of the World: A Universal Anthology,* edited by Ninian Smart and Richard D. Hecht (New York: Crossroad, 1982), pages 348, 15, and 383–384 respectively.

The extract in the sidebar on page 43 is quoted in *Eerdmans' Handbook to the World's Religions* (Grand Rapids, MI: Wm. B. Eerdmans Publishing Co., 1982), page 63.

Chapter 3

The extract on page 68 is from *Orthodoxy,* by Gilbert K. Chesterton (London: John Lane the Bodley Head Ltd., 1908), page 83.

Chapter 4

The story on page 71 is from *The Upanishads,* translated by Juan Mascaro (Baltimore: Penguin Books, 1965), pages 117–118; quoted in *The Hindu Tradition,* Religion in Human Culture series (Niles, IL: Argus Communications, 1978), page 14.

The quotation on page 72 is from the *Bhagavad Gita,* in *Sacred Texts,* edited by Smart, page 195.

The quotation on page 76 is from *Building the Earth,* by Pierre Teilhard de Chardin (Wilkes-Barre, PA: Dimension Books, 1965), page 97.

The extract on page 78 is from the *Bhagavad Gita* 11:52–54, in *Hindu Scriptures,* translated by R. C. Zaehner (New York: Dutton, Everyman's Library, 1966).

The extract on page 80 is from *Declaration on the Relation of the Church to Non-Christian Religions,* 28 October 1965, no. 2; in *Vatican Council II,* edited by Flannery.

The extract in the sidebar on page 81 is from *All Men Are Brothers: Life and Thoughts of Mahatma Gandhi as Told in His Own Words,* edited by Krishna Kripalani (New York: Columbia University Press, UNESCO, 1958), page 63.

The extract on page 85 is from *The Upanishads,* in *Springs of Indian Wisdom* (New York: Herder Book Center, 1965).

Chapter 5

The extract on page 91 is from *Vinaya Pitaka* (London: Pali Text Society); quoted in *Buddhism Made Plain: An Introduction for Christians and Jews,* by Antony Fernando with Leonard Swidler (Maryknoll, NY: Orbis Books, 1985), pages 18–19.

The quotation on page 93 is from *Declaration on the Relation of the Church to Non-Christian Religions,* 28 October 1965, no. 2; in *Vatican Council II,* edited by Flannery.

The extract on page 97 is from *The Asian Journal of Thomas Merton* (New York: New Directions, 1973), pages 233 and 235.

The verse attributed to Bodhidharma on page 99 is quoted in *Buddhism: A Way of Life and Thought*, by Nancy Wilson Ross (New York: Alfred A. Knopf, 1980), page 147.

The *haiku* by Basho on page 101 is quoted in *Many Peoples, Many Faiths: An Introduction to the Religious Life of Mankind*, by Robert S. Ellwood, Jr. (Englewood Cliffs, NJ: Prentice-Hall, 1976), page 203.

The extract on page 102 is from *Thoughts in Solitude*, by Thomas Merton (New York: Farrar, Straus & Cudahy, 1958), page 83.

Chapter 6

The extract in the sidebar on page 109 is from the *Huai-nan Tzu*, in *Sacred Texts*, edited by Smart, page 293.

The three quotations in the sidebar on page 112 are from *The Analects of Confucius*, translated by Arthur Waley (London: George Allen & Unwin Ltd., 1938), 2:15, 2:17, and 4:17.

The extract on page 112 is from the *Analects* 2:4; quoted in *The World's Great Religions*, by the editorial staff of *Life* (New York: Golden Press, 1958), page 73.

The quotation on page 114 is from the *Analects* 15:18–21,36; quoted in *Religions of the World*, by John A. Hardon (Westminster, MD: The Newman Press, 1963), page 154.

The first extract on page 116 is from *The Sayings of Lao Tzu*, Wisdom of the East series, [translated] by Lionel Giles (London: John Murray, 1905), no. 78; quoted in *Man's Religions*, by John B. Noss (New York: Macmillan Publishing Co., 1980), page 251.

The second extract on page 116 is from *The Way of Life: According to Lao Tzu*, translated by Witter Bynner (New York: The John Day Co., 1944), pages 26–27; quoted in *Many Peoples, Many Faiths: An Introduction to the Religious Life of Mankind*, by Robert S. Ellwood, Jr. (Englewood Cliffs, NJ: Prentice-Hall, 1976), page 168.

The quotation in the caption on page 116 is from *Tao Teh Ching*, by Lao Tzu [unknown trans.], no. 25.

The extract on page 119 is from *The Great Learning;* quoted in *The Religions of Man*, by Huston Smith (New York: Harper & Row, 1958), page 181.

Chapter 7

The extract on page 128 is from *The National Faith of Japan*, by D. C. Holtom (London: Kegan, Paul, Trench, Trubner and Co., 1938), page 49; quoted in *Man's Religions*, by John B. Noss (New York: Macmillan Publishing Co., 1980), page 311.

The extract on page 130 is quoted in *The Long Search*, by Ninian Smart (Boston: Little, Brown and Co., 1977), page 278.

Chapter 8

The extracts on pages 135 and 138 are from the *Yasna* 33:3–6 and 46:1; quoted in *Religions of the World*, by John A. Hardon (Westminster, MD: The Newman Press, 1963), pages 192 and 189.

Chapter 9

The extract from Hosea on page 155 is from the Revised Standard Version of the Bible.

The extract in the sidebar on page 163 is quoted in *Religions of the World*, by John A. Hardon (Westminster, MD: The Newman Press, 1963), page 247.

The first extract on page 170 is from *Declaration on the Relation of the Church to Non-Christian Religions*, 28 October 1965, no. 4; in *Vatican Council II*, edited by Flannery.

The second extract on page 170 and the quotation on page 171 are from *The Writings of Martin Buber*, edited by Will Herberg (Cleveland: The World Publishing Co., 1956), pages 275 and 296.

Chapter 10

The story on pages 173–174 is from *The Way of the Sufi*, by Idries Shah (New York: E. P. Dutton & Co., 1969), page 74.

The prayer on page 181, the four extracts from the Koran on pages 179 and 185, and the extracts from the Hadith on pages 184 and 185 are quoted in *The Islamic Tradition*, Religion in Human Culture series (Niles, IL: Argus Communications, 1978), pages 51, 16, 13, 88, 88–89, 89, and 89, respectively.

The six extracts from the Koran on pages 184, 186, and 187 are from *The Koran*, translated by J. M. Rodwell (New York: Dutton, Everyman's Library, 1909).

The extracts in the sidebar on page 190 are from *Ibn 'Ata' Illah: The Book of Wisdom*, translated by Victor Danner (New York: Paulist Press, 1978), nos. 8, 13, 49, and 94–95.

The first extract on page 191 is quoted in *The Black Muslims in America*, by C. Eric Lincoln (Boston: Beacon Press, 1961), page 219.

The second extract on page 191 is from *The Autobiography of Malcolm X*, with Alex Haley (New York: Grove Press, 1964), pages 343 and 368.

Chapter 11

The quotation from Romans on page 201 is from the Revised Standard Version of the Bible.

The sidebar on page 204 is from *The Book of Catholic Worship* (Washington, DC: The Liturgical Conference, 1966).

The quotation from James on page 212 is from the Revised Standard Version of the Bible.

The extract in the sidebar on page 212 and the extract on page 213 are from *Sermons*, edited and translated by John W. Doberstein, vol. 51 of *Luther's Works* (Philadelphia: Fortress Press, 1959), pages 110 and 189.

The quotation on page 214 is from *Calvin: Institutes of the Christian Religion*, edited by John T. McNeill, translated by Ford Lewis Battles, vol. 21 in the Library of Christian Classics (Philadelphia: The Westminster Press, n.d.), page 926.

The extract on page 214 is quoted in *John Calvin and the Calvinistic Tradition,* by Albert-Marie Schmidt, translated by Ronald Wallace (New York: Harper & Brothers, 1960), page 67.

The two quotations on page 216 are from *John Wesley,* edited by Albert C. Outler (New York: Oxford University Press, 1964), pages 205 and 435.

The quotation on page 219 is from *Dogmatic Constitution on the Church,* 21 November 1964, no. 18; in *Vatican Council II,* edited by Flannery.

The first extract and quotation on page 221 and the first extract on page 222 are from *Decree on Ecumenism,* 21 November 1964, nos. 1, 9, and 15–16; in *Vatican Council II,* edited by Flannery.

The last quotation on page 221 is from *Directory Concerning Ecumenical Matters: Part One,* 14 May 1967, no. 62; in *Vatican Council II,* edited by Flannery.

The first quotation on page 222 is from *The Common Declaration of Pope Paul VI and Patriarch Athenagoras I,* 7 December 1965, no. 4; in *Vatican Council II,* edited by Flannery.

The last extract on page 222 is quoted in *1985 Catholic Almanac,* edited by Felician A. Foy (Huntington, IN: Our Sunday Visitor, 1984), page 301.

The extract on page 223 is from "Address to the Secretariat for Promoting Christian Unity," by John Paul II, 8 February 1980; quoted in *Origins* 10, no. 24 (27 November 1980), page 384.

Epilogue

The first quotation on page 229 is by David Breese, and the second quotation on page 229 is from *These Also Believe,* by Charles Braden (New York: Macmillan, 1949), page *xii;* both are quoted in *Strange Gods: Contemporary Religious Cults in America,* by William J. Whalen (Huntington, IN: Our Sunday Visitor, 1981), pages 3 and 4.

Photo Credits

Cover: Taurus Photos (left); Mimi Forsyth (top, right); Museum of Fine Arts, Boston (middle, right); Art Resource, Inc., (bottom, right).

Half-title page: Mimi Forsyth.

Title pages: James L. Shaffer (far left), Taurus Photos (left), Mimi Forsyth (right).

Copyright pages: Frost Publishing Group, Ltd.

Contents pages: Mimi Forsyth.

Dan Alf: pages 153, 156 (bottom).

Art Resource: pages 27, 36, 39, 44 (top and right), 46, 47, 48, 72, 111, 134, 135, 139 (left), 157, 166 (above), 176, 178 (top and bottom), 194, 201 (top), 204, 206 (above), 214.

Bettmann Archives: pages 8, 17, 22, 25, 28, 30, 32, 37, 42 (top), 43, 44 (bottom), 51, 52, 57, 59, 60 (bottom), 61, 69, 74, 75, 76, 79 (bottom and left), 80 (top), 81, 82, 84, 91, 97 (top), 98, 105, 106, 107, 110 (right), 115 (bottom), 117, 120, 123, 124 (bottom and right), 127 (bottom), 128, 129, 130, 133 (top, left; and bottom, left), 137, 138, 139 (below), 141, 143, 146, 158 (top), 159 (bottom), 161 (top), 162, 164, 165, 166 (right), 168, 169, 170, 174, 179, 181 (top), 182 (bottom), 183, 189, 190, 195, 196, 197, 201 (bottom), 202, 205, 209, 210, 211, 213, 215 (top), 216, 217, 219, 220, 221, 223, 226, 228 (above), 229, 230, 232, 233, 238.

EKM-Nepenthe: pages 12, 13 (left), 20, 21, 29, 54, 56 (bottom), 62 (top two), 64 (above), 65, 71, 73, 80 (bottom), 102, 150, 167 (left), 206 (right), 227, 228 (right), 232 (below), 234, 235, 236.

Mimi Forsyth: pages 11 (top), 16, 69 (bottom), 86, 87, 93, 95 (bottom).

Frost Publishing Group, Ltd.: pages 11 (bottom), 13 (right), 24, 26, 31, 63 (bottom), 69 (top), 79 (top), 83, 95 (top), 97 (bottom), 99, 100, 101, 103, 113, 118, 124 (top and bottom), 125, 127 (top), 126, 127 (right), 131, 144, 147, 149, 156 (top), 181 (bottom), 182 (top), 192.

Dettie de Jesus: page 121.

Jean Claude Lejeune: page 19.

Gene Plaisted: pages 14, 19, 66, 67, 133 (top, right), 198.

James L. Shaffer: pages 15, 19 (bottom, left).

Taurus Photos: pages 9, 23, 33, 42 (bottom), 55, 56 (top), 60 (top and right), 62 (bottom two), 63 (top), 64 (right), 88, 96, 109, 110 (above), 114, 116, 151, 152, 158 (bottom), 159 (top), 161 (bottom), 167 (right), 172, 173, 178 (right), 187, 208, 218.

Bill Thomas: page 70.